CAMBRIDGE STUDIES IN RUSSIAN LITERATURE

Vladimir Nabokov

CAMBRIDGE STUDIES IN RUSSIAN LITERATURE

General editor HENRY GIFFORD

Vladimir Nabokov
A critical study of the novels

DAVID RAMPTON

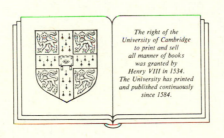

The right of the
University of Cambridge
to print and sell
all manner of books
was granted by
Henry VIII in 1534.
The University has printed
and published continuously
since 1584.

CAMBRIDGE UNIVERSITY PRESS

CAMBRIDGE

LONDON   NEW YORK   NEW ROCHELLE
MELBOURNE   SYDNEY

Published by the Press Syndicate of the University of Cambridge
The Pitt Building, Trumpington Street, Cambridge CB2 IRP
32 East 57th Street, New York, NY 10022, USA
296 Beaconsfield Parade, Middle Park, Melbourne 3206, Australia

© Cambridge University Press 1984

First published 1984

Printed in Great Britain at
the University Press, Cambridge

Library of Congress catalogue card number: 83-23212

British Library Cataloguing in Publication Data
Rampton, David
Vladimir Nabokov. – (Cambridge Studies
in Russian Literature)
1. Nabokov, Vladimir – Criticism and
interpretation
I. Title
813'.54   PS3527.A15Z/
ISBN 0 521 25710 7 hard covers
ISBN 0 521 27671 3 paperback

CE

Contents

Preface

'Writing is that neutral, composite, oblique space where our subject slips away, the negative where all identity is lost, starting with the very identity of the body writing.' Thus Roland Barthes, in one of contemporary criticism's most famous threnodies, announces 'The Death of the Author' for modern readers and critics. The implications of this death are far-reaching, says Barthes. Because all personal, 'antecedent' relations between author and text no longer exist, '*writing* can no longer designate an operation of recording, notation, representation, "depiction"'. What was once considered to be, say, a realistic novel is now simply a verbal form 'in which the enunciation has no other content (contains no other proposition) than the act by which it is uttered'. The critic's task changes accordingly: 'the space of writing is to be ranged over, not pierced', because ideas about 'levels of meaning', or 'depth', or 'profundity' are as dead as the author. 'Writing', says Barthes, 'ceaselessly posits meaning ceaselessly to evaporate it, carrying out a systematic exemption of meaning'. Barthes's views still do not command anything like universal assent, but a majority of the most influential literary critics writing today holds some version of them. For these critics, the autonomous author, the consciousness who creates a world and the origin of truth and meaning, seems well and truly dead.

In this book I have set out to study the novels of Vladimir Nabokov in precisely the way that Barthes obliterates so effortlessly here, and to make a case for the kind of criticism that he dismisses as moribund. What kind of reality do they depict? What kind of meaning do they posit? What kind of truth do they tell about Nabokov and about the world? These are the sorts of question I have set out to answer. A great deal of criticism that 'ranges over' Nabokov's writing without attempting to 'pierce' it already exists: books that attempt to disentangle the complex patterns in his novels, to describe the self-referential nature of the aesthetic objects he creates, or to define their significance in terms of an internal system of relations. In his particular case, a more traditional approach begins to look like something of an innovation.

The other justification for another book on Nabokov is also related to the 'Death of the Author' movement in contemporary criticism. One does not have to read very far in someone like Barthes to realize that the obsequies that have been performed are somewhat selective. When he cites Mallarmé to support the view that the writer has no authority (i.e., he does not 'own' his language; not he but it speaks), it becomes clear that Barthes is concerned only with the death of a certain type of author. Others, with very definite ideas about the nature of literary art and about how it should be discussed, are very much alive, and they continue to exercise considerable influence and to attract dedicated defenders.

Nabokov is one of these writers. He acquired a large readership and a reputation in academic circles only in the late 1950s. The great pioneering studies of the sixties sought to celebrate a major new talent, to atone for the fact that he had been neglected, and to enlist him as a leader in a movement that advocated a new kind of novel. This was no more than he deserved; but it led to an oversimplified view of his fiction, and the critics who have gone on to extend our knowledge of Nabokov's work have, with a few notable exceptions, mainly contented themselves with preaching to the converted. Nabokov's ideas about fiction are not self-evidently true; nor are his novels good novels because they illustrate what the critic takes to be Nabokov's aesthetic views. In a sense, this modern author is not yet dead enough.

These two reasons then constitute the justification for this particular book: the predominant interest in the formal aspects of novels which I shall argue are expressions of a personal view of the world suggests that a study with a different emphasis might be useful; and given the extent to which Nabokov has determined how his novels should be discussed, the time seems right for tempering admiration for his mastery and brilliance with a little respectful scepticism.

My choice of which novels to concentrate on has been influenced by my desire to question the critical assumption that content is of strictly secondary importance in any account of Nabokov's work. Although one critic has argued that Nabokov's first novel, *Mary*, is an initial experiment in self-reflexive fiction, and another has exhibited considerable ingenuity in proving that *Pnin* was written to prove that Pnin does not exist, basically critics agree that novels like *Mary* and *Pnin*, *The Defence* and *Glory*, are to be read as representations of various human worlds. (Of these novels only *Pnin* has received substantial critical attention.) I have organized my study of Nabokov around novels in which such a content is not granted primary status, being regarded as less significant than the complex formal arrangements and self-reflexive strategies that make the fiction quintessentially Nabokovian. In an introductory chapter, I argue that his ideas about literature and its obligations are less narrow than some have supposed. I then offer readings of three early novels to show what happens when the parodic and self-referential elements are seen as part of a larger design that involves Nabokov in traditional representational art and all that that implies. In Chapter Two, I analyze *Invitation to a Beheading* and *Bend Sinister* for what they have to tell us about the author's view of totalitarianism. In Chapter Three, I consider *The Gift* as a history of Russian literature and culture. No one has explored these issues in any detail, and therefore these discussions fill distinct gaps in Nabokov criticism. Chapter Four, on *Lolita*, is different: it is an attempt, in the light of the way criticism of the novel has developed, to say something new about the moral and aesthetic problems it raises. In the last two chapters, I examine the claims of those who see the late fiction as the triumph of Nabokovian artifice, and try to discover what sort of content is there in the novels for the reader determined to approach them in the traditional way.

Throughout what follows, then, the stress is on things like human drama and ideas and the complex ways in which Nabokov's self-conscious artistry actually affects the reader's sense of the characters and events being depicted. He believed that art was not just a game, but a 'divine game', because 'this is the element in which man comes nearest to God through being a true creator in his own right'. He could say near the end of his career that 'the main favor' he asked of 'the serious critic' was 'sufficient perceptiveness to understand that whatever term or trope I use, my purpose is not to be facetiously flashy or grotesquely obscure but to express what I feel and think with the utmost truthfulness and perception'. I have tried to say something about how perceptive Nabokov was, and about what kind of truth his novels tell.

I should also like here briefly to record my thanks for all the assistance I have received in writing this book. It is a pleasure to acknowledge what I owe to the many critics whose works have been so helpful to me, both as information and provocation. In the notes, I have tried to give some idea of the range and the nature of my indebtedness. The British Library and the Widener Library at Harvard University kindly made much early Nabokov material available to me. This book began life as Doctor of Philosophy dissertation at the University of Sussex, where several years of research were made possible by grants from the Social Sciences and Humanities Research Council of Canada. Special thanks go to Mrs M. Framroze and Mrs J. Benning in the Interlibrary Loan section at the University of Sussex Library, and to all the staff in Reader Services: the more difficult the problem, the more determinedly they set about solving it. Dr Lawrence Mathews of the University of Alberta gave me valuable encouragement at every stage of this project, and saved me from many blunders. My supervisor at Sussex, Dr Cedric Watts, saw the dissertation through several drafts, made innumerable helpful suggestions, and waited patiently while I struggled to find my own way. It could not have been written without him. Mr Terence Moore of Cambridge University Press has been very patient and helpful, and Mrs Lynn Hieatt did a superb job as subeditor. Finally, I would like to thank my wife Elizabeth, to whom this work is dedicated. She dedicated herself to it: she listened and advised and prodded, kept the demons away, and kept the faith.

Notes on the text

I have used a modified version of British Standard 2979, 1958. The modifications are: ё and з are transliterated as *e* (the one exception is the name of the hero of *The Gift*, which I have written not 'Fedor' but 'Fyodor', as it appears in the English version of that novel); й becomes *i*; ь is ' as in British Standard, but I have omitted it in proper names; ъ is not transliterated; -й, -ий, -й, and -ый become -*y* at the end of proper names.

All translations from French and Russian texts are mine, unless otherwise indicated.

1
Introduction

In *Speak, Memory*, Nabokov summarizes the critical reaction to the novels of his favourite émigré author, V. Sirin. It seems that there were two schools of thought. Those who criticized him did so because of the novels' content: 'Just as Marxist publicists of the eighties in old Russia would have denounced his lack of concern with the economic structure of society, so the mystagogues of émigré letters deplored his lack of religious insight and of moral preoccupation.' Those who admired him were impressed by the formal qualities of his work, by his 'unusual style, brilliant precision, functional imagery', and by 'the mirror-like angles of his clear but weirdly misleading sentences'. They realized, says Nabokov, that the 'real life' of Sirin's books 'flowed in his figures of speech'.[1] The joke on the reader here is that 'Sirin' was Nabokov's pseudonym: his account of the 'loneliest and most arrogant'[2] of the young émigré writers is a self-description. But I have quoted these remarks, not to comment on one of his dead-pan deceptions, but to take up this question of Sirin's critical reception. In fact, those who wrote about his novels do not divide up quite so neatly as Nabokov suggests. Many praise the content of his fiction, with particular emphasis on the way he uses it to comment on contemporary life. Mikhail Osorgin reads *Korol', Dama, Valet* as an indictment of the dehumanization of the European bourgeoisie, and commends its author for his representation of 'the real horror of the epoch'.[3] Vladislav Khodasevich says that Nabokov employs cinematographic effects in *Kamera Obskura* to illustrate 'the terrible danger hanging over our whole culture, distorted and dazzled by various forces among which the cinematographic, though of course far from being the strongest, is perhaps the most characteristic and significant'.[4] And Wladislav Weidlé links Nabokov with writers who depict 'the disintegration of spiritual life' and who reflect 'the contemporary state of the world, as much by their themes as by their narrative and stylistic devices'.[5] Sometimes this praise is coupled with an awareness of contradictory tendencies in the novels themselves. Speaking of *Korol', Dama, Valet*, M. Tsetlin observes that Nabokov, knowing that any intimate knowledge of German everyday life (*byt*) is impossible for an outsider, does not try to represent that life in a traditional way. But he goes on to point out that the soullessness and automatism of contemporary life is what Nabokov wants to depict, that 'The author feels the ugliness and vulgarity, the nightmare atmosphere of a large city, in this case Berlin, its everyday life [*byt* again], streets, night clubs, large stores.'[6] Even Georgy Adamovich, one of the critics, referred to by Nabokov in the remarks quoted above, who thought that literature had to be something other than just literature, will condemn Nabokov in one review for writing about nothing,[7] yet insist in another that it is wrong to consider him a mere technician or virtuoso.[8] So the idea of two groups of critics, one stumbling around in Nabokov's labyrinths, checking rusty compasses and denouncing the constructor for not building according to accepted specifications, the other easily finding its way through the maze because it has come prepared for 'mirror-like angles' and a skilful arrangement of traps and diversions, is not completely accurate. Nabokov's émigré critics discussed the form and content of his novels together.

It is important to understand this in order to appreciate the shift that has occurred, for modern critics of Nabokov's novels, if one were to sum up their interests in a single sentence, have placed the emphasis squarely on the formal qualities of his work. Tracing image patterns, explaining the significance of allusions to mirrors or spirals or chess or butterflies, discussing 'the art theme', concentrating on details with a view to demonstrating how the whole complex structure of a given novel hangs together – it is this kind of very useful activity that characterizes much of the criticism devoted to his work. But even more striking are the claims made by many of his critics about the ways in which Nabokov's novels subvert any attempt to read them as representations of, or commentaries on, various aspects of reality. Sometimes this takes the form of assertions that his fiction proves that there is no such thing as reality *tout court*, by showing us in novel after novel how the human imagination creates its own reality by giving order and meaning to a raw material that only automata and dull critics take to be something fixed, stable, objectively knowable. The referential drops out because there is nothing left to refer to.[9] But far more often

Nabokov's critics argue for the autonomy of his creations by stressing the ways in which he reveals his novels to be self-reflexive forms that constantly advertise their own artificiality. In *The New York Review of Books*, his fiction has been described this way: 'Art to Nabokov is entertainment and his characters are pieces he manipulates on a chess board, devising problems for the absorbing, challenging, clever game of which he is a master'; and 'His novels are demonstrations, overt or implicit, of his conviction that art and life have little, if anything, to do with each other.'[10] In the journals of literary criticism, he is viewed in similar terms: 'His novels', writes Charles Russell in *Modern Fiction Studies*, 'are totally self-absorbed, self-referential linguistic games claiming no entrance into, no involvement with, the phenomenal world.'[11] An American novelist, William Gass, claims that Nabokov shares all the essential characteristics of the American 'fabulators' who acknowledge him as master. His novels impress Gass precisely because they have no content in the traditional sense:

They were not stuffed, like geese, with journalistic observations, deter-mining and moralizing milieus, intensely instructional entanglements, those shifty banalities that do credit to their authors and also to mankind ... One did not hear the tinny click and whirr of toy psychologies as the eyes and loins of the characters lit up, wet, or otherwise expressed themselves, or find the weight of sex and class was heavier than shoulders.[12]

And Alfred Appel, the annotator of *Lolita* and perhaps Nabokov's most influential critic, sums up the novels this way:

'All reality is a mask', he writes (p. 148 [*Nikolay Gogol*]), and Nabokov's narratives are masques, stagings of his own inventions rather than re-creations of the naturalistic world. But, since the latter is what most readers expect and demand of fiction, many still do not understand what Nabokov is doing. They are not accustomed to 'the allusions to something else behind the crudely painted screens' (p. 142), where the 'real plots behind the obvious ones are taking place'. There are thus at least two 'plots' in all Nabokov's fiction: the characters in the book, and the consciousness of the creator above it – the 'real plot' which is visible in the 'gaps' and 'holes' in the narrative.[13]

In various ways, then, the idea that Nabokov's novels are best understood as self-contained artefacts has become the central assumption in most of the criticism devoted to his work. In the present book, I want to quarrel with this assumption. I think that tracing image patterns and explaining allusions is only a necessary first step in dealing with these novels, that the game metaphor does not account for every aspect of Nabokov's work, that the choice between 'staging of his own inventions' and 're-creations of the naturalistic world' has an either/or quality which is not really very helpful when we try to come to terms with this author, that the 'obvious' plot of the novels is something other than a collection of 'crudely painted screens', and that his characters tell us at least as much about Nabokov and his view of man as the 'gaps' and 'holes' in which he reveals himself as the artificer responsible for manipulating events.

Before I give some examples, using three of Nabokov's early novels, of what an approach with a different emphasis might entail, I want to say something about Nabokov's own views on literature in general and on the novel in particular. For the great advantage of talking about formal qualities, and about games and puppets and painted screens where this author is concerned, is that one does so with the express approval of Nabokov himself. After all, isn't he the writer who never tired of insisting that art means nothing to society, that terms such as 'real life' and 'reality' should never appear in print unless mocked and jostled by inverted commas, that what seemed to be one of his political novels was really only a collection of 'absurd mirages' that fade away when he 'dismiss[es] the cast',[14] that the settings of his novels were invented and unimportant, that their 'worlds' were 'fantastic and personal'?[15] Of course Nabokov wrote much more about the work of others than he did about his own. Here too the critic primarily interested in the form of his work and in the way that it sabotages the ostensible content can find a great deal of support for his approach. In his study of Gogol, Nabokov pours scorn on the idea that a novel like *Dead Souls* has anything to tell us about nineteenth-century Russia, and insists that Gogol's achievement is 'a phenomenon of language and not one of ideas'.[16] In his lectures, he says that Flaubert is a great novelist, not because he wrote realistic novels, but because he wrote a great 'fairy tale' like *Madame Bovary*;[17] and he goes on to claim that *À La Recherche du Temps Perdu* is a 'pure fantasy on Proust's part, just as *Anna Karenin* [the English title Nabokov prefers] is a fantasy, just as Kafka's "The Metamorphosis" is fantasy' (*Lectures on Literature* (*LL*), p. 210). As far as contemporaries are concerned, our critic can argue that it is Borges and Beckett and Robbe-Grillet, writers who have forced us to rethink the relation between fiction and reality, whom Nabokov singles out for special praise. As for the novelists who incur his particular contempt, doesn't he reserve his disdain precisely for those who want their novels to be judged in mimetic terms, who assume that they have something to tell us about human life, and who use their fiction to work out a set of human values? Dostoevsky's 'journalese,' 'sentimentality' and 'tedious and muddled' soul-searching,[18] the 'easy platitudes' of D. H. Lawrence,[19] Faulkner's 'belated romanticism and quite impossible biblical rumblings and "starkness" (which is not starkness at all but skeletonized triteness)'.[20] Pasternak's 'melodramatic and vilely written' *Dr Zhivago*,[21] – the list is a long one. What Nabokov calls 'Literature of Ideas' does not fare any better. He calls it 'topical trash coming in huge blocks of plaster that are carefully transmitted from age to age until somebody comes along with a hammer and takes a good crack at Balzac, at Gorky, at Mann'.[22] No one could ask for a more forthright expression of the 'aesthetic' attitude than this.

Since my whole argument is based on making a case for a view of Nabokov's art that places the emphasis squarely on ideas and human values and what his novels are 'about', all the things he disposes of so scornfully here, I want to start by trying to show that he was much more interested in such things than the above account implies. The place to begin is not the interviews of the sixties and seventies, nor the lectures of the forties and fifties in America, but the criticism he wrote in the decades of European exile, mostly in the form of book reviews which helped supplement the meagre income he gained from teaching and from writing fiction.

It is true that much of Nabokov's early criticism is devoted to formal matters. He praises writers like Khodasevich[23] and Ladinsky[24] for their masterful use of language. He lectures poets for inappropriate rhymes[25] and for 'slovenly' attempts to make lines scan by adding non-existent syllables to words.[26] He commends someone for avoiding political themes,[27] criticizes someone else for writing about them,[28] and blasts another émigré poet for indulging in 'general ideas' and the 'cheap poetical pessimism' of the age.[29] But there is a different strain running through Nabokov's reviews of the period that deserves our attention. Here is an excerpt from a 1927 review:

A plot is as necessary to a poem as it is to a novel. The most beautiful lyric poems in Russian literature owe their strength and delicacy to the way in which everything in them moves agreeably toward some inevitable, harmonious *dénouement*. Poems in which there is no unity of imagery, no distinctive lyric plot but only a mood, are as fortuitous and short-lived as that mood itself. If, let us say, a poet, having decided to describe his sadness, does not have in mind a single definite image in which to embody that sadness, then something diffuse and irresponsible occurs, the poem is aimless, neither saying nor showing anything. Such a poem is boring.[30]

Here it sounds as if Nabokov thinks that an author, provided he finds the appropriate form, can use his work to communicate something. A true adherent of an art for art's sake position would scoff at this notion of a lyric poem's expressing a poet's sadness; and committed fabulators, who take plot to be the enemy,[31] could hardly speak about it in this way. When Nabokov reviews a collection of short stories by Kuprin, he places even more emphasis on the content of the work: 'when', he writes, 'not simply a Russian man but a Russian writer, having received a generous gift from God, speaks of what he knows and loves, of his passion, perpetual in its tenderness and strangeness, then you can imagine the accuracy and purity of expression that animate his words'.[32] He dismisses some stories published in an émigré journal by saying that 'aesthetes' will like them,[33] condemns Tsvetaeva for writing for herself and not for the reader,[34] wishes Damanskaya would write more descriptive stories based on real life,[35] and praises Bozhnev for the 'thought' in his poetry.[36] In his review of Nina Berberova's first novel, after stressing the importance of the plot and its 'musical development', he applauds her for having extracted from the cacophony of everyday life one of its crucial aspects, the émigré's yearning for a settled way of life.[37] In another review, he celebrates ancient legends for their representational qualities, their 'mysterious perspectives of ancient thought, landscapes ennobled by vistas, symbols which in their time were full of fragrance and meaning', criticizes Remizov because his stories do not resemble these, and accuses him of playing boring games in his fiction.[38] He tells young poets generally that the more they care about creating impressions of the 'living world', the more alive their poetry will be.[39] Perhaps most revealing in this regard is the article he wrote in 1930 about Soviet literature. Instead of simply denouncing writers for allowing their art to be contaminated by ideology, he attacks Soviet literature by arguing the view of man expressed in it is untrue. Nabokov notes that he personally feels no class hatred whatever for those better off than he is, for the gold-toothed, champagne-swilling stockbrokers who play the villains in the new revolutionary novels. 'However,' he goes on:

the discerning and honourable Soviet critic will answer that a humanistic, classless approach to things is absurd, or, more accurately, that this very impartiality in appraisal is itself a disguised form of bourgeoisness. This claim is extremely important, for from it follows the conclusion that the staunch communist, the descendant of the proletariat, and the impetuous property owner, the descendant of the gentry, perceive differently the most simple things in the world: the pleasure of a drink of cold water on a hot day, the pain of a hard blow on the head, the irritation from a tight-fitting shoe, and many other human sensations which are similarly peculiar to every mortal. In vain would I begin to claim that the responsible worker sneezes and yawns just like the irresponsible bourgeois; it is not I who am right, but the Soviet critic.[40]

Nabokov concludes that a 'class' way of thinking is a sort of 'spectral luxury, something highly spiritual and ideal', which the Soviets have invented to save the worker from the despair of having a bourgeois skeleton in a body constructed according to a bourgeois model, doomed to live out its days under 'the bourgeois blueness of the sky'.[41] How far is he willing to take this idea of a shared humanity? Could it be that Nabokov's reality is not so 'fantastic and personal' after all? What alternative to the idealized Soviet view of man does he propose? I do not pretend that these questions have simple answers; but I think that they are genuine questions, and that this kind of criticism bespeaks an interest in aspects of literary art which Nabokov is often supposed to have regarded with supreme indifference.

This brief summary of an important element in Nabokov's early critical views should make us take a fresh look at his recently published lectures. Many reviewers understandably seized on what is undoubtedly their most striking feature – Nabokov's claim that novels are not statements about things as they are but supreme fantasies – as his basic message. Peter Prescott, for instance, calls the lectures 'virtually avant-garde in their author's insistence on divorcing the worlds that novelists create from what dull readers call "real life"'.[42] And John Updike notes in his Introduction to the first volume that 'in any decade Nabokov's approach would have seemed radical in the degree of severance between reality and art that it supposes' (*LL*, p. xxv). Once again, I want to argue for a complementary view that is at least as important as the generally accepted one. To simplify matters I shall concentrate on the lectures devoted to Dickens's *Bleak House*.

Nabokov singles out this novel in his introductory remarks as 'a fantastic romance within a fantastic London' that has nothing to tell us about life in that city in the last century (*LL*, p. 2). He begins the lectures themselves by asking: is *Bleak House* a satire? Hardly: legal cases like Jarndyce vs Jarndyce had ceased to exist by the 1850s; and as 'an indictment of the aristocracy the description of the Dedlocks and their set is of no interest or importance whatsoever' (*LL*, pp. 64–5), because Dickens knew very little about aristocrats. An exposure of the abuses of child labour then? No; Dickens's children are all borrowed from previous literature, and anyway, their persecution takes us back to the author and his own childhood, not the 1850s. Conclusion: only the enchanter in Dickens is immortal, keeping him 'above the reformer, above the penny novelette, above the sentimental trash, above the theatrical nonsense . . . It is in his imagery that he is great' (*LL*, p. 65). Now this is by no means as straightforward as it sounds. We note the implication that had Dickens known more about the aristocracy he could have written a more incisive critique, and the claim that part of his novel, like the lyric poet's meditation on grief, is a transmutation of his own personal experience. But the general thrust of Nabokov's argument is clear. Presumably a detailed discussion of the structure of the novel, its imagery, and its complex web of internal cross-references is what follows. We know what kind of critic we are dealing with.

Yet as we read on we realize that Nabokov, for all his interest in explaining the great formal artistry of Dickens in *Bleak House*, is also very keen to talk about content, specifically the conflict between good and evil. He says that some of the characters are 'symbols of greater, more universal forces', and that some are on the side of the Devil, but 'Dickens was too much of an artist to make all this obtrusive or obvious. His people are alive, not merely clothed ideas or symbols' (*LL*, p. 69). Again the dual emphasis, again the concern with the vitality of the embodiment that we remarked on in the reviews of émigré literature. Nabokov is particularly intrigued by what he calls 'the child theme' (*LL*, p. 91); but instead of developing his idea about the literary antecedents of these figures, he spends his time explaining what makes the depiction of the children in *Bleak House* so real and so moving, and how

Dickens opposes those who persecute the helpless and those who defend them. To illustrate this he quotes the long passage in which John Jarndyce and Esther visit Charley and her 'children', the brother and sister whom she must look after. 'Now, please,' says Nabokov, 'note the intonation of pity and of a kind of tender awe in Mr Jarndyce's speech', and quotes the exchange ending: '"And how do you live, Charley? O! Charley", said my guardian, turning his face away for a moment, "How do you live?"' (*LL*, p. 86). According to the criteria laid down in his introductory remarks about how one should read a novel, Nabokov ought to warn his students here not to fall for Dickens's blatant appeal to the reader's sympathy. But, as if anticipating being charged with inconsistency, he goes on to say: 'I should not like to hear the charge of sentimentality made against this strain that runs through *Bleak House*. I want to submit that people who denounce the sentimental are generally unaware of what sentiment is' (*LL*, p. 86). The passage illustrates, he goes on, not Dickens's emotional indulgence but the importance he attaches to 'keen, subtle, specialized compassion, with a grading and merging of melting shades, with the very accent of profound pity in the words uttered'. Only then does Nabokov mention the author's choice of 'the most visible, most audible, most tangible epithets' (*LL*, p. 87) to communicate this compassion. But the crucial point, the reason for dwelling at such length on 'the child theme', seems to be what the author's treatment of it tells us about ourselves. Nabokov contends that 'despite all our hideous reversions to the wild state' (*LL*, p. 87), modern man is better than ancient man or medieval man because he is capable of this special kind of feeling. He contrasts the cruelty and squalor of the ancients, redeemed only by the greatness of their art, with our own age, and uses the world represented in Dickens and those of Homer and Cervantes to prove his point. Whatever we finally decide about these propositions, they should make one thing clear: Nabokov thinks that an author conveys a certain view of man in a work of fiction, and that readers are entitled to comment on it and to judge it.

This is not just an isolated case, a brief interlude between disquisitions on style. Nabokov spends four more pages on the death of Jo to underline his point about cruelty and compassion, and when he reads aloud the famous passage in which Dickens indicts the whole of Victorian society, the interspersed observations show how interested Nabokov is in every aspect of Dickens's art. In a parenthesis he describes Tom-all-Alone's as 'the frightful slum' where Jo lives (*LL*, p. 93), a remark which sounds, coming as it does after he has quoted Dickens on how 'civilisation and barbarism walked this boastful island together' (*LL*, p. 92), like Nabokov's recognition of the fact that the author of *Bleak House* does have something to tell us about nineteenth-century England. Then comes the end of that scene, which Nabokov handles this way:

And now listen to the booming bell of Carlyle's apostrophic style: 'The light is come upon the dark benighted way. Dead!
'Dead, your Majesty. Dead, my lords and gentlemen. Dead, Right Reverends and Wrong Reverends of every order. Dead, men and women, born with Heavenly compassion in your hearts. And dying thus around us every day.'
This is a lesson in style, not in participative emotion.   (*LL*, p. 94)

Having warned his listeners against the emotional response to fiction, the lecturer feels obliged to alert them to the cool, clinical task he is actually performing. But the passage cannot be read effectively without the feelings being swayed, and the whole idea of 'performing' Dickens in this way, of taking one's students slowly through Jo's halting attempt to say the Lord's Prayer and so on, is bound up with sniffling audiences and emotional displays. Oscar Wilde's remark about being unable to read the death scene of little Nell without laughing reminds us of what critics who concern themselves exclusively with style have made of such scenes. Nabokov quotes this one at length to make a point about Dickens's impressive cadences, and to show how fiction can move us and communicate all the more powerfully what it has to say when it does so.

The other lectures are full of evidence supporting this view of Nabokov as a critic who is as interested in the content of a novel as he is in its form. He says that 'inspiration' helps the author 'to recapture and reconstruct the world' (*LL*, p. 379), that 'the art of not only creating people but keeping created people alive within the reader's mind throughout a long novel' is 'the obvious sign of greatness' (*LL*, p. 123), that 'even more important' than the author's ability to create his own world is 'how plausible he has succeeded in making it' (*Lectures on Russian Literature* (*LRL*), p. 106), that imagery is the evocation of something that is meant to appeal to the reader's senses 'in such a way as to impress upon his mind a picture of fictitious life that becomes to him as living as any personal recollection' (*LRL*, p. 199). His commentary on these living pictures, created people and plausible worlds occupies many pages. He discusses 'philistinism' in *Madame Bovary* and the 'vulgar cruelty' (*LL*, p. 142) of its chief representatives. He examines in great detail the moral argument in works by Tolstoy and Kafka. Even if, he says, a certain kind of subject matter can become dated – for example, the debate in *Anna Karenin* about agriculture in the 1870s – the 'thrill of Anna's or Kitty's emotions and motives' is 'eternal' (*LRL*, p. 143). Chekhov can write like a journalist at times, but his genius reveals itself in 'the association of odd little details which at the same time are perfectly true to life' (*LRL*, p. 282), and in his ability to disclose 'more of the blackest realities' of peasant Russia than writers who 'flaunted their social ideas' (*LRL*, p. 254). Joyce is as likely to be praised for putting in the mouth of Stephen Dedalus 'a wonderful squelching answer to bourgeois anti-Semitism' (*LL*, p. 300) as he is to be commended for his prose. And in a fascinating conclusion to the first volume of lectures, Nabokov sums up his eclectic approach by opting for the 'much abused ivory tower' as the writer's fixed address, providing it does not prevent him from collecting 'the treasures of observation, humor, and pity which may be professionally obtained through closer contact with his fellow men' (*LL*, p. 371). In short, he talks surprisingly often about novels and novelists in the way that critics and readers generally have done since people have considered novels to be worth talking about. Some of the generally accepted notions about Nabokov's views on fiction need to be revised.

I have not yet said anything about his views on his own fiction during these years because he did not have much to say about it. In a 1932 interview, there are some interesting remarks about how characters suffer in his novels because suffering reveals a certain kind of truth about human nature.[43] In an early letter to Edmund Wilson, he calls *Podvig* an example of his *blevotina* (vomit).[44] He admitted to an American interviewer in 1951 that he thought *Laughter in the Dark* was 'a little crude'.[45] But of course he did not really get a chance to say anything in print about his own novels until people became interested in what he had to say. In the last two decades of his life, he got his chance. I take up his comments on individual novels in my own discussions of them; all I want to do here is examine some of his views on how his novels should be read.

First, Nabokov on 'ideas' in his work. He has a great deal to say on this subject: he does not waste his time on 'illustrated catalogues of solemn notions and serious opinions';[46] only 'mediocrity thrives on "ideas"';[47] anything in his fiction that resembles an idea has nothing whatever to do with the 'general ideas' found in other novels, those 'bloated topicalities stranded like dead whales'.[48] His position is summed up in this answer to an interviewer who asked about the lack of ideas in his work:

The middlebrow or the upper Philistine cannot get rid of the furtive feeling that a book, to be great, must deal in great ideas. Oh, I know the type, the dreary type! He likes a good yarn spiced with social comment ... If American, he has a dash of Marxist blood, and if British, he is acutely and ridiculously class-conscious; he finds it so much easier to write about ideas than about words; he does not realize that perhaps the reason that he does not find general ideas in a particular writer is that the particular ideas of that writer have not yet become general.[49]

This is the argument as Nabokov usually states it, but it makes for certain problems. He never bothers to distinguish between generally accepted ideas ('Individual liberty must be subject to some constraints if society is to function'), ideas related to the generality ('Marxism', 'class'), and general, i.e., commonplace or banal, ideas. He often seems to be saying that any ideas about class or politics or society that find their way into fiction inevitably become undigested and indigestible lumps of cliché and platitude. But what about all the novelists who acquire a readership and a reputation precisely because their 'general ideas', their visions of the world, are so different from the generally accepted view, both when their work is published and when it is read by subsequent generations? Nabokov's remarks about the 'topical trash' of Balzac, Gorky and Mann and the 'easy platitudes' of D. H. Lawrence indicate what his answer would be, but these are glib dismissals, not arguments. These are authors interested in ideas related to the generality, but what they have to say about these things is particular, not general. And the aesthetic use they make of them is obviously very different: few would want to argue that *Père Goriot, Women in Love*, and *The Magic Mountain* are thesis novels in the sense that Gorky's *Mother* is. I do not want to trade value judgments with Nabokov about these authors; I do want to point out that his case against the 'Literature of Ideas' suffers from not being more carefully formulated. If the 'particular ideas' in his work turn out to concern general questions as seen from his particular point of view, we should not be too surprised. Some of his other statements on this subject are not quite so unequivocal as they first appear either. When he says that ideas given his characters may be 'deliberately flawed'[50] he intends to forestall inquiry, but I think he actually encourages it. What are these ideas? How are they flawed? How do they relate to Nabokov's own views, so forthrightly expressed in his discursive prose? Again, he insists that there are no 'main ideas' in a given novel that could be stated in fewer words than he used to write it;[51] but this is a general idea that has been used by authors to thwart critics for rather a long time now, and it doesn't seem to have prevented many of them from going about their useful business.

Nabokov's claim that art, particularly his art, is of no use whatever to society[52] is another of his absolute aesthetic positions that requires some qualification. Society for him is a group, not of individuals, but of non-individuals. His repeated denials of any satiric intent, for example, constitute his refusal to admit that he could ever be of 'use' to that group, ever tell it some harsh truths about itself or suggest ways in which it might change. (He does admit though that he mocks popular trash in his novels because 'a good laugh is the best pesticide'.)[53] 'Social comment' is anathema to him for the same reason: it means to be 'useful' and his novels are not to be used. If we consider the 'topical trash' trio again, we can see another reason why Balzac, Gorky and Mann were chosen. Marx and Engels used Balzac and his insights into the society of his time for their analysis of socio-economic forces in nineteenth-century Europe. Soviet critics used Gorky to help create the myth of the new Soviet man. Lukács used Mann's *Dr Faustus* to make his case against modernism and the bourgeoisie, and for the triumph of the people's democracies. And yet ... Even Nabokov cannot delimit his fiction in a way that prevents people from reading it as a commentary on human life and from drawing conclusions about the man who wrote it. He maintains that his only purpose in composing his novels is 'aesthetic bliss', and that a book's capacity to instil that feeling in the reader is all that matters.[54] Most readers seem to think otherwise. John Bayley, in an article devoted to some of Nabokov's critical views, puts it well (he has just been discussing Nabokov's contempt for the idea that Gogol was a 'social satirist'):

Art has no job, insists Nabokov. Fine: only it just happens to have done one – in *Lolita* no less than in *Dead Souls*. If Nabokov were not so deliberately combative, he would grant that, instead of insisting that there is only one proper end result – the purr of beatitude. For this is as absurd as saying that art gives us a message. In all great art the message is dissolved in the beatitude; we only know we have received it when we begin to realize how good the work is.[55]

Finally, and perhaps most importantly, we should note that during these decades when Nabokov had the opportunity to speak his mind and when his own fiction became more openly self-reflexive, he offers relatively little support in his literary critical remarks for the 'self-referential linguistic game' theory of his novels. He is perfectly willing to talk about the importance of riddles and deception and insincerity in fiction; but he is reluctant to allow his works to become 'anti-novels', i.e., he does not want them to be used in that way either. Of course this does not prove that they cannot be, but his general attitude to what was happening in fiction in the nineteen sixties and seventies should give pause to those who are set on making Nabokov their ally in the battle over what kind of novel is appropriate in our age. As late as 1966 he told an interviewer that he was not acquainted with the work of Barth or Pynchon.[56] In 1965 he called Updike and Salinger 'by far the finest artists in recent years',[57] and in later years continued to praise their work effusively.[58] Beckett was high on his list, but not for anything he said about the inexpressiveness or impenetrability of art. Nabokov liked the trilogy, particularly *Molloy*, for its 'limpness', but he dismissed the plays as 'wretched'.[59] Although Borges was a favourite for a while, by 1969 Nabokov decided that he was one of those authors who promises more than he delivers.[60] Robbe-Grillet he admired enormously, but thought of him as a psychological novelist, albeit at a certain remove. His theories? 'preposterous'.[61] The French new novel? The stalwart defenders of the *status quo* in France would have been heartened to learn that Nabokov thought its practitioners a bunch of 'banal scribblers whom a phony label assists commercially'.[62] In other words, substantial differences exist between Nabokov's views on fiction and those of some of his famous contemporaries, and critics should ponder the implications of this.

This summary of six decades of Nabokov's criticism suggests that a major reassessment of his ideas about what novels do and what they ought to do is in order. But what about his own novels? In the third section of this chapter, I want to discuss three of them, *Korol'*,

Dama, Valet, Kamera Obskura, and *Otchayanie*,[63] Nabokov's second, sixth, and seventh novels, with a view to discovering whether some of the ideas he expresses so forcefully in his criticism can be found in his fiction, and whether another image of Nabokov that is rather different from the generally accepted one emerges when we read his work with all of his critical precepts in mind. Is there, for instance, a link between the critic who is interested in how a novel expresses the author's vision of a human world or a proposition about the moral health of modern man, and the novelist? Can the self-referential devices in these novels be seen as a means by which he illustrates the fictional nature of fiction *and* as part of a Nabokovian commentary on things as they are? What happens if we insist on placing the emphasis primarily on the content of these novels?

First *Korol', Dama, Valet*. Nabokov's own remarks on this book don't augur well for our attempt. In the Foreword to the English translation, he says he set his novel in Germany in the 1920s because 'the lack of any emotional involvement and the fairytale freedom inherent in an unknown milieu answered my dream of pure invention'(p. vi). Discussions of the novel concentrate on the allusions to literature and the cinema, the presence of the author-equivalents, the puppet-like quality of the characters, the deliberate exposure of the mechanisms of the plot, and on how all these things remind us that the book we hold in our hands is a fiction, Nabokov's 'dream of pure invention'. Andrew Field says that *Korol', Dama, Valet* is not a satire on German life, not Berlin seen through Russian eyes, and that 'any other set of characters could be led over Nabokov's carefully placed chalk marks'.[64] Alfred Appel stresses the importance of the parody, the 'infinite regress' and the 'anthropomorphic deity' at the 'nucleus' of the 'perform-ance'.[65] And L. L. Lee calls it 'in large part, a series of parodies that suggest that all art is irrational'.[66] I do not deny how crucial all the self-referential aspects of Nabokov's novel are for anyone inter-ested in making sense of it, but I don't think they are there simply to remind us of how the artist manipulates his material; nor am I convinced that they prevent us from reading *Korol', Dama, Valet* as an attempt to expose evil in the same way that (say) Dickens does, or as an expression of the author's contempt for certain kinds of people and values.

Take Franz, for example. Why is he as two-dimensional as the image on a court card? So that Nabokov can use him to work out a detailed parody of the *Bildungsroman*? The young provincial who comes to the big city to earn his fortune but never does see the world or learn anything about it could be seen as a comic version of a Julien Sorel or a Rastignac. He is even more plausible as a parody of Dreiser's Clyde Griffiths, another timid, ambitious and dangerous character who plots a murder by drowning, although Nabokov denies any such intention (p. viii).[67] But we do not have to read many pages to realize that satire is the more appropriate word for what Nabokov is usually doing with this character. Franz is his unnatural natural man, uneducated, uncivilized, inarticulate. The physical world is not a place in which he lives, but a chamber of horrors in which he exists, full of grey sandwiches, stained walls, puddles of vomit, discarded condoms, and so on. Sexual desire is not something he feels, but a force that possesses him and occasions a predictable series of squalid consequences. Violence and cruelty are not something he engages in now and then, but the natural expression of his inner essence. Like any good satirist, Nabokov hammers away at the repulsive physicality and automatism of Franz's world to drive home his point about how those with little imagination and no mind are condemned to live. How significant is it that Franz is a German youth? I take up this question of Nabokov and the Germans in more detail in Chapter Three; but for now let me note that his claim that he could have staged the novel in 'Rumania or Holland', and that it was only his knowledge of the geography and the weather of Berlin that determined his choice of a German milieu (p. vi), is somewhat disingenuous. He wants to talk about Germany, its crudity and savagery, telescoped in little vig- nettes like the one about how hard Franz's mother hits him for not wanting to eat the chocolate his sister has licked. In revising *Korol', Dama, Valet* for translation he made it more German and Franz's childhood more violent.[68] The novel is set, not in an imaginary country that happens to be called Germany, but in an alien world which Nabokov himself was obliged to inhabit. 'Germany' is short- hand for 'evil' because this is, on the whole, what he saw in that country. And the appearance of the author *in propria persona*, though it may well remind us that the story is just a fiction, accentuates this distinctly Russian view of the Germans. Nabokov and his wife, the young couple that Franz sees at the dance near the end of the novel, are an irritating mystery for him partly because they are speaking 'a totally incomprehensible language' (pp. 240/254). This suggests the unbridgeable gap separating him and them. Nabokov adds to the English version that the man is 'contemptuous of everything on earth' except the woman he's with (p. 254): Germans were high on that long list.

With Martha, Nabokov takes aim at vulgarity, malevolence and soullessness on a different social level. He wants to deride the convention-bound existence of the wife of a 'wealthy businessman' (p. 36) ('a reasonably wealthy German businessman in the nineteen-twenties' (p. 35) in *King, Queen, Knave*), so he makes Martha a two-dimensional character in a three-dimensional world. We learn about how she decorates her home, treats her servants, dreams about money, decides to commit adultery, and so on. There is parody here, of course, particularly in details like the allusions to *Madame Bovary*: Martha borrows Emma's piano teacher as a cover for her sessions with Franz, and wears Emma's slippers when she visits her lover.[69] But the main reason Nabokov devotes a major part of his novel to this adultery is not to imitate comically one of fiction's stock plots but to depict the sordid nature of their affair; hence Martha's botched attempts at seduction, the messy consummation, the tawdry trysts – all described with a sort of loving horror. Even when he adds to the English version a remark like 'She was no Emma, and no Anna', he follows it up by informing us that Martha is guilty not of adultery but 'harlotry' (p. 101). In this way, Nabokov uses authorial commentary to point out the literary weight on the shoulders of anyone writing this kind of novel in the twentieth century, but he is also making a conventional sort of comment to clear up things for any readers who might be in doubt about where he stands. Martha says something 'softly' (p. 240) in the original; Nabokov removes this adverb in the translation (p. 255): dehumanizing her like this makes her more of a puppet and shows how Nabokov wants to direct our sympathy. But doesn't he underline the fictional status of his murderess at the expense of everything else, especially when he has her die so conveniently at the end? Appel suggests that this death is as corny as her murder plots, Nabokov's deliberate attempt to confound 'the expectations of the old-fashioned reader'.[70] Yet this can also be taken in two ways. Nabokov consulted a doctor in early 1928 about ways of killing off his character,[71] so he must have wanted a certain kind of verisimilitude, and he adds several references to Martha's heart

condition in *King, Queen, Knave* to make the death more plausible.[72] Even without these hints, the increasingly obsessive nature
of her desire to murder a man who simply refuses to be murdered
actually prepares us for her sudden demise. In moral terms her
death is not a shock, not an affront to our expectations at all, but the
obvious conclusion to the straightforward moral logic of the tale.

As a satiric portrait, Martha is somewhat less successfully drawn
than Franz, because the relentless exposure of her shallowness and
villainy makes Nabokov seem rather heavy-handed at times.
Weird, farcical humour gives way to some fairly obvious irony: for
example, Martha's response to the atmosphere in the train: 'It is
supposed to be stuffy in a car; that is customary and therefore good'
(pp. 13/10). The authorial commentary sometimes overmakes a
point: 'Martha really did believe that her marriage was no different
from any other marriage, that discord always reigned, that the wife
always struggled against the husband' (pp. 66/65). One thinks of
Nabokov's remark about Dickens's being too much of an artist to
make things too 'obtrusive or obvious'. The novel's view of the
provincial and the bourgeois is powerfully realized but partial, and
it inevitably reminds us that others have done a better job of what
Nabokov, at least part of the time, is attempting to do here. The
limitations of *Korol', Dama, Valet* are not less real for being
self-imposed. Another problem involves the 'banality of evil'
thesis, which sometimes makes the aesthetic critique of human
depravity read like a critique of a mediocre murder mystery. 'That's
just the point', some of his critics would respond, but criticizing
such things is a delicate business best left to those who really know
the genre. In this case Nabokov is better on human failings than on
literary ones. The links between the hackneyed conventions of
some literature and those of real life are genuine enough, but they
do not take him as far as he wants to go.

What does it mean to see life as an artist sees it? Nabokov uses the
third figure in his trio to provide some tentative answers to this
question. Of course it could be argued that by making Dreyer an
artist figure who tries to create people out of wax and fails dismally,
Nabokov images the novelist's own enterprise here and exposes its
pathetic inadequacy. But even the artist as failure is a positive, vital
figure in this novel, a pointed contrast with Franz and Martha, a
symbol of the kind of life that is opposed to their non-existence. A
sense of humour, a whimsical attitude to making money, an ability

to recognize vulgarity for what it is, a penchant for wondering about the secret professions and desires of passers-by – Nabokov gives his 'King' these qualities to make him sympathetic and different. Yet Dreyer's chief drawback is that the creative imagination that gives him a human dimension is ultimately responsible for confining him to a self-created world of escapist fantasy. For it is of no use to him in the human relations part of real life which is so important in Nabokov: his egocentricity militates against feeling. He registers a strange 'melancholy' that recurs (pp. 223/235, 239/253), but he cannot understand it. He is embarrassed for the off-key singer in the dance hall, but he feels no compassion for her, none of that sympathy which Nabokov praises in Dickens's characters, for example. Without that feeling, the artistic imagination can too easily see life as merely a collection of inchoate designs which it can revise at its leisure, inventing innumerable possibilities but realizing none, turning the lives of others into a romance or a farce or a series of nightmarish adventures as it sees fit. The idea is only touched on in *Korol', Dama, Valet*, but Nabokov was to develop it in *Kamera Obskura* and *Otchayanie*, and all three of these novels lead in the end to *Lolita*.

What can we learn from *Kamera Obskura*, which came out in 1933, and from its substantially revised version, *Laughter in the Dark*, published five years later, by looking at them from a similar standpoint? Germany and Germans once again, the setting and the actors in another portrayal of adultery and degradation, plus the same strange *mésalliance* between the crude natural energy of the provincial and the jaded appetites of the middle class with its unfulfilled yearnings and conventional outlets. Magda is Franz with good skin and some cunning, brought up in the same atmosphere of casual violence by parents with the same almost religious awe for money. Her brother and his friends supply the hoodlum element in the novel's collection of 'naturals' that Magda, for all her viciousness, cannot quite convey. The series of parallels between Martha and Kretschmar, her counterpart in this novel, is even more instructive. Like her, he is delighted at the prospect of unlimited illicit sex, and doomed to discover that this is the key to a happiness that will turn out to be very short-lived. Both of them attempt to repay the 'natural' with a little bourgeois 'civilization': Martha makes doilies for Franz's room; Kretschmar has Magda shave her armpits, and, embarrassed, tries to buy off her bullying brother with a little money. And both end up being loathed and rejected by the object of their desire. He lives the same kind of life, taking as little account of other people's feelings as she does. He dies the same kind of death, destroyed by his own hatred. But Nabokov's exposure of his moral nullity is more subtly managed, and more devastating. Though he plots no murder, he is indirectly responsible for the death of his daughter who, weakened by her illness, comes to the window to look for him, catches a chill and dies. The real condemnation lies, not in this fateful sequence of events, but in Kretschmar's actions once Irma is taken ill. When he learns that she is unwell, he is reluctant to leave his jealous mistress to go to the bedside of the dying girl. And, in one of those 'moment of decision' scenes that Nabokov is so good at depicting, so forcefully does he bring home to us the way in which a seemingly trivial physical movement or act can determine the whole future course of a man's life, Kretschmar chooses not to go to his own daughter's funeral so that he can stay at home and play with his new 'child'.

In this novel, Nabokov makes even clearer the links between desire and violence, sex and death. Magda confesses to having 'deceived' Kretschmar, i.e., lied to him about her background, and he instantly takes this to mean that she has another lover. A revealing reaction, but, more strikingly, this conviction immediately translates itself into a desire to kill her. 'Death', says Kretschmar to himself (p. 68; 'she must die', in *Laughter in the Dark*, p. 64), like some sultan pronouncing sentence on a wayward concubine. All the violence that follows is really a development of this idea, the violence of attempted possession, the violence that turns people into objects, the desire that is corrupt at its very source.[73] We begin to understand why a critic like Adamovich can say that Eros is absent from the world of these novels,[74] if we take Eros to mean something other than the need of certain organs to be stimulated more or less constantly (blind Kretschmar hears the creak of bedsprings coming from Horn's room even at 1:30 in the morning). *Lolita* was to be Nabokov's complex answer to this kind of criticism.

But what about the form of *Kamera Obskura*, all the allusions to and imitations of films, or the way it mimics 'the conventions of the thriller'?[75] How do these things fit in with my view of it as an anatomy of sexual desire and an exposure of moral turpitude? Don't the cinematized lives of the characters make *Kamera Obskura* another parody, in which the author is repeatedly reminding the reader that he (the reader) is 'confronting an imaginary creation that has its own principles of reality that do not ask to be viewed from the same perspective one takes on other aspects of his life?'[76] Has Nabokov so vividly imagined his characters – Kretschmar, working off his wedding ring with his thumb, his hand hidden in his raincoat pocket; Magda, forcing herself to drink the beer which she has paid for so that Otto and his friends will not get any of it – only to undermine their reality by alerting us to its artificial nature? His own comments on the novel do not shed very much light on this problem. He said in one interview that in *Kamera Obskura* 'I tried to express a world in terms as candid, as near to my vision of the world, as I could. If I was cruel, I suppose it was because I saw the world as cruel in those days.'[77] This offers some support for the case I have been making; yet Nabokov has made another comment on the novel that at least partially undercuts this assertion. Appel reports the following exchange between himself and Nabokov about this book: '"It's my poorest novel", he says. "The characters are hopeless clichés." But isn't that part of their characterization? "Yes, perhaps, but I 'succeeded' all too well. They are clichés nonetheless."' Appel concludes that 'Nabokov's low opinion of the novel in all its versions tacitly acknowledges his failure to control or realize fully its "cinematic pattern"',[78] but Nabokov may have meant that the characters were not complex or convincing enough for the cruel 'vision of the world' that he had tried to convey.

I think the function of the self-referential in the novel can be clarified if we consider the major difference between *Korol', Dama, Valet* and *Kamera Obskura*: the principal artist figure is now the 'Knave' rather than the 'King' in this new triangle, and the 'hideous reversions to the wild state' are not the result of the dead soul of convention but of the studied inhumanity of an artist. Horn is clearly a portrait of the artist as indifferent god, toying with his amusing, helpless creatures. As he himself suggests, the old-fashioned God 'understands nothing about the new art' (p. 124; this phrase is omitted in the English version), and that is why he has been superseded by someone who has the power to create a new world according to his own laws. Once again, Nabokov's point is quite clearly a moral one: total detachment and indifference to suffering in the interest of furthering certain 'artistic' designs can lead to a kind of sadism. But some of Nabokov's early critics were troubled by his own cold brilliance and indifference to his characters; *Kamera Obskura* risked alienating them still more. I think he was aware of these dangers and moved to forestall this kind of criticism in two ways: first, by showing his readers a specific example of the forces for good that are pitted against Horn's kind of evil; and second, by contrasting Horn's aesthetic attitudes with those of another artist figure, Segelkranz, and then sharpening the contrast in the revised version which opposes Axel Rex's views on art and Udo Conrad's.

Nabokov's 'candid' vision of a 'cruel' world is counterbalanced by the stress he lays on the simple domestic virtues represented by Kretschmar's family. This is why his wife and child are presented to us with a certain reserve, even a gentleness; why Nabokov notes the way in which Annalisa's pregnancy separates her from her husband's world, making her calm and reflective while he is tormented by strange desires; why he mentions the ability of both mother and child to take 'a quiet delight' in their own existence (pp. 12/12).[79] It is not enough to save them in this novel, but it is what makes people worth saving. Annalisa's brother Max is also singled out for special consideration. We are treated to details of his gloomy love life and scenes from his life as a comfortable burgher, but when he denounces Kretschmar as a scoundrel, he is speaking for Nabokov himself.[80] Those concerned about authorial coldness in the novel should re-read the scene in which this man, 'who had never in his life hit a living creature', catches up with the fleeing Horn and cracks him on the head with Kretschmar's stick (pp. 195/178). Horn's unexpected reaction, an attempt to cover his nakedness, and the explicit allusion to Adam after the Fall help to make clear the significance of what has happened: the artist who has played at being a god is only a man after all, and a remarkably vulnerable one at that. In *Laughter in the Dark*, Nabokov makes Elizabeth and Paul even more sympathetic. Without sentimentalizing or idealizing these figures, he shows us all the ways in which they care about each other, a quiet family gathering in the midst of an orgy of egocentricity.

Nabokov also attempts to forestall criticism with his other artist figure. Segelkranz is as involved in Kretschmar's plight as Horn is detached from it. When he learns that, by reading his friend a sketch which includes a scene between Magda and Horn that he happened to witness, he has informed Kretschmar about the true state of his amatory affairs, Segelkranz groans through clenched teeth, condemns his literary methods, and, unwilling to face Kretschmar, flees to the Pyrenees for a month. When he returns and learns of the accident with the car, he is in such a state of 'nervous terror' that he thinks he is going out of his mind, and tears up his manuscript so violently that he almost dislocates his fingers (p. 177). The implication is that his excessive involvement with the events in which his art has entangled him, his hypertrophied sense of responsibility for Kretschmar's tragedy, is what makes him a good human being but a distinctly minor artist. Nabokov evidently decided that he could use this figure to better advantage. When he revised the novel, he cut out all these details, made his new writer only partly responsible for Albinus's enlightenment, and emphasized not his emotional involvement with the poor victim but his cool detachment. When Albinus, having heard how Margot and Axel Rex behaved on the bus, rushes off to find and kill his mistress, Udo Conrad simply says: 'I wonder whether I haven't committed some blunder', and reflects on the 'nasty rhyme' (p. 143). Even before this he displays his detachment, not just from Albinus's problems, but from those of Humanity in general. Here he strikes some familiar notes. The writer who contends that 'when a literature subsists almost exclusively on Life and Lives, it means it is dying', who doesn't like Freudian novels, who is incensed to see 'the books that are being taken seriously' (p. 139) – this is clearly an authorial self-portrait. But how do these attitudes differ from those of a Horn who professes complete indifference to the sufferings of the guinea-pigs whose plight he is asked to publicize with his cartoons, or from those of an Axel Rex who particularly enjoys the ingenious cruelty of the practical jokes life plays on people? The difference is this: a commitment to aesthetic objectivity can produce a Robert Horn/Axel Rex, but it doesn't have to. It can also produce a writer like Udo Conrad, who can view the world with detachment (unlike Segelkranz), but is able to see it in other ways as well. This attitude is only one of the tools of an artist, something he can use to write novels about conjurers and vanishing tricks, as we are told Conrad does, or to write one like *Kamera Obskura/ Laughter in the Dark*, in which one artist's objectivity is analyzed and judged by an author who sees the potential dangers of the aesthetic attitude.

I have to admit that I am not quite convinced by my own argument here. Nabokov's case for aesthetic objectivity is less vividly realized than the cruelty. The ability to feel compassion is a positive in his view of the world, but it is also what makes people the helpless victims of fate's pitiless manipulations, which, as he often reminds us, are the author's manipulations dressed up in the guise of fate. With this novel, Nabokov forces us to think up explanations like the ones I just propounded to rationalize the attractiveness of aesthetic representations of suffering. This is of course where the 'Nabokov stresses the non-referential, fable-like aspects of the novel to release us from these concerns' argument comes in. Yet isn't that to take the easy way out, to assume he has nothing to tell us about the potential cruelty of the objective attitude in both author and reader? Consider a 1928 poem of his called 'The Wasp':

> Your armour, yellow and brilliant,
>   I pierced with a pin
> and I heard your cry ascending,
>   your utterly transparent hum.
>
> With blunt scissors the sting
>   I pinched – and here
> I cut it off ... How you began to drone,
>   how your abdomen arched!
>
> Now the buzzing was thick,
>   and the wings more quickly
> I snipped off, almost without a crunch,
>   at their very roots.
>
> And the noiseless body
>   stretched out six legs
> Turned like a goggle-eyed head ...
>   And I lit a match, –
>
> – to see how you would thrash about [*vskipish' burlivo*],
>   as soon as I raised the flame ...
> Thus a patient boy torments
>   a beautiful wasp;
>
> Thus, sharpening hearing and vision,
>   cutting up, plucking at [*terebya*], –
> – My living inspiration,
>   I tormented you![81]

I think Nabokov plays with the reader here by shocking him first with an account of methodical sadism and then with the audacity of the conceit. An early exercise in self-referentiality, perhaps, but it works only because the torments are imagined so vividly. So too in *Kamera Obskura*: the author sometimes treats his characters as the boy does the wasp; the reader is shocked by the suffering, but he enjoys the account of Kretschmar's anguish in the same way that he enjoys the cool accuracy of the epithets and the suspense in the poem. When Nabokov reminds us of these things he does it, not to resolve the tension, but to make us think.

Appel suggests that *Laughter in the Dark*, which has sold more copies than any Nabokov novel except *Lolita*, is popular because 'Nabokov's own attitude toward its popular ingredients was not sufficiently highlighted by irony or parody.'[82] But I think Nabokov's attitude to 'popular ingredients' throughout his career was always more ambivalent than this implies. He uses them in this novel to tell a story about a certain kind of obsessive desire and about the different ways in which human experience can be aestheticized. The inevitability of the development, the vitality of the embodiment, and the range of questions raised by the novel's content are not examples of his pandering to low-brow tastes, but a challenge to elitist assumptions about his fiction.

Does Nabokov's next novel, *Otchayanie*, take up the same problems and shed some new light on them? Are we right to see it as primarily a psychological study of considerable power, a refinement of his ideas about evil and the aesthetic attitude, and a portrayal of another of those 'hideous reversions to the wild state' he mentions in his Dickens lectures? If such a view is defensible, how does it square with critics' claims that in this novel 'The essential thing is how the artist's memory associates objects and events, how it shapes *Despair* itself',[83] and that it is 'a compendium of parody' in which 'Nabokov's constant flirtation with the tour de force most closely approaches a full-blown affair'?[84] Or perhaps this either/or formulation is itself misleading?

Let us begin by looking more closely at this problem of the relation between Nabokov's novel and previous literature. In 1939, Jean-Paul Sartre wrote a review of *Despair* in which he accuses the author of being a spiritual and artistic descendant of Dostoevsky, discontent with the old ways of writing novels but unable to create new ones: 'He mocks at the devices of the classical novel', says Sartre, 'but in the end he himself uses the same ones.'[85] Nabokov's critics have given this review a rough ride. Field calls it 'a splendidly low watermark in the critical literature on Nabokov and on Russian

émigré writing in general'.[86] More recently, Stephen Suagee has
suggested that Sartre, with his 'carefree invocation of weighty
ideas', completely missed the point of *Despair*.[87] Both critics' point
is that Nabokov has found other 'devices'; that he has used parody
to liberate himself from the 'classical novel'; and that, far from
being a spiritual descendant of Dostoevsky, he is a novelist who
mocks the emotional excesses and the philosophizing of his Russian
forebear by giving us a comic imitation of a Dostoevskian novel.
And not just Dostoevsky: Field goes so far as to claim that *Despair*
is actually Nabokov's critique of the traditional novel's most basic
assumptions, that Hermann's idea of re-creating himself in the form
of another man is 'an allegory of the absurd pretension of realistic,
"representational" art'.[88] I want to argue that Sartre's view of the
novel is not patently ridiculous, and that the defenders of *Despair*
are at least as misleading about its relation to previous literature as
he is.

To clarify this question of the effect of the self-referential in the
novel, let us try a brief comparison. Here is Hermann Karlovich,
Nabokov's acutely self-conscious hero:

> March 31st. Night.
> Alas, my tale degenerates into a diary. There is nothing to be done, though;
> for I have grown so used to writing, that now I am unable to desist. A diary,
> I admit, is the lowest form of literature. Connoisseurs will appreciate that
> lovely, self-conscious, falsely significant 'Night' (meaning readers to
> imagine the sleepless variety of literary persons, so pale, so attractive). But
> as a matter of fact it *is* night at present.   (pp. 199/218)

– and here is one of the 'pale', 'literary' figures, also at the end of his
story, from John Barth's *Lost in the Funhouse*:

> O God comma I abhor self-consciousness. I despise what we have come to;
> I loathe our loathsome loathing, our place our time our situation, our
> loathsome art, this ditto necessary story. The blank of our lives. It's about
> over. Let the *dénouement* be soon and unexpected, painless if possible,
> quick at least, above all soon.[89]

In this story by Barth, literary self-consciousness reaches its limits.
The baggage of traditional fiction is now an intolerable burden, a
bunch of old words, and the reaction against it seems equally
unattractive. New art is still-born from this futility. In the excerpt
from *Despair*, literature is not a stultifying weight but a frame which
gives words a context and a meaning. The word 'Night' looks rather

hackneyed in the old frame but Hermann needs it, so he revivifies a cliché by putting a new frame around it. The reader is left with a complex double awareness: the referential function of words is questioned but not abolished; the voice that articulates its own dilemma forces us to attend to it. The problem with talking about the pre-eminence of parody in Nabokov or about his exposure of the 'absurd pretension' of representational art is that one makes (relatively) early Nabokov sound like late Barth, and one forgets about this voice and the strange, hypnotic cadences that keep us constantly in the grip of a maniacal story-teller, trying to fathom him and the world he creates for us. This is why I think Sartre is at least partly right in relating Nabokov to the *roman classique*. Sartre goes wrong in assuming that Nabokov wants to free himself from all the old devices, but he is right to say that he uses them.

Of course even the sound of a human voice that I have been praising is an illusion, and Hermann himself remarks on the spurious sense of intimacy created by this 'fictitious' device (pp. 43/53). But this is the least interesting thing about it. In *Korol', Dama, Valet* and *Kamera Obskura*, we saw how figures outwardly resembling people gradually reveal themselves to be mere collections of violent impulses. In the end they are all deprived of language: Martha delirious, Franz emitting hideous laughter, Kretschmar rendered almost inarticulate on the telephone by the knowledge that Magda is in the flat, and condemned to play the last scene in pantomime with his intended victim. In *Otchayanie*, Nabokov takes the same instincts, the sexual desire that has gone awry, the nonchalant cruelty, the twisted desire for peace and harmony that turns out to be a kind of death wish, gives them to a civilized subject and charts his progress. The result is just as disastrous, but in this novel there can be no silence. For Hermann, with his hyperactive imagination and his love–hate affair with words, always has something else to say. The Russian version of the novel ends with 'How about opening the window and making a little speech' (p. 202), the English, with that speech itself (p. 222). It is not only Nabokov's 'representational art', the skill with which he re-creates that voice and the character it speaks for, that makes the novel so impressive, but also the scornful and derisive and enormously entertaining view of the world that it articulates. Hermann's detailed meditations on all sorts of human conduct and ideas – the scatterbrained nature of a bourgeois housewife; the parasitic existence of a bohemian artist and his set; the avarice, amorality, stupidity, and sentimentality of another Nabokovian 'common man'; the plebeian swarm awaiting us in the Christian version of heaven – these, together with his descriptions of the strange phenomena and objects in his unnatural world, twisted out of true by the nature of his obsession, are the very source of the novel's driving energy and of its claims to greatness.

When we consider these things and add to them the scrupulous attention to everyday speech and gesture, the sequence of events involving a human conflict and its resolution, the recognizable albeit somewhat nightmarish setting, the pre-eminent concern with the presentation of character, we can see just how committed to the representation of a world Nabokov is in this novel. This at any rate is what Tom Stoppard and Rainer Werner Fassbinder evidently decided when they went to work on the movie version of *Despair*. The parodic allusions to literature are still there ('Too bitter or not too bitter? that is the problem', says Hermann about his chocolate at one point), but the drama plays itself out against a real-life background of economic chaos, Nazi brutality, and social unrest. Although there are few specific references to such things in the novel, if we open it at random, we inevitably come upon some detail from one of Hermann's weird encounters or monologues that helps create the same kind of atmosphere that Fassbinder, with his overt social and political references, seeks to convey. He was right to take the novel seriously.

But what about Dostoevsky? Surely here Sartre has missed the point, since Nabokov has not imitated the Russian writer but in various places written a quite deliberate parody of him, which makes Nabokov a curious spiritual descendant indeed. Yet I wonder whether the influence of Dostoevsky on Nabokov's novel can be dismissed so easily. Consider the following excerpt from Nabokov's lectures on him (*LRL*, pp. 106–7):

when an artist sets out to explore the motions and reactions of a human soul under the unendurable stresses of life, our interest is more readily aroused and we can more readily follow the artist as our guide through the dark corridors of that human soul if that soul's reactions are of a more or less all-human variety . . . We can hardly accept as human reactions those of a raving lunatic or a character just come out of a madhouse and just about to return there.[90]

By this criterion, Nabokov insists, Dostoevsky and his epileptics, hysterics, and psychopaths stand condemned. Even if we want to quarrel with this reading of Dostoevsky, it may provide an insight into the problem Nabokov set himself in *Otchayanie*: how to write a novel about a madman, guide us 'through the dark corridors of that human soul', and make the result relevant to human experience in a way that, in his opinion, Dostoevsky had not succeeded in doing. But this particular Russian novelist is not to be laid to rest so easily. Nabokov rejects 'the ghastly *Crime and Punishment* rigmarole',[91] the whole idea that a horrible crime might be profoundly significant for our understanding of human nature; and yet Hermann's assertions of individual freedom, his rejection of his society's system of values in favour of the one that he will create, and his ability to use his perverse intelligence to confound our theories about him, involve us just as surely in the areas of human character that Dostoevsky explores.

Furthermore, Nabokov's murderer inspires as many different feelings in the reader as someone like Raskolnikov does. Of course Hermann is a villain, and Nabokov wants us to hold him in utter contempt. The murder scene makes this very clear. The painstaking detail with which all of Felix's gestures and movements are described just before Hermann shoots him is there to accentuate the difference between a human being and a 'murder victim'. Like George Orwell, who in an essay on capital punishment writes about how, on seeing a man being led to the gallows step aside to avoid a puddle, he realized what is so abhorrent about killing a human being,[92] Nabokov wants us to visualize what taking someone's life actually means, right down to the shuffling motions of the dying man in the snow. This death is very different from Martha's off-stage removal, and even Kretschmar's death is 'staged', inevitable, acceptable in a way that Felix's is not. Its ugly reality reveals Hermann's artistic aspirations for what they are, part of an insane attempt to impose an aesthetic pattern on real life, a 'beastly reversion to the wild state' by a man as unfeeling as Robert Horn. Nabokov puts the moral in the mouth of the murderer's victim, the simple truth which mad Hermann cannot see, that one man is not the same as another. As G. M. Hyde observes, the novel suggests 'the moral pattern inevitably enacted by true art (Nabokov has no false modesty about making this claim for his work) in total disregard of the immoral pretensions of the bogus artist-hero'.[93] And yet . . . The same Felix dismisses philosophy, religion, and poetry (and presumably morality) as inventions of the rich, and the elegance and skill with which Hermann conducts the case for the defence makes his view of things a potent adversary for the simple truth his story tells. Besides, Nabokov's 'true art' is inextricably bound up with the scorn he gives to his 'bogus artist-hero', and what liberates his imaginative powers is the portrayal of energetic evil. Having finished a book like *Despair*, we feel his contempt for Hermann, yet it is hard not to sense that the novelist feels an instinctive sympathy for the confidence trickster he has created. In this regard, I was struck by something Nabokov said in an interview about how much he would have liked to have been a reporter covering the Charles Manson trial: 'I have a taste for case histories', he added, 'and it would have interested me greatly to look for one spark of remorse in that moronic monster and his moronic beast girls.'[93] This is the moral Nabokov speaking. 'Moron' is an ethical term in his work: with it, he expresses his abhorrence for what Manson did, and reiterates his assertion that all brutal crime is unutterably banal. But I suspect that what intrigued him so much about Manson was that he was not a moron, not a crude, dull, willing-to-go-along killer like Franz, but a madman like Hermann, a figure who had a magnetic attractiveness and who tried to reshape the world according to his own fantasies.

There is more to be said about these novels, but I hope with these observations to have made a case for the approach I have chosen. In the next chapter, I want to study in more detail Nabokov's vision of good and evil, and the forms he chose to embody that vision. In the political satires, he anatomizes the 'hideous reversions to the wild state' that affect a whole society.

2

Invitation to a Beheading and *Bend Sinister*

Nabokov took two different positions on the political content of *Priglashenie Na Kazn'* and *Bend Sinister*. In the Foreword to the translation of the first, *Invitation to a Beheading*, he calls it a 'violin in a void' (p. 7), and denies that it has anything in common with the works of 'popular purveyors of illustrated ideas and publicistic fiction' (p. 5).[1] Enlarging upon this theme in the Introduction to *Bend Sinister*, he scoffs at 'literature of social comment', insists that he has no satiric or didactic purpose, and adds that the influence of the epoch upon his book has been 'negligible'.[2] In both the Foreword and the Introduction, George Orwell is singled out as the sort of mediocre novelist whose clichés are just what Nabokov has taken great pains to avoid. The other position is exemplified by Nabokov's claim that *Invitation to a Beheading* depicts a 'Communazist state' which persecutes 'a rebel' by putting him in prison,[3] and by his description of both novels as 'absolutely final indictments of Russian and German totalitarianism'.[4] Émigré critics are similarly divided. Some, like Sergey Osokin[5] and Georgy Adamovich,[6] think that Nabokov does have a satiric purpose in *Invitation to a Beheading*, but are not convinced that it has been realized. Others endorse his first position: Khodasevich, for example, talks about the events of the novel as 'the play of devices and images that fill the creative consciousness or, rather, the creative delirium' of the central character, and suggests that its ending represents 'the return of the artist from creative work to reality'.[7] More recent critics of both novels tend to avoid any detailed discussion of them as social or political commentary, treating them instead, if not as 'violins in a void', at least as works that are essentially about something other than twentieth-century politics.[8] D. Barton Johnson says in one article that *Invitation to a Beheading* is 'about language and art, literature and the *littérateur*'.[9] Julia Bader insists that 'the artistic imagination combining and recombining its themes' is the 'main subject' of *Bend Sinister*, adding that its events may be just the hero's 'bad dreams'.[10] And Alfred Appel has suggested that in both novels Nabokov develops the absurd logic of the police state 'into an extreme and fantastic metaphor for the imprisonment of the mind, thus making consciousness, rather than politics, the subject of these novels'.[11] Other critics have concentrated on the element of play in these works. 'We *must* treat as a joke, an indulgence, novels like . . . *Invitation to a Beheading*, where reality is a stage-set which ultimately crumbles to nothing', writes Mark Lilly in a collection of articles about Nabokov's work published in 1979.[12] And in the special number of *Modern Fiction Studies* devoted to him, David Sheidlower, discussing the chess-game patterns in *Bend Sinister*, justifies his approach this way: 'If we choose to read a Nabokov novel and are willing to deal with it on the author's terms, then he rewards us by planting meaning in his details which produce satisfying solutions to the literary puzzles which he has devised.'[13] Even Robert Merrill, in an article written to deplore the excessive emphasis on Nabokov the artificer and puppeteer, confines his commentary on *Invitation to a Beheading* and *Bend Sinister* to a consideration of the formal effects Nabokov orchestrates to expose the artificiality of his creations, and concludes that 'these two novels read rather like medieval dream-visions, or even fantasies'.[14] What follows is an attempt, not to refute everything these critics have to say about the novels, but to make a case for a view with a different emphasis. The consensus seems to be that if Nabokov's novels are the 'final indictments' he says they are there is not much more to be said about that particular aspect of them. I think there is, and most of this chapter is devoted to saying it.

Before proceeding with that, I want to take up the question of what effect the form of the novels actually has on their subject matter. Obviously Nabokov has distanced himself from the traditional novelist in many important ways, and the critics I have just mentioned have explored in great detail what these ways are. They often see Nabokov's 'flaunting of artifice'[15] as his attempt to break with the nineteenth-century novel and its restrictive conventions. Ellen Pifer, for example, argues that 'For Nabokov, the "so-called 'realism' of old novels" falsely promotes average reality as though it were true reality.' Or again: 'Because Nabokov does not seek to make his literary artifice continuous with natural laws, he can make distinctions that are unavailable to the realist. He does not have to credit average reality, or its approximation, with "real, authentic" reality.'[16] This idea of the old-fashioned novelist, confined to reproducing the stock perceptions and generally uninspired existence of some moribund majority, may seem a rather limited one; but it does have the explicit support of Nabokov, since he encourages in the novels themselves this distinction between what he does and what a mere realist does. In *Invitation to a Beheading*, one of the books in the prison library that Cincinnatus reads is *Quercus*, the biography of an oak, and an account of all the historic events it has witnessed over some six hundred years:

> It seemed as though the author were sitting with his camera somewhere among the topmost branches of the Quercus, spying out and catching his prey. Various images of life would come and go, pausing among the green macules of light. The normal periods of inaction were filled with scientific descriptions of the oak itself, from the viewpoints of dendrology, ornithology, coleopterology, mythology – or popular descriptions, with touches of folk humour. Among other things there was a detailed list of all the initials carved in the bark with their interpretations. And, finally, no little attention was devoted to the music of the waters, the palette of sunsets, and the behaviour of the weather.   (pp. 125–6/111–12)[17]

Robert Alter remarks that this novel is

> the *reductio ad absurdum* of the naturalistic novel and of the principle of exhaustive documentary realism ... Such photographic realism, in other words, is mindless, formless, pointless, infinitely tedious, devoid of honesty. It denies imagination, spontaneity, the shaping power of human consciousness; subverting everything art should be, it produces the perfect novel of a totalitarian world.[18]

But photographic realism is 'mindless, formless, pointless', etc. only in Nabokov's exaggerated version of it. It could just as easily be, like a great photograph, intelligent, sensitively composed, richly significant, and so on. *Quercus* is approved by the management of the prison; but it can hardly be 'the perfect novel of a totalitarian world', which title must surely be reserved for tracts about tractors and kolkhozes and the importance of fulfilling quotas, or novels that analyze society in a way that enables the revolutionary masses to draw the politically correct conclusions. If with *Quercus* Nabokov takes aim at 'documentary realism' he misses his target. Marx preferred Balzac to Zola, and Lenin would have thought *Quercus* as tedious and irrelevant as Nabokov does.

Bend Sinister continues this commentary on realistic art. The 'white-bearded waltwhitmanesque' (p. 85) painter working at his sunset the morning after he began it, filling in what he was unable to complete, copies real life in much the same way that the author of *Quercus* does, but he too ends up with dead art. The sunset is the artist's cliché, and the wrong aesthetic creates nothing but a banal after-image. Besides, the man who resembles the writer whose credo committed the poet to 'flood himself with the immediate age as with vast oceanic tides'[19] is doubly mocked, since he paints on in blithe ignorance of the real-life drama going on around him: on one side a grieving couple, on the other a student leader being criticized for his cowardice. The novel's other direct comment on realistic art is more tendentious. It comes while Krug is looking through a collection of odd bits of information he once made for an essay:

> Speaking of Roman *venationes* (shows with wild beasts) of the same epoch [the first century A.D.], we note that the stage, on which ridiculously picturesque rocks (the later ornaments of 'romantic' landscapes) and an indifferent forest were represented, was made to rise out of the crypts below the urine-soaked arena with Orpheus on it among real lions and bears with gilded claws; but this Orpheus was acted by a criminal and the scene ended with a bear killing him, while Titus or Nero, or Paduk, looked on with that complete pleasure which 'art' shot through with 'human interest' is said to produce.   (p. 138)

Important to note here is the unusual use of the phrase 'human interest'. We normally associate it with journalistic endeavours to supply athletes or astronauts with a family and a background so that they seem more human to those who follow their exploits. But Nabokov evidently wants it to stand for any kind of art in which real life impinges too crudely on our sensibilities. Yet his colourful example should not distract us from the rather large gaps in the argument here. The digression on Roman amusements is a condemnation of the obscenity of a pseudo-art in which the potential cruelty of hyper-aestheticism is fully realized. We take his point, but it is a more limited one than he wants us to believe.

I do not think it is surprising that these forays into literary criticism are so inconclusive. We saw in the last chapter how varied Nabokov's actual views are on these matters, and how often the novels qualify his more absolute declarations about what he is doing in his own fiction. *Invitation to a Beheading* and *Bend Sinister* are no different. For sooner or later we have to come to terms with the fact that they resemble the traditional novel in some crucial ways, and that these resemblances are finally much more important than the literary critical discussions in the novels themselves. Like the traditional novelist, Nabokov has organized his material around the unfolding of a series of events in which human conflict, psychology, and motives play a central role. Let us dwell on this rather obvious point for a moment; it may compel us to regard the effect of our author's formal innovation rather differently.

Consider Nabokov's problems in writing these two books. He starts with a hero against whom a vast array of forces is lined up, but these forces are, in human terms, extremely negligible. This is a rich source of comedy, but it makes for a paucity of serious dramatic scenes and a potential lack of conflict. Most of the time the main character is isolated: Cincinnatus usually refuses to talk to anyone, and Krug stays just as aloof. Both are potentially tragic figures, yet Nabokov's tragic options are limited. All the emotions required – indignation or pride or defiance – depend on the hero's acquiring the kind of stature that is difficult to generate in these circumstances. Nabokov solves his problem by focussing his narrative, staying inside the head of his character in order to communicate his ideas and emotions. For every instance in which Nabokov reminds us that his hero is only a puppet, there are a dozen in which he stresses his human complexity. He often does this simply by having him look at some object and respond to what he is seeing. The energy and richness of the descriptions that result inevitably become associated with the hero's response. Their metaphors are his emotions, and the Nabokov style the index of his perceptiveness and sensitivity, the symbol of his humanity itself.

Here are some examples of how this works. Take this passage from *Invitation to a Beheading*, in which Nabokov uses an exotic image of something precious but remote to express his hero's sense of yearning, a desire whose hopelessness is transposed for the reader by the imaginative richness of its expression:

stol podnimalsya, kak pologaya almaznaya gora, i v tumanakh plafonnoi zhivopisi puteshestvovala mnogorukaya lyustra, plachas', luchas', ne na-khodya pristanishcha.   (p. 182)

the table seemed to slope up like a diamond mountain, and the many-armed chandelier journeyed through the mists of plafond art, shedding tears, shedding beams, in vain search of a landing.   (p. 171)

In the Russian this chandelier is, like Cincinnatus, looking for a *pristanishche*, a 'refuge' or 'haven', not a 'landing'; and *luchit'sya* is usually used for eyes, which, again, humanizes the non-human in a way that 'to shed beams' does not. But the main effect in both versions is the same: the images characterize the observer, evoking his desire to escape and his preoccupation with a strange beauty that transcends the banality surrounding him. Although critics have argued that similar passages in *Bend Sinister* are actually part of Nabokov's self-referential game, because by drawing attention to the author's style they suggest 'that the mode of telling, rather than the tale itself, must remain our proper focus',[20] in that novel too they can be seen as a means of creating the kind of 'human interest' Nabokov approves of. The first chapter provides a whole series of examples. It begins with Krug's looking at the view from a hospital window:

An oblong puddle inset in the coarse asphalt; like a fancy footprint filled to the brim with quicksilver; like a spatulate hole through which you can see the nether sky. Surrounded, I note, by a diffuse tentacled black dampness where some dull dun dead leaves have stuck. Drowned, I should say, before the puddle had shrunk to its present size.   (p. 5)

Sentence fragments for mental fragments, giving the impression that perception is somehow free, that the details are just being reported, not forced into specific relations and syntactic units immediately. But the flurry of metaphors is already suggesting a whole matrix of relations. In fact, the language is so metaphorical it implies that all those mental associations are 'out there', that the commonsense assumption about reality as a collection of neutrally perceived hard objects is a public fiction, created to limit the spread of metaphorical seeing. Critics have made much of the role of fantasy in *Invitation to a Beheading* and *Bend Sinister*, fantasy meaning 'a whimsical or visionary notion or speculation' (*OED*). But both works offer sustained examples of another kind of fantasy, the one which, in scholastic psychology, meant the 'mental apprehension of an object of perception', or 'the faculty by which this is performed' (*OED*). It often seems as if Nabokov is determined to bring the old and the new meaning together. How, he asks himself, can I prove that the fantastical imagination is actually a part of the perceptual process? Those leaves are 'shuddering three-legged bathers coming at a run for a swim' (p. 5), that line of lights is 'a metrical incandescence with every foot rescanned and prolonged by reflections' (p. 9). And to those who say that this leisurely opening *tour de force* is Nabokov's way of demonstrating

how unimportant the story in *Bend Sinister* actually is, we can reply
that Nabokov is getting on with the story. Look again at that
opening paragraph, the skilful play of imitative rhythms in 'diffuse
tentacled black dampness', the monotonous beat of those 'dull dun
dead leaves', the rhymed finality of 'surrounded' and 'drowned'.
All these underline the fragility of Krug's emotional state and hint
at his menaced position. Far from being mere static virtuosity, the
whole scene works dramatically because the repetition of seemingly
disconnected impressions begins to create considerable tension, a
tension finally confirmed by the telegram Nabokov sends the
reader – 'The operation has not been successful and my wife will
die' (p. 6) – in the middle of Krug's musings.

The point is that even at his most self-conscious Nabokov is
involved in some kind of representation. In another scene in *Bend
Sinister*, Krug, dreaming of his youth, finds himself in an old
classroom, unprepared for an exam. A demonstration is arranged
for one of the questions. It turns out to be his dead wife, taking off
her jewels after a ball. She removes her necklace, and the narrative
voice makes an oblique allusion to de Maupassant's 'Le Collier'.[21]
Then she removes her head; and Krug, faced with the prospect of
her complete disintegration and simultaneously aware that his
dream has changed her into a 'tall cold stripteaser', wakes up 'with a
horrible qualm' (p. 74). Maurice Couturier notes that the 'phenomenon of writing' is in the ascendant here, that all these 'stories'
could not exist in the head of a single subject, and concludes: 'one
has to fall back on the text and say that it is in it that everything
happens. It does not mimic nor does it represent anything.'[22] And
yet, this is a classic anxiety dream that conveys useful information
about the psychological distress of the hero, telling us, for example,
that in his mind the horror of death is linked with sexual fears and
fear of failure.[23] The different voices and the bizarre details may
remind us that we are reading a fiction, but they also mimic dream
dislocations. The world that all this self-referential language points
to will not go away.

But what about explicit authorial interference at the end of both
novels? Doesn't this reveal the fictionality of what we had taken to
be real and clearly establish these texts as fabulations, inventions –
anything but representations of a world? After all, *Invitation to a
Beheading* ends with Cincinnatus walking off a disintegrating stage-
set; and *Bend Sinister* concludes in the author's own room, where

Nabokov himself muses about the significance of his invented ending and signs off with an enigmatic phrase, 'A good night for mothing' (p. 211), which many no doubt read as 'A good night for nothing', i.e., a good night for finishing a book about nothing by making the reader aware that that is all he is holding in his hands. Once again, I would argue that our responses to such manipulations are various and contradictory. The Greeks must have watched the conclusion of a Euripides play thinking that the author needed the *deus ex machina* to get him out of a tight spot, without supposing for a moment that its intervention effectively cancelled all their earlier responses to the play. There is no reason to suppose that our reaction to Nabokov's endings is necessarily different. He has put a special frame around his narrative, one that requires the critic to change the form of some of his standard questions about the depiction of human life but leaves the relevance of those questions unchanged.

So if the novel's content is not completely undermined by its mode of presentation, we are presumably entitled to ask how the author uses that content to communicate something about the subject he has chosen. Do the novels present us with a set of attitudes or ideas that can be retrieved and discussed as 'the author's'? Someone like Couturier, the author of the first full-length study of Nabokov in French and a critic influenced by recent developments in French criticism, is not very encouraging about the prospects of such an attempt. He says:

There certainly was at one time an author who, in a burst of inspired madness, composed this text and provided us with all the materials on the basis of which our practise is developed, but this personage is forever inaccessible to us, so complex and contradictory are the materials which he has scattered on our way. It would be madness to try to reconstruct his discourse.[24]

And Nabokov claims that 'There exist few things more tedious than a discussion of general ideas inflicted by author or reader upon a work of fiction.'[25]

Keeping these warnings in mind, I have tried in what follows to 'reconstruct' a Nabokov 'discourse'. The discussion is divided into three sections. In the first, I suggest that both novels implicitly defend a certain social class and the set of social attitudes that belongs to it; in the second, that Nabokov repeatedly involves himself in the most direct way with the important figures and events of twentieth-century history; and in the last part, I argue that, far from presenting us with a madcap fantasy and inviting us to accept it as the product of some 'inspired madness', Nabokov endorses all kinds of moral norms which will make him seem surprisingly old-fashioned to some, reassuringly humane to others.

I begin with a passage from *Speak, Memory* about the role played by leisure in the evolutionary scheme of things (the 'you' is Nabokov's wife Vera):

'Struggle for life' indeed! The curse of battle and toil leads man back to the boar, to the grunting beast's crazy obsession with the search for food. You and I have frequently remarked upon that maniacal glint in a housewife's scheming eye as it roves over food in a grocery or about the morgue of a butcher's shop. Toilers of the world, disband! Old books are wrong. The world was made on a Sunday.[26]

A clever inversion, and we want to believe it, so persuasively and charmingly has Nabokov proposed his counter-revolutionary project. It is not, as conventional wisdom has it, the search for food that makes men struggle and fight to earn a living; it is that unseemly battle which makes them less than human, mere toilers. Only two kinds of man could argue like this: a member of the leisure class or someone skilled enough to live by his wits. Nabokov was both. Behind these remarks stand the land-owning ancestors in fifteenth-century Russia, the German barons on his grandmother's side of the family, the grandfather who was offered the title of Count by Alexander the Third, the Nabokov country estate at Vyra, the childhood holidays in Biarritz, the servants, the inheritance of property worth millions of dollars at the age of sixteen. In the years of exile he lived by his wits. They were hard years; but Nabokov managed to get by as a teacher and a writer, until America gave him a modicum of security and *Lolita* restored him to the style of life to which he had once been accustomed. I mention these well-known biographical facts here because they remind us that Nabokov was a special case. For the majority of people the evil is not the battle or the toil, but material conditions that turn men into beasts. And the world of long hours of dull work and a little time off is still more of a reality for the rest than Nabokov's tempting creation.

What does all this have to do with the novels? Nabokov's heroes are sometimes allowed to borrow various things from their creator's lineage, but Cincinnatus is not an aristocrat. Quite the opposite: he is the son of 'a tramp' or 'a fugitive' (pp. 134/121) and a midwife, grows up in the suburbs, and marries a factory girl. Or is he? His father's identity is actually unknown, and mysterious births usually augur well for fictional characters, particularly those who, like Cincinnatus, feel somehow out of place in surroundings everybody else takes for granted. More importantly, he has dreams of a world 'ennobled, spiritualized' (pp. 97/82), where 'time takes shape according to one's pleasure' (pp. 99/85), and where children wander and play in magic gardens. In the sections devoted to Leshino in *The Gift* and to Vyra in *Speak, Memory*, this golden age and these special gardens find their full expression. About Krug's childhood we learn only a few nightmare details, but the adolescence of the woman he loves is re-created in one of his reveries:

You crossed the porch; stopped; gently worked open the glass door by means of your elbow; made your way past the caparisoned grand piano, traversed the sequence of cool carnation-scented rooms, found your aunt in the *chambre violette* –
I think I want to have the whole scene repeated. Yes, from the beginning. (p. 120)

The scene is repeated, in other novels, other stories: she is walking through the Nabokov house, carrying a hawk moth back to another Nabokov garden. These are odds and ends, but they are part of a coherent pattern whose significance is clear. Once upon a time there was a garden, and a cool house, and a warm summer. Children played there and grew up slowly. Then there was a fall and they were ejected. They succeeded well enough in their new world, although they always felt out of place in it and dreamed of getting back to the one they had lost. In the end they could not, but a unique combination of imagination and desire made it possible to 'get back' by re-creating it in a medium where 'time takes shape according to one's pleasure'. Nabokov did not think much of 'mythic criticism', but this myth, with its suggestion both of triumphant recovery and the difficult acceptance of inevitable loss, informs everything he wrote.

Its consequences in *Invitation to a Beheading* and *Bend Sinister* are not just a few autobiographical details and some vague parallels. Both Nabokov's view of society and his view of human nature are influenced by it. What does it mean to talk about the myth of the Fall in Nabokov's view of society? Two things: first, that his hero embodies many of the qualities of the pre-lapsarian world. He displays a childlike sense of awe about the mysteries that surround him; his goodness makes him a trifle naïve about certain kinds of evil; and he has a special relationship with his creator. And second, that this figure finds himself in a fallen world, which Nabokov anatomizes with great skill and considerable aristocratic disdain. The chief representative of this world is the average man. He is practically everyone and everywhere in *Invitation to a Beheading*: M'sieur Pierre, the prison director, the civic officials, Cincinnatus's in-laws – all these and others combine to give the reader a composite portrait. He is a philistine in his artistic tastes, a glutton in his culinary ones, hopelessly vulgar, sexually warped, pathologically obsessed with conforming, fantastically insensitive to the reality of suffering and death. But what does it mean to say that the novel is an attack on the 'fallen world' or 'the average'? Are these figures supposed to represent Nabokov's view of a certain aspect of human society, or are they just the ghoulish inhabitants of his fictional creation? He said in one interview that 'average reality begins to rot and stink as soon as the act of individual creation ceases to animate a subjectively perceived texture', which does suggest a certain amount of scorn for the masses, since he seems to think that most people most of the time are incapable of this 'act of individual creation', and content themselves with living in a world of 'general ideas, conventional forms of humdrummery, current editorials'.[27] Yet some of his critics have pointed out that his contempt could be taken another way. Perhaps he means that everyone's vision is animated by this 'act of individual creation' by definition, that there is no such thing as an average man, except in demographers' studies and news reports, that we are all Cincinnatus fighting to assert our individuality in a society which keeps trying to turn us into abstractions.[28] This makes the food sliding out of the prison director's mouth as he eats, and M'sieur Pierre's speech on the pleasures of sex, and the family send-off for the youth on his way to his first execution ('this day he had reached execution-attending age' (pp. 212/202)), the stuff of pure comic fantasy, with no specific human referent involved. For the moment we shall reserve judgment.

In *Bend Sinister*, Nabokov seems to endorse this second interpretation. In the discussion of 'Mr Etermon', the cartoon version of the Ekwilists' Everyman, he points out that the flaw in the whole notion of an average man is that it confines us to generalizing about

mere externals. Viewed from the inside, any Etermon may have a
secret passion or a forbidden dream that belies the bland sameness
the world perceives. He concludes: 'No, the average vessels are not
as simple as they appear: it is a conjuror's set and nobody, not even
the enchanter himself, really knows what and how much they hold'
(p. 72). But this comes after a couple of pages of quite merciless
satire of this very figure, Mr Etermon, who seems suspiciously like a
vehicle for Nabokov's attack on the American middle class, casu-
ally imported into Paduk's distinctly European country: 'a visit to
the movies, a raise in one's salary, a yum-yum something for dinner
– life was positively crammed with these and similar delights,
whereas the worst that might befall one was hitting a traditional
thumb with a traditional hammer or mistaking the date of the boss's
birthday' (pp. 70–1). Even if we decide that this is just Nabokov's
light-hearted look at comic strip versions of American society, what
are we to make of the following passage, which seems to be a
preview of the 'grunting beast' world that he alludes to in the
excerpt from *Speak, Memory* quoted above:

He remembered other imbeciles he and she had studied, a study conducted
with a kind of gloating enthusiastic disgust. Men who got drunk on beer in
sloppy bars, the process of thought satisfactorily replaced by swine-toned
radio music. Murderers. The respect a business magnate evokes in his
home town. Literary critics praising the books of their friends or partisans.
Flaubertian *farceurs*. Fraternities, mystic orders. People who are amused
by trained animals. The members of reading clubs. All those who *are*
because they do *not* think, thus refuting Cartesianism. The thrifty peasant.
The booming politician.   (p. 13)

This kind of list shows us Nabokov's greatness and his limitations.
For sheer invigorating readability, there is nothing like his invective, cutting a swath through a whole society, assembling a veritable
menagerie of *bêtes noires*, creating its own momentum as it goes.
But – 'members of reading clubs'? 'thrifty peasants'? If these people
are all imbeciles and the objects of his disgust, there is not much
hope for the rest of us. And there is another problem here. The
liberal Nabokov has taken aim at tyranny in these novels while the
ethical one conveys his distinctly patrician contempt for vulgarity.
The tyranny is Fascist or Communist, but the vulgarity is American:
the juke-box lovers and the people who swill beer in pubs happen to
be the ones who fought totalitarianism in the Second World War.
By folding half the world over on the other half, he lessens the

political impact of his work.[29] In any event, these are not scientific abstractions or editorialists' inventions that Nabokov wants to repudiate; they are people he wants to ridicule. He is after more than just the generalizers: he wants to savage what he sees as the vulgarity and emptiness of much of contemporary life.

I am not saying that Nabokov does not have some valid points to make on this score. I just do not think that in these contexts we should judge him differently from the way we would any other satirist, and this means not always simply taking his assumptions for granted. However naïve it might sound, 'Is it true?' is a question Nabokov critics should ask more often. For surely his view of the individual and society in these two novels is in one sense superficial. Aristocratic scorn for the boorishness of all groups without exception, the lauding of the few individuals independent enough to resist the urge to cluster together in sticky lumps – these attitudes sometimes threaten to become mere romantic clichés. When Nabokov extols the virtues of proud defiance in the face of the most hideous oppression, he is more convincing because such tyranny is as obnoxious as he makes it out to be. 'Let the proletarian and the bourgeois speak of fraternity and equality', he often seems to be saying to us, 'the aristocrat will speak of liberty, because that is what he has known and what must never be compromised.' But to believe that society and its group instincts are as potent a menace as political tyranny requires a rather large leap of faith on the part of the reader. Critics are sometimes reluctant to admit this, as the following remarks about the hero's narrow escape at the end of *Invitation to a Beheading* suggest:

Misapplying the magic of his creative perception, Cincinnatus nearly brings the parody to life and power. From this Nabokovian perspective, we might suggest that those who take too seriously and too much to heart the current issues and ideological slogans that plague an era – sacrificing their rare and special energies (and their lives) to the general and sometimes mad social machine – may invite their own kind of beheading. They may destroy the possibilities for a classless, unclassifiable, wholly unique experience of life itself.[30]

This is certainly a plausible reading of the novel, and it sounds like the Nabokov program,[31] but is it true? Shouting ideological slogans may be a kind of beheading, but the same can hardly be said for taking 'current issues' seriously. And can we really agree to this absolute distinction between the obligations of living in a society and those of our private lives? This 'wholly unique experience of life itself', this 'classless, unclassifiable' thing sounds like a formulaic endorsement of a somewhat hackneyed notion of personality, and there is nothing more banal than constantly savouring one's own uniqueness. No, ideas about the intrinsic emptiness of social commitment and its dangers for the integrity of the individual are just assumptions, and Nabokov's case against the tyranny of contemporary society remains unproved.

The fairly rigid division between an idealized world and a fallen one on the social level is reproduced in Nabokov's depiction of his heroes' individual make-up. None of his protagonists is entirely at home in his own body: they are patrician ghosts in distinctly plebeian machines. Cincinnatus's passion for his grotesquely promiscuous wife causes him endless pain and frustration. And the freedom he longs for is graphically depicted as an escape from he body and a union with the insubstantial elements: 'He took off his head like a toupée, took off his rib cage like a hauberk ... What was left of him gradually dissolved, hardly colouring the air' (pp. 44–5, 29). Only by leaving his body on the block, walking away from it while the headsman's axe descends, does he move toward some kind of genuine freedom. Krug has similar problems. He describes sex as 'the convulsion men value most' (p. 9), and the body as a 'dungeon' (p. 153) from which the prisoner may escape at death when the walls crumble. Sexual desire threatens to turn this gentle, civilized man into a mere brute. This is doubly embarrassing because it assails him just when he is trying to soar on the wings of his fabulous intellect, dragging him back to earth. Nothing very new here for the comic writer, but it is the way Nabokov has Krug express his desire that is so striking. To his slatternly maid's enticing invitation he says: 'You know too little or much too much ... If too little, then run along, lock yourself up, never come near me because this is going to be a bestial explosion, and you might get badly hurt. I warn you. I am nearly three times your age and a great big sad hog of a man. And I don't love you' (p. 172). An extraordinary speech. Why 'bestial' and why 'hog'? Despite all the talk about being an 'indivisible monist',[32] Nabokov is an operative dualist: the conflict between elegant mind and farcical bodily desires eventually became one of his essential themes.

Conjecture about the role played by Nabokov's upbringing in all this must remain highly speculative, but it is at least worth noting a hint of the same attitude in the *Speak, Memory* account of his youthful interest in sex. He says that he talked about women with his friend Yuri, but: 'The slums of sex were unknown to us. Had we ever happened to hear about two normal lads idiotically masturbating in each other's presence . . ., the mere notion of such an act would have seemed to us as comic and impossible as sleeping with an amelus.'[33] And when he asks his parents about the cause of erections, his father describes the phenomenon as 'another of nature's absurd combinations, like shame and blushes, or grief and red eyes'.[34] 'Slums of sex', 'idiotically', 'comic', 'absurd': this kind of language helps explain Krug's predicament. Nabokov's dualistic view could also have its roots in some of his adolescent reading. One of his favourite authors was H. G. Wells, whom he referred to with immense respect and admiration all his life.[35] The works he particularly liked were the scientific romances, and they may well have had considerable influence on him. Think of the opening pages of *War of the Worlds*, where the narrator talks about the Martians as having 'minds that are to our minds as ours are to those of the beasts that perish, intellects vast cool and unsympathetic', and then goes on to describe the chaos when the 'inferior animals' are faced with the devastating Martian invasion.[36] Or that wonderful sequence in *The First Men in the Moon*, in which Professor Cavor describes how the Selenites do without books by evolving bigger brains: 'With knowledge the Selenites grew and changed; mankind stored their knowledge about them and remained brutes – equipped.'[37] But wherever Nabokov got his dualistic view, its consequences are important, as we shall see.

I want to turn now to the specific links between these novels and twentieth-century history. This second section is divided in the following way: first, the question of aristocratic attitudes and the 'beastly' element in revolutionary events in Russia; second, the more general problem of seeing totalitarianism in our century in terms of a ridiculous farce; third, the special concerns of the literary artist who has to write about horrors that exceed the wildest nightmare of the most jaded satirist; fourth, some thoughts on the risks involved in underestimating the power, complexity and attractiveness of authoritarian regimes; and finally, the theory of history that Nabokov propounds based on the rise and fall of these regimes.

In November 1917, just after the Bolshevik *coup*, Nabokov and his brother Sergey travelled from Petrograd to the Crimea in a first-class sleeper. During that trip there were two incidents that tell us something about how Nabokov saw the revolution. The first occurred when the train stopped for a moment:

A milky mist hung over the platform of an anonymous station – we were somewhere not far from Kharkov. I wore spats and a derby. The cane I carried, a collector's item that had belonged to my uncle Ruka, was of a light-colored, beautifully freckled wood, and the knob was a smooth pink globe of coral cupped in a gold coronet. Had I been one of the tragic bums who lurked in the mist of that station platform where a brittle young fop was pacing back and forth, I would not have withstood the temptation to destroy him.[38]

Sensitive to the contrast between the poverty around him and the luxury of an elite which exists alongside it, Nabokov shows here an engaging ability to get outside himself and see the world as others see it. The story he goes on to tell about almost missing the departing train in order to rescue the cane after dropping it confirms our impression that an objective and perceptive observer has re-created the scene. Both the ridiculous yet entirely human *amour propre* of the young fop and the curious impression he must have made on the onlookers are successfully conveyed. The other incident involved an encounter with some soldiers on the same train and the Nabokov brothers' attempt to keep their compartment for themselves. Nabokov observes that the soldiers were 'either "deserters" or "Red Heroes", depending upon one's political views'.[39] Here he shows less understanding. With a peace about to be negotiated and the Russian military position a complete shambles, these men could hardly be called deserters, and not many people were talking about the soldiers as 'Red Heroes' in 1917. Something like 'human beings intelligent enough to save themselves from the war and its senseless slaughter' seems fair, but Nabokov excludes this possibility.

I mention these two incidents to show how he can be both detached and committed concerning such matters. Yet in *Invitation to a Beheading* and *Bend Sinister*, his satiric purposes dictate that detachment be jettisoned. Here the soldiers are all beasts or dunces. They wear dog masks in *Invitation to a Beheading*. In *Bend Sinister* they get to talk, but only so that they can serve as straight men for Krug:

'What's this?' asked the fatter of the two, marking a word with the nail of the thumb he was pressing against the paper. Krug, holding his reading spectacles to his eyes, peered over the man's hand. 'University', he said. 'Place where things are taught – nothing very important'.

'No, this', said the soldier.

'Oh, "philosophy". *You* know. When you try to imagine a *mirok* [small pink potato] without the least reference to any you have eaten or will eat.'

(p. 10)

'Is that all the revolution was?' someone is bound to ask. 'Illiterate soldiers harassing witty academics? Nabokov even misses the irony of what he mocks here, since it was their very lack of education that made such men so susceptible to the slogans and promises of the Bolsheviks.' But he doesn't care about this. He wants to make a point about anarchic violence and the beast our culture is trying to civilize. Such soldiers killed a lot of people for the sake of a cause that in the end replaced a repressive, autocratic regime with something far worse; therefore they stand condemned.

We know how important Nabokov's father was in shaping his son's views on these matters,[40] so it is of particular interest to find something similar in his own account of the events in 1917. Of the Bolsheviks' failed insurrection in July of that year, he wrote that the soldiers he saw in the street had 'the same dull, vacant, brutal faces that we all remembered from the February days'.[41] These faces became the canine masks and pock-marked mugs in his son's novels. The 'February days' that V. D. Nabokov refers to were the days of the February revolution, during which the same soldiers were instrumental in wresting power from the Tsar. Almost a thousand of them died fighting against the last defenders of the old order. A political commentator like Trotsky is quick to pounce on something like this. He quotes Nabokov's remark about the soldiers in his *History of the Russian Revolution*, and points out that the February uprising was 'the very revolution which the liberals had officially pronounced glorious and bloodless'.[42] Trotsky wants his readers to ponder just where all the liberals and their supporters in the Provisional Government would have been without the soldiers' sacrifice, and to remember that the ruling classes bought their new freedom at a particular price.

Critics who bother about these things generally locate Nabokov somewhere in the political centre, and he called himself an 'old-fashioned liberal'.[43] With regard to his general views on human

rights and freedoms this is undoubtedly correct. But everything in
his life prior to the revolution encouraged him to make certain
assumptions about the way a society was organized and divided,
about the natural rights of an elite, and the essential traits of all
those who do not belong to it. In the end it is hard to escape the
feeling that for Nabokov the revolutionary upheavals in twentieth-
century society left the brutish existence of those who stood to
benefit from them basically unchanged. In his autobiography, he
talks about looking out the schoolroom window and seeing 'ker-
chiefed peasant girls weeding a garden path on their hands and
knees or gently raking the sun-mottled sand', then adds in a
parenthesis: 'The happy days when they would be cleaning streets
and digging canals for the State were still beyond the horizon.'[44] The
position of this 'old-fashioned liberal' and that of the monarchists
vis-à-vis the masses were not all that different.

For stupid and brutal followers, a supremely stupid and brutal
leader. Nabokov's various tyrants all resemble each other in this
crucial sense. Though he imagines himself to be a genius, Salvador
Waltz, the would-be ruler of the world in *The Waltz Invention*, is a
crude, cruel, foolish man, who in the end turns out to be a lunatic
who has only fantasized the despotic persecution that we thought
was actually occurring. In a short story called 'Tyrants Destroyed',
Nabokov makes a detailed study of this embodiment of dullness and
cruelty: this tyrant is a 'coarse, little-educated man – at first glance a
pigheaded, brutal and gloomy vulgarian full of morbid ambition'.[45]
And though relatively harmless, the director of the prison in
Invitation to a Beheading, the man responsible for the rule which
prohibits 'nocturnal dreams whose content might be incompatible
with the condition and status of the prisoner' (pp. 59/43–4), is
clearly a member of this group. Nabokov brilliantly exploits all this
for comic purposes, and many would argue that he deliberately
focuses on this aspect of the typical totalitarian regime in order to
free himself from historical reality and get on with his tasks as a
comic writer. But he did not see it this way. When asked questions
about current political affairs, he dismissed real-life dictators in
identical terms. 'Tyrants and torturers will never manage to hide
their comic stumbles behind their cosmic acrobatics', he said in one
interview,[46] and called them 'les bouffons de l'histoire' in another.[47]

I am interested in the validity of this view and in how convincingly
Nabokov makes his case for it in his fiction. The satirist can alter

and exaggerate as much as he likes, but he is still obliged to tell his own special kind of truth and must be judged accordingly. We are not likely to get very far until we sort out who, if anyone, Nabokov had in mind when he wrote a novel like *Bend Sinister*, his most detailed study of the tyrant as the 'bouffon de l'histoire'. He says that the dictator in both 'Tyrants Destroyed' and the novel is a composite: 'Hitler, Lenin, and Stalin dispute my tyrant's throne in this story and meet again in *Bend Sinister*, 1947, with a fifth toad', he claims in an introductory note to 'Tyrants Destroyed',[48] but as far as that story is concerned his claim doesn't really stand up to any scrutiny. A man who encourages a fantastic personality cult; who turns a 'wild-flowery country into a vast kitchen garden, where special care is lavished on turnips, cabbages, and beets'; who interviews one of his subjects who has succeeded in growing 'an eighty-pound turnip' and, after hearing the story of its planting and extraction, says: 'Now that's genuine poetry ... Here's somebody the poet fellows ought to learn from'; and who inspires the narrator, bent on destroying him, to indulge in a witty parody of an abject recantation ('Execute me – no, even better, pardon me, for the block is your pardon, and your pardon the block')[49] – this is not Lenin or Hitler or a composite, but 'le petit père des peuples' himself. I think the same man was on Nabokov's mind when he wrote *Bend Sinister*. In 1945, just before starting work on the novel, he wrote a letter to Edmund Wilson in which he suggests that the Stalin in the press photographs of the Yalta conference is 'not the real Stalin, but one of his many duplicates'. He goes on:

I am not even sure whether this tussaudesque figure is real at all since the so-called interpreter, a Mr Pavlovsk (?), who appears in all the pictures as a kind of Puppenmeister, is obviously the man responsible for the uniformed doll's movements ... I am thinking of writing a full account of the business, because it was really beautifully ingenious – especially when the dummy circulated and jerkily drank 34 toasts. Mr Pavlovsk is a great conjuror.[50]

Bend Sinister is presumably his 'full account of the business'. A beautification session with a mortician, eyes that 'snap open again' (pp. 127–8) after being closed, the jerky speech – Nabokov gave all these to his dummy and made himself the conjuror.

But can an actual case be made for seeing Stalin as a buffoon and a hopeless mediocrity? How does thinking of him in these terms help us understand what he did? On intellectual grounds, the verdict is clear. His forays into linguistic matters, the gross simplifications of his account of Communist Party history in the famous *Short Course*, his support for Lysenkoist biology, and the general level of his cultural interests, for which Milovan Djilas's account of being forced to listen to a recording of some dogs howling along with a coloratura soprano while Stalin guffawed may serve as an example,[51] all lend support to the Nabokov view. We read about these things now with real awe, thinking of a whole generation of artists and scientists condemned to howl along with him. And Nabokov's satire, because it has a solid basis in history, draws some real blood here.

The same is true for his study of the consequences of having this kind of 'intellect' at the head of a country. The historian Alec Nove has pointed out how important the disdain of the Stalinists for the intellectuals was as a cause of the Great Terror, how 'They enjoyed kicking the educated classes into the swill, forcing them to tell lies and to denounce fellow intellectuals.'[52] Nabokov portrays their sadistic violence and their contempt for someone like Krug in Mac, the policeman who arrests him and beats him up with a methodical ferocity. This virulent anti-intellectualism, along with the hallowed image of the Leader as sage and spiritual guide, had considerable popular support as well. Nabokov's comment on this aspect of the typical totalitarian state is the harangue of the shopkeeper who walks across the bridge with Krug. He decries the 'millions of unnecessary books accumulating in libraries' (p. 21), specialized scientific research, foreign languages and museums ('one long hoax' (p. 21)). In place of all these he wants common sense and the collected speeches of Paduk: 'I shall always remember – and shall pass it on to our grandsons – what he said that time they arrested him at the big meeting in the Godeon: "I", he said, "am born to lead as naturally as a bird flies." I think it is the greatest thought ever expressed in human language, and the most poetical one' (p. 20). Lest Nabokov be accused of excessive hyperbole here, I should point out that this man is alive and well and occupying positions of power in the Soviet Union. Listen to the current head of a large collective farm on the subject of Joseph Stalin:

I was in love with that man, and I still am. I love him like I can never love another. The day he died, I wept like a baby. I own his collected works, and I read them again and again for my inspiration. His *Short Course* is the most brilliant and humane analysis I've ever seen.

I love him for his mind, his logic, his manliness – above all, his courage.[53]

This is not some cretinous party hack talking, but a decent, hard-working, fun-loving human being, good to his family, fair with his workers, interested in arguing with those who disagree with him. One can laugh at the fool in *Bend Sinister*, but one hardly knows what to do with his real-life counterpart.

But Nabokov is writing a political satire as well as an intellectual one, and he conveniently ignores some unpleasant political truths about a dictator like Stalin. His skills were not just the natural expression of a sadistic brutality but the manifestation of a remarkably acute intelligence. In his excellent biography of Stalin, Ronald Hingley claims that 'In his own highly specialized and essentially destructive field, Stalin was indeed a genius – no less so, perhaps, than a Mozart or an Einstein.' He was able to manoeuvre 'sections of a large, potentially harmonious community into an orgy of mutual annihilation', says Hingley, because he had 'the wit to discern that humanity's collective brain can often be most effectively bamboozled by the crudest of tricks and the simplest of verbal devices'.[54] The 'crudest of tricks'. In *Bend Sinister*, these prove that such regimes are made up of fools and incompetents, responsible for ludicrous ploys that anyone can see through in a second: a spy disguised as a tailor's dummy, Paduk himself impersonating one of the Valkyries in Krug's prison cell. Under Stalin, the very crudity of all the plots and the fabrications was the result of his astute assessment of what was needed and the mocking symbol of the success of his oppression. If we fail to grasp this key point and simply dismiss cruel tyranny as farcical stupidity, our intellectual condescension will make us vulnerable to it.

Nabokov's most dedicated defenders cannot simply reply that it is not the business of the literary artist to go into such matters; he has gone into them. But they might say, with some justification, that history has so far outstripped the satiric novelist that he is obliged to misrepresent it. Merely heaping up horror stories will automatically turn the most fervent denunciation into Gothic absurdity; therefore, some other way of communicating the necessary contempt must be found. At the end of 'Tyrants Destroyed', the narrator uses precisely this argument: 'I see', he says of his depiction of the tyrant, 'that, in my efforts to make him terrifying, I have only made him ridiculous.'[55] I think this fact of literary art does determine to a large extent Nabokov's approach to such matters. In another story written in the thirties, 'A Russian Beauty', he introduces the biographical sketch of his émigré subject this way: 'Everything happened in full accord with the style of the period. Her mother died of typhus, her brother was executed by a firing squad. All these are ready-made formulae, of course, the usual dreary small talk, but it all did happen, there is no other way of saying it, and it's no use turning up your nose.'[56] Writing is 'small talk' (*govorok*) in comparison to what actually happened. List the historical details if necessary, but get on with what is personal and therefore more interesting. If you try to be serious about such events, you will end up being solemn and trite.[57]

But I am not sure that Nabokov is right about the necessary incompatibility of literary art and appalling suffering. As a test, let us consider a famous example from *Nineteen Eighty-Four*. Winston Smith, bound to a chair in the dreaded Room 101, is trying to hold out against what he fears most, the rats about to be released from the cage just in front of his face:

Suddenly the foul musty odour of the brutes struck his nostrils. There was a violent convulsion of nausea inside him, and he almost lost consciousness. Everything had gone black. For an instant he was insane, a screaming animal. Yet he came out of the blackness clutching an idea. There was one and only one way to save himself. He must interpose another human being, the *body* of another human being, between himself and the rats ... It was not relief, only hope, a tiny fragment of hope. Too late, perhaps too late. But he had suddenly understood that in the whole world there was just *one* person to whom he could transfer his punishment – one body that he could thrust between himself and the rats. And he was shouting frantically, over and over:

'Do it to Julia! Do it to Julia! Not me! Julia! I don't care what you do to her. Tear her face off, strip her to the bones. Not me! Julia! Not me!'[58]

I have chosen this particular passage for three reasons: first, the Nabokov who ridiculed any idea of a comparison between himself and Orwell might have used just such a passage to illustrate Orwell's inferiority as a novelist; second, I think it does show how vulnerable someone like Orwell is to the points Nabokov makes against this kind of writing; and third, it proves that in the last analysis such objections are not as conclusive as they might at first seem.

In one sense Orwell has produced the Gothic melodrama Nabokov warns against: the clichés, all those italicized words and exclamation marks to counterfeit passion, and that laborious prose, so painfully inadequate for conveying the mental processes and emotional reactions of someone in a state of pure terror. Yet the scene has a kind of crude power that we cannot ignore, and what makes this power so remarkable is that it is bound up with what seems least convincing. Winston Smith's saving idea cries out to be dismissed as a contrived piece of authorial heavy-handedness, but we cannot bring ourselves to do it. Perhaps it is the black parody of Christ's sacrifice;[59] or the fact that millions of people in Soviet Russia did betray the people closest to them; or simply Orwell's dogged sincerity. Just before this scene O'Brien forces his victim to look at himself in a mirror: his back is bent, his teeth are rotting, his hair is coming out in clumps. 'If you are human', says O'Brien, 'that is humanity.'[60] Using the same crude technique, Orwell forces his reader to think about what he sees in the mirror the satirist holds up for him.

Compare his scarifying approach with what Nabokov does when his heroes come to their 'Room 101'. In *Invitation to a Beheading*, Cincinnatus becomes more determined to conquer his fears, his persecutors become more ridiculous, the setting more unreal, the staged quality of the whole execution more obvious. His chamber of horrors can be escaped by a simple act of self-assertion. So too in *Bend Sinister*. Krug's 'Room 101' is the abduction and murder of his son, but as events become more and more horrible for him the comedy becomes more and more frenzied, creating a wild counterpoint to the human drama. Mac's 'pig-iron paw' (p. 175), Mariette's 'burning rose' (p. 178), Linda's account of Hustav's strangulation, Konkordiĭ Filadelfovich Kolokololiteĭshchikov ('they call me Kol' (p. 183)), the 'very special' execution offer, 'not likely to be renewed' (p. 200) – all this riotous farce pushes the torture and death right off stage. Instead of using the 'death of the child' scene as a means of engaging the reader's sympathies, Nabokov has Krug's son destroyed by the patients at an 'Institute for Abnormal Children' so that he can get in a savage parody of advanced psychology. Here the intrinsic obscenity of what is being described makes the humour so black that the comic point is almost obscured, and the distinctly American nature of the parodied object confuses things still more. An unfocused and disconcerting sense of horror results, but Nabokov has avoided Orwell's mistakes in the 'big scene' by refusing to write it. This means he has to create the emotive effects he relies on in other ways, but it saves him from lapsing into the banality he so hated.

I want to turn now to some of the implications of Nabokov's view of tyranny. Perhaps the principal message of these two novels is that in political terms there is an absolute difference between 'us' and 'them'. The world that Cincinnatus goes toward at the end is different in kind from the one full of cardboard people and unreal cities that he leaves, as is the country beyond the border that Krug has visited and dreams of escaping to. Where they are going, the respect for human rights and freedoms is absolute. This is the Nabokov view of the way the world divides up politically. He saves his most withering contempt for those who compare Stalin and McCarthy or insist that 'We all share in Germany's guilt.'[61] Asking ourselves searching questions about the implications of what has happened in our century, and altering our view of human nature accordingly, seems to him ludicrous, because explaining is the first step on the road to excusing, or worse, self-accusing.[62] There are two points at issue here, and I think Nabokov is absolutely right about one, not quite so convincing about the other. Surely he is justified in deploring the slick way we use ready-made formulae to avoid having to think about something or to indulge in a little harmless self-flagellation. But as soon as we begin to feel as morally superior as Nabokov wants us to feel, the nagging doubts begin. Soldiers using bayonets on defenceless women and children to force them into trains headed for concentration camps, administrators sending millions of people to almost certain death, whole nations breaking all kinds of moral and international laws for the sake of some 'final solution' that they felt obliged to carry out – this we cannot be said to 'share' with Germany. Yet it is precisely these things that were done when the Allies forcibly repatriated millions of Soviet citizens at the end of World War Two, all gruesomely documented in Nicholas Bethell's *The Last Secret* and Nikolai Tolstoy's *Victims of Yalta*.[63] No one who has read these accounts can ever again be quite so eager to make automatic assumptions about 'our' moral superiority.

Another consequence of insisting on this absolute difference between 'us' and 'them' is that the rightness of 'our' position is assumed to be self-evident and 'theirs' self-evidently absurd. Nabokov sometimes tries to bully the reader into assenting; he substitutes bluster for argument. For example: he borrows parts of the Soviet Constitution for Paduk's regime, includes them in a long 'explanation' of that constitution, and then has Krug think: 'I shall have it treated by some special process which will make it endure far into the future to the eternal delight of free humorists' (p. 147). One of the things he quotes is a defence of the 'freedoms' guaranteed by the state: 'our citizens have free access to the papers, a state of affairs which is unknown anywhere else. True, in other countries there is a lot of talk about "freedom" but in reality lack of funds does not allow one the use of the printed word. A millionaire and a working man clearly do not enjoy equal opportunities' (p. 146). This may be a superficial objection to western democracy, but it is not patently stupid. In *The Times* of London a few years ago, Bernard Levin created considerable controversy when he set about refuting the claims of a young man, unemployed, who had used a version of the same argument about freedom, wealth, and unequal opportunities, as part of his explanation of why he would willingly trade off the individual freedoms he enjoyed in England for the job security of less free but more equal people in Eastern Europe. Those who responded to Levin's column, and there were many, almost without exception disagreed with him and supported the young man's position.[64] That these were all *Times* readers as opposed to subscribers to the *Socialist Worker* suggests that the issues are not so clear cut as one might think. Add to this the fact that about a third of the world is officially committed to the proposition that documents like the Soviet Constitution are right about this question of freedoms, and the importance of making clear just why such ideas have had such appalling consequences for free expression becomes all the more obvious. Scornful laughter is not enough.

Another consequence of underestimating the complexities of the issues raised by totalitarianism is that some of its most active supporters do not get treated as harshly as they deserve. I am thinking particularly of the intellectual's role in these matters. Let us review how Nabokov depicts him in the two novels. Cincinnatus is one type, the honest searcher after truth, the one who succeeds after many false starts in writing 'something', in crossing out the word 'death' (pp. 201/190), and thus symbolically assuring himself immortality in the form of posterity and a readership. Then there is the Librarian. He is different from all the idiots who surround the prisoner: he doesn't want to get involved, but he does answer some of Cincinnatus's questions; he offers no sympathy, but he does suggest that the prisoner might find some consolation in a book 'about gods' (pp. 177/165); he attends the execution along with everyone else, but he alone sits 'doubled up, vomiting' (pp. 217/207) as the head rolls. In other words, he is not like all the brutes who persecute Cincinnatus, but he is so weak and withdrawn that he cannot stop them. *Bend Sinister* follows the same pattern. Krug is the honest searcher after truth here, although, rather disappointingly in view of the fact that he is a famous philosopher, he does not turn up much of interest. Then we have Krug's colleagues, aptly characterized by him as estimable 'because they are able to find perfect felicity in specialized knowledge and because they are not apt to commit physical murder' (p. 54). True, they go along with Paduk, but only because they are above politics. If the University stays open their research can continue. One signs the statement supporting the Toad because he wants to get his book published, with 'the footnote on page 306 that would explode a rival theory concerning the exact age of a ruined wall' (p. 50). The zoologist on the faculty, a natural scientist like Nabokov, signs his unread copy of the same statement while speculating about the possibility of collecting animals in Egypt. Dr Alexander actually works for the government, but he is just a clever opportunist and he dismisses Paduk's regime as 'whimsical' (p. 54). In this way Nabokov manages to convey the idea that the tyrant, the lackeys who carry out his commands and the people who enthusiastically sing his praises inhabit a world from which the intellectual, with a smile or a slight shudder, utterly absents himself. As an intellectual he ignored an important truth; as a satirist he missed a great chance. What about Sartre, who said that if the great Purge Trials really were faked, the French proletariat should not be told because it would dishearten them? Or Brecht, who said of the accused in the same trials: 'The more innocent they are, the more they deserve to die'?[65] Perhaps I have rigged the case by choosing writers with specific political interests. But many of the pronouncements about Stalin's Russia by a great range of literary and other figures of that time do not make very pleasant reading these days; and someone like George Watson has gone so far as to claim that 'Between 1933 and 1939 many (and perhaps most) British intellectuals under the age of fifty, and a good many in other Western lands, knowingly supported the greatest act of mass-murder in human history.'[66] Again, it is simply not true to say that Nabokov was not interested in these questions. His letters to Wilson are full of attempts to explain what American intellectuals had not understood about the Russian Revolution, and what brutality and cruelty they were in fact condoning. The writers and academics were not all on one side or above the fray, and he knew it. To take this up in the novels might have upset their schematic neatness, but it would have made them more like the 'final indictments' he wanted them to be.

Nabokov has a theory of history to accompany this view of tyrants as buffoons. It is hinted at in the warning given to Cincinnatus by the narrator when he tries to make sense of what is happening to him: 'Involuntarily yielding to the temptation of logical development, involuntarily (be careful, Cincinnatus) forging into a chain all the things that were quite harmless as long as they remained unlinked, he inspired the meaningless with meaning, and the lifeless with life' (pp. 155/143). And it gets its full expression in *Bend Sinister* as 'Krugism':

To try to map our tomorrows with the help of data supplied by our yesterdays means ignoring the basic element of the future which is its complete non-existence. The giddy rush of the present into this vacuum is mistaken by us for a rational movement. . . . To those who watch these events [accompanying a dictator's rise to power] and would like to ward them, the past offers no clues, no *modus vivendi* – for the simple reason that it had none itself when toppling over the brink of the present into the vacuum it eventually filled.   (pp. 41–2)

Mere literary whimsy? If it is, Nabokov is remarkably persistent in putting it forward.[67] His argument is basically a variation of the old 'How do we know that the sun will rise tomorrow?' problem. Those who argue against inductive logic, like Nabokov's Krugian historian, cannot be logically refuted. As A. J. Ayer points out, we can tell a person who denies us the right to form expectations of the future that he is being irrational, but 'this will not worry him; our standard of rationality is just what he objects to. Our only recourse is to point out . . . that the proof that he requires of us is one that he makes it logically impossible for us to give.'[68] But history itself seems to have refuted Nabokov's theory. Revolutions do not just pop up in the way that his professor suggests they do. When a certain level of material deprivation, a revolutionary intelligentsia and a weak and unpopular central government come together at the same time, the kind of upheaval that Lenin and the Bolsheviks exploited so successfully tends to occur.

As a refutation of the Marxist theory of history, Krugism works together with 'Ekwilism', Nabokov's parody of Marx's social doctrines. The founder of Ekwilism, Skotoma, thinks that 'At every given level of world-time' there is 'a certain computable amount of human consciousness distributed throughout the population of the world. This distribution was uneven and herein lay the root of all our woes' (pp. 67–8). Nabokov scores wittily and repeatedly off the utopian aspirations of old Skotoma, but behind this comic strength lurks a certain theoretical weakness. He concentrates on the utopian aspects of Marxist thought because they are the easiest to ridicule, but he has taken the line of least resistance here. His letter to Wilson about the explanation of Marxism in *To the Finland Station* is revealing: 'your "clearing up" of Marxism's difficulties . . . would have maddened Marx. Personally I find that you have simplified his idea a little too drastically. Without its obscurities and abracadabra, without its pernicious reticences, shamanic incantations and magnetic trash, Marxism is not Marxism.'[69] But Marx on the working conditions in the nineteenth century, the inequities of capitalism, the sources of proletarian discontent – this is the essential Marx, and what he has to say about these things now seems so obvious that no one would think of arguing against it. Paduk organizes the school misfits, works out a ludicrous credo based on the mumblings of a crackbrain and seizes power. Nabokov makes the whole sequence look like a historical accident, but here at least he is writing a satire of a fantasy.

Yet despite all its obvious inadequacies, I think he touches on something important with his theory of history as a creation of unpredictable chance and personal whim. Stalin succeeded Lenin, and the whims of one man really did come to mean more than the concrete historical situation or the progress of the class war. We want this not to be true; we want Nabokov to be wrong so that all that suffering will have meant something. If it didn't, then our only consolation is that, again according to Nabokov's theory, there is no reason to assume that the future will throw up something like it again.[70]

To conclude this chapter, I want to suggest what Nabokov sees as the weapons of the forces for good in the battle against tyranny, and what kind of future his two dystopias anticipate for us.

In these two novels, Nabokov organizes his ethical scheme around something as simple and basic as compassion and the importance of certain kinds of human relations. At first *Invitation to a Beheading* looks like a direct challenge to this idea. Cincinnatus's pathetic desire for his wife represents one of his real weaknesses, and M'sieur Pierre's attempt to establish a *Bruderschaft* with his victim seems to symbolize just how repellent all human links are in this novel. But one relation in Nabokov is always sacrosanct, the one between parent and child, and this is true even in Cincinnatus's strange world. Nabokov himself hinted at this in an interview when he observed that Cincinnatus dismisses his mother as 'a parody' (pp. 136/122) 'not quite fairly'.[71] She is foolish and garrulous and somewhat cowardly, but the author takes care to distinguish her in all sorts of ways from the 'spectres' (pp. 51/36) that haunt his hero. She mouths no comforting platitudes about his imminent execution. She seems to be genuinely alive in some sort of natural world, which she describes in terms that echo her son's dreamy evocations of the Tamara Gardens. Life baffles her: 'it always seems to me', she says, 'that a marvellous tale is being repeated over and over again, and I either don't have the time to, or am unable to grasp it, and still somebody keeps repeating it to me, with such patience!' (pp. 135/122). This kind of speech is always code for 'good person' in Nabokov. The identity of life and art can lead, as it does in M'sieur Pierre's conception of an execution as a dramatic performance, to a superficial aestheticizing of life and art, but it does not have to. It can increase our sense of wonder at both. Most importantly, unlike everyone else in the prison, she is not in collusion with the authorities. In fact, the prison director is very upset by her visit and unceremoniously evicts her, all the time insisting that 'this little midwife presents no danger to us' (pp. 138/124). But she does present a danger, and her last moments with Cincinnatus suggest what it is. He begins to ask her if she knows about his impending execution, but his question breaks off:

He suddenly noticed the expression in Cecilia C.'s eyes – just for an instant, an instant – but it was as if something real, unquestionable (in this world, where everything was subject to question), had passed through, as if a corner of this horrible life had curled up, and there was a glimpse of the lining. In his mother's gaze, Cincinnatus suddenly saw that ultimate, secure, all-explaining and from-all-protecting spark that he knew how to discern in himself also ... The spark proclaimed such a tumult of truth that Cincinnatus's soul could not help leaping for joy. The instant flashed and was gone. Cecilia C. got up, making an incredible little gesture, namely, holding her hands apart with index fingers extended, as if indicating size – the length, say of a babe ...   (pp. 137–8/123–4)[72]

The reader's natural inclination here is to classify this with all the other false hopes – Emmie and the promised escape, the knocking on the wall that turns out to be M'sieur Pierre – and dismiss it as a fictional cliché of the 'messenger transmits mysterious life-giving sign to condemned man in his hour of need' type. But unlike the other signs that Cincinnatus tries to interpret, this one is never shown to be delusory. So what does it means? His mother is a midwife: perhaps the gesture she makes with her hands is her way of reassuring her son about what is going to happen to him, of hinting that it will be not a death but a birth, an escape from a dark, confusing world into a new and different one. Or perhaps it is something that cannot be put into words, something more important than messages and meanings. At any rate human contact has been made, *can* be made, and that is the essence of the secret the authorities are so afraid of. The equivalent in *Bend Sinister* is of course the relationship between father and son, what Krug calls the 'agony' of loving a person created 'by the fusion of two mysteries, or rather two sets of a trillion of mysteries each' (p. 163). Nabokov, the father of a son whom he doted on, calls this love the 'main theme' of the book.[73]

I have dwelt on this aspect of the novels because it suggests that in some fundamental ways Nabokov is unlike many of the novelists with whom he is often compared. Since Kafka's name comes up so frequently in relation to these works, especially *Invitation to a Beheading*,[74] let us put him and Nabokov side by side for a moment. It may make us think again about the advisability of using words like 'post-modern' for those who happen to come after. In a novel like *The Trial* or *The Castle*, the hero's quest eventually causes him to modify the assumptions with which he began, and the nature of his 'Prozess' changes accordingly. The labyrinth takes on new configurations as he ceases to be preoccupied with getting out of it. The world looks like an alien and artificial structure to the Nabokov hero as well; but instead of interrogating it in order to understand it better, he creates his own world and then tries to keep it safe from the hostile elements that surround him. Kafka's heroes must come to terms with guilt and despair; Nabokov's must reject such feelings. Think too of the difference in the confidence with which the narrative voice speaks in both writers. Roland Barthes notes that Kafka's fiction authorizes 'a thousand equally plausible keys, which means that he validates none'.[75] Despite all the ambiguities in

Nabokov, he is an author who 'validates', and a man who could write, as Kafka never could: 'In the final analysis everything in the world is very simple and founded upon two or three not very complicated truths.'[76] In short, Nabokov believes in the basic human decencies, and he thinks that it is relatively easy to communicate some sort of basic truth about them. Are we likely to conclude the same about Kafka after reading one of his stories? The answer to this apparently rhetorical question is that Nabokov did precisely what it implies is impossible. I quote from the lectures on 'The Metamorphosis':

It should be noted how kind, how good our poor little monster is. His beetlehood, while distorting and degrading his body, seems to bring out in him all his human sweetness. His utter unselfishness, his constant preoccupation with the needs of others – this, against the backdrop of his hideous plight comes out in strong relief. Kafka's art consists in accumulating on the one hand, Gregor's insect features, all the sad detail of his insect disguise, and on the other hand, in keeping vivid and limpid before the reader's eyes Gregor's sweet and subtle human nature.[77]

This reading of Kafka tells us rather more about the man who wrote it than the one being written about. Gregor's 'human sweetness' was probably not uppermost in Kafka's mind when he wrote the story, but Nabokov's unequivocal view of good and evil enables him to assume that it was. These two writers saw the world very differently.[78]

But there is no need to invoke Kafka to show how enthusiastically old-fashioned Nabokov was in these matters. Someone like Orwell can help put his moral vision in perspective. In *Nineteen Eighty-Four*, Winston Smith thinks: 'Nothing was your own except the few cubic centimetres inside your skull.'[79] Samuel Hynes argues that this is 'the base on which Orwell's whole morality rests': 'Starting from the proposition that personal identity is fixed and private, one can go on to other propositions: that the past is unchangeable, that truth is objective, that words have fixed meanings. And that love is possible.'[80] These claims define a conception of reality that is not so very different from the one Nabokov assumes in these novels. But Hynes goes on to point out that *Nineteen Eighty-Four* is 'horrible because in it every one of these propositions is denied'.[81] In *Invitation to a Beheading* and *Bend Sinister*, Nabokov never turns the conventional view upside down quite like that.

And now, in conclusion, the future prospects of the forces for good and of the regimes opposed to them. As a student at Cambridge, Nabokov once participated in a Union debate at which he spoke against the new tyranny in Russia. To prepare for that debate, he memorized most of a lecture about the future of Russia given by his father at King's College, London on January 16, 1920. In that lecture, V. D. Nabokov has this to say about the Bolsheviks: 'To live they have to use violence and oppression and these lead inevitably to the ruin of the vital forces of the country'; and: 'Bolshevism can live, but its life is death to civilisation, to progress – as it has been proved by Russia's terrible experience.'[82] His son's writings on the same subject throughout his career reiterate the same basic point. Yet both V. D. and V. V. Nabokov reject despair. In his stirring conclusion, the father quotes Pushkin:

> But in the test of long chastisement,
> After enduring the blows of fate,
> Russia was strengthened. Thus under a heavy hammer
> Glass is shattered but steel is forged.

And he insists that 'in the ultimate result victory will be secured by those forces which have their source in the higher aspirations of human nature'.[83] The conclusions of *Invitation to a Beheading* and *Bend Sinister* tentatively reaffirm this kind of optimism. And Nabokov says in the Chekhov lectures that because men full of 'fire of abnegation, pureness of spirit, moral elevation' have lived in Russia and perhaps still live there, there is 'a promise of better things to come for the world at large'.[84] (Winston Smith, it will be remembered, contends that 'It is impossible to found a civilisation on fear and hatred and cruelty', and that there is 'something in the universe', 'some spirit, some principle' which will never be overcome.)[85] It is still too early to make a definitive judgment, but so far neither the pessimistic nor the optimistic view has been decisively confirmed. For the truth is that Bolshevism has survived, and civilization and progress have survived along with it. The cost has been terrible, more terrible than V. D. Nabokov, making his grim prediction in 1920, could ever have imagined. But the boot that Orwell saw 'stamping on a human face forever'[86] stamps only intermittently now. An important literature has re-emerged alongside *samizdat*. The idea of a Russian nation with a special destiny is as strong as ever. Some of this may be only a temporary thaw, the slight melting of an immense glacier, with the threat of another ice age hovering ominously. It does tell us though that 'the vital forces of the country' have proved stronger than the forces of oppression, which is a hopeful sign.

A last word from Nabokov on these matters? – 'symptoms of "thaw" in Soviet Russia, the Future of Mankind, and so on, leave me supremely indifferent'.[87] I have tried to suggest that he was never 'supremely indifferent', that in these novels he created, not just fictional artefacts, but a discourse. This has been an attempt to reconstitute and comment on an important part of it.

3

The Gift

The Gift is a key novel for anyone interested in Nabokov. Its detailed and provocative discussion of Russian literature and culture provides us, as one critic has said, with 'basic insights into Nabokov's views on the uses of literature and literary criticism and contains an explanatory key to many of Nabokov's controversial literary, political and social opinions'.[1] This, combined with the fact that it is usually described as the best of his Russian novels, might lead one to suppose that a considerable amount of criticism devoted to the issues raised in the novel already exists. Yet surprisingly little has been written about *The Gift*. While it was still coming out in serial form in *Sovremennye Zapiski* (1937–8), Khodasevich predicted that there would be a stormy response to things like the presentation of the nineteenth-century radical critics in the novel: 'All disciples and worshippers of the progressive thought police, watching over Russian literature since the 1840s, will fly into a rage', he wrote in *Vozrozhdenie*.[2] But few of them did, at least in print. By refusing to publish Chapter Four, the biography of Chernyshevsky which raises so many crucial questions about the role of Russian literature and the role of its 'thought police' in the last century and in our own, the editors of the most important émigré journal effectively stifled the debate before it got started. The novel did not receive any substantial critical attention until 1963, when Simon Karlinsky published his brief but penetrating analysis of it.[3] Since then various summaries of *The Gift*'s contents have appeared, and many interesting observations about it have been made in passing; but only Field and Hyde, in their studies of Nabokov, have made important contributions to our understanding of the novel, and we still have no comprehensive account of the literary and social questions raised by Nabokov in it. What follows is an attempt to fill part of this gap, and in so doing to make a case for laying the emphasis squarely on the novel's content. Inevitably, it has been re-read in the light of Nabokov's late fiction. Julia Bader calls it one of 'the most apparently "artificial" of his novels'.[4] John Stark says that of the novels written between *Mary* and *Lolita*, *The Gift* most closely resembles *Pale Fire*, *Ada*, and *Transparent Things*.[5] And Alfred Appel has stressed its self-reflexive qualities, noting that it begins on April Fool's Day,[6] and that certain aspects of its structure call into question our most basic assumptions about fiction and reality: 'If it is disturbing', he writes, 'to discover that the characters in *The Gift* are also the readers of Chapter Four, this is because it suggests, as Jorge Luis Borges says of the play within *Hamlet*, "that if the characters of a fictional work can be readers or spectators, we, its readers or spectators, can be fictitious" '.[7] My interests are rather different.

This chapter is divided into three parts. In the first, I examine the portrayal of Nikolay Chernyshevsky and the discussion of his ideas. Chapter Four of *The Gift* provides us with another opportunity for observing how Nabokov the novelist deals with real historical people and events. In the second part, I explore some of the ramifications of the debate about the Russian literary tradition, with specific reference to the discussion in the novel of 'committed' and 'uncommitted' literature. In the final section, I discuss some of the things that *The Gift* has to tell us about Nabokov's own relation to Russian literature.

Most of the novel's critics agree that the biography of Chernyshevsky, for all its irreverence, gives us the real human being instead of the public cliché the man so quickly became. Field suggests that 'By means of a revolutionary overthrow of the basic premises of the art of biography, the revolutionary criticist has been made to live', saved from 'the dust pile of history and his own prose'.[8] Lee argues that 'Fyodor's (Nabokov's) strikingly original work makes Chernyshevsky a truly sympathetic, if foolish, man and rescues him from politics in the sense that he becomes human and not a symbol.'[9] And Couturier makes a similar point when he says of him: 'Nabokov brings the character to life again, all the while stripping him of the political and literary dimension which tradition had willingly attributed to him: the man revives, the myth dies.'[10] Let us take a look at this process in action.

Consider the treatment of Chernyshevsky's early years. Fyodor covers the first twelve years in two short paragraphs and the next six in three, and the tone is intermittently parodic ('very sweet in his homemade little coat and nankeen breeches' (pp. 239/203)).[11] This is important for the Nabokov reader, because it means that he should prepare himself for a certain kind of development. This will be one of those characters whose childhood barely exists, and whose consciousness of the past, always a quintessentially human trait in Nabokov, is therefore hopelessly impoverished. Nabokov would argue that this is only verisimilitude, since these years were one long non-event in Chernyshevsky's life, and experienced with so little sensitivity that they must be consigned to oblivion. At eighteen, we are told, he went from Saratov to St Petersburg, his first long journey, and 'The whole way he kept reading a book' (pp. 241/205). Fyodor even adds a paragraph deploring the fact that this dullish introvert, lost in his own imaginary world, never had a word to say about the landscape he would have seen had he looked up from his book. It is interesting to juxtapose this and an excerpt from one of Chernyshevsky's letters, written on May 23, 1846, the fifth day of his month-long journey:

Only now have I come to my senses after the rapture caused by the view of Atkarsk [a city en route] with its countless pools, recalling the lagoons of Venice ... and its innumerable choruses of frogs, which have I think this rather important advantage over nightingales, that they sing all summer and spring and autumn, day and night, and don't shun people, don't flee from them into a thicket, like nightingales, but peacefully sing in every swamp, even if it's in the middle of noisy, populous, busy Atkarsk, seething with life and movement.[12]

A rare example of Chernyshevsky's responsiveness in an otherwise barren youth? But he wrote nine letters home during the trip, and in each he is excited about what he has seen and eager to describe it. In one he even lectures his brother, who has complained in a letter that life in Saratov is boring, about the infinite riches of the natural world, describing how a single drop of water on a leaf comes alive under a microscope, how one can see 'a whole world' in that drop, and how life is an endless series of discoveries of this kind (vol. XIV, pp. 12–13). Still, doesn't the letter about Atkarsk show Chernyshevsky to be less interested in the world than in theories about it? Perhaps it even contains the first hint of his proletarian leanings, an early preference for an earthy batrachian realism rather than the aesthetic narcissism of the nightingale. But this prejudges the case just as surely as Fyodor's thesis has done. The real Chernyshevsky, in this instance anyway, must struggle for existence with the preconceived notions about him.

What about his attempts to cope with the alien being that was his own body? Does Fyodor's discussion of Chernyshevsky's sexual problems, his 'uneven struggle with the desires of the flesh, ending in a secret compromise' (pp. 247/210), make him more human? At least Fyodor has some real evidence this time, and he quotes from the diaries to support his case. What could be more pathetic than the following attempt to account for a desire by means of a theory? Infatuated with the wife of his friend Lobodovsky, Chernyshevsky decided to compare her with some portraits of women:

he was now able by experimental means to test something which love had suggested to him: the superiority of Nadezhda Yegorevna's beauty . . . that is, Life, to the beauty of all other 'female heads', that is Art ('Art!').

On the Nevski Avenue poetic pictures were exhibited in the windows of Junker's and Daziaro's. Having studied them thoroughly he returned home and noted down his observations. Oh, what a miracle! The comparative method always provided the necessary result . . . Life is more pleasing (and therefore better) than painting. (pp. 250–1/212–13).

The use of indirect discourse is particularly clever here, because it subtly blends what actually happened with Fyodor's additions. The 'experimental means', the anti-art theory, the rapturous exclamation when the suspicions are confirmed – all this is Fyodor's own creative distortion. The twenty-year-old Chernyshevsky did go to look at the pictures, and did decide that Nadezhda Yegorevna was more beautiful than the women pictured there, but he was interested in women, in his feeling for this woman in particular, not theory. In one of the diary entries devoted to these excursions, he describes sexual arousal as 'stupid', 'vulgar', and 'base', adding that he believed 'those thoughts' had been left behind (vol. I, p. 83). The feelings caused by Chernyshevsky's inhibitions are extremely muddled, but I think the homely circumlocutions he uses to explain those feelings to himself give us the man in a way that Fyodor's brilliant pastiche, for all its vitality, does not:

It's strange: are all these thoughts that wander through my head serious, or do I consider them simply as a dream, delirium, romance – this is impossible to say, this I can't decide; . . . although these thoughts don't excite me, still it's strange, you see they all crowd into my head and it's impossible to say that they hardly occupy me; of course they don't occupy me excessively but you know I do think of them. What a strange man I am, most incredibly funny. (vol. I, p. 159)

Instead of the shrill voice of the pseudo-aesthetician, the pathos of the mixed-up kid. But what difference does all this make, someone might object, since Chernyshevsky was foolish enough to compare people and portraits, and actually did spend a considerable part of his M.A. dissertation proving that life was more lifelike than art? Only this: the emotionally immature youth, going through the kind of experience that practically every young man goes through, is ignored in Fyodor's biography because the same facts can be manipulated in order to create a more amusing 'literary' character.

Fyodor uses Chernyshevsky's diary of his courtship for the same purposes, comparing it to 'an extremely conscientious business report' (pp. 257/218), and then proceeding to extract all of its comic contents. Perhaps a man who would draw up a list of reasons for and against marriage to help him decide what to do deserves this kind of criticism, but reading through the diary one is struck, not so much by Chernyshevsky's pedantic attempts to rationalize his passion, as by his need to be loved, his naïve faith in the existence of the simple truth in the world of deceptive appearances which his coquettish fiancée inhabits, and his uncertainty about the efficacy of writing it all down as a means of dealing with his problems. Once again, some all too human emotions. 'I feel', he writes, 'that if I let slip this chance to marry, then with my personality perhaps another chance will not soon present itself, and I'll spend my youth in arid loneliness' (vol. I, p. 414). The fact that he can come to a decision about marriage means that he really is a man like other men and not merely *dryan'*, 'rubbish', 'a good-for-nothing' (vol. I, p. 480). Fyodor's 'business report' turns out to be a hundred pages of the most intimate kind of self-portraiture possible.[13]

Such a figure could have been depicted, the combination of arrogance and self-doubt in Chernyshevsky could have been analyzed, but that would have meant psychology, ambiguity, contradiction. Fyodor evidently feels that if he indulges too often in this kind of thing, Chernyshevsky will end up escaping him altogether. If he allows his subject to engage our sympathy too frequently, the clown with the painted grin will be forgotten. So except for rare occasions, as when Chernyshevsky is allowed to declare his love for his wife with the kind of simplicity and directness that Nabokov usually reserves for his favourite heroes, Fyodor avoids the details that don't fit the aesthetic design he has in mind for his subject. When Chernyshevsky's other passion, his revolutionary fervour, fails to take him to the gallows to die for the cause, Fyodor cannot help regretting the fact that the convicted man did not receive the death penalty, thus avoiding the 'twenty-five insipid years' (pp. 314/267) he still had to live. His life would have been more plausible if it had had an aesthetic shape. It didn't, so his biographer has to supply it with one.

The dismissal of the last years of Chernyshevsky's life means that they will be, not ignored, but accounted for by the 'themes' which organize the first half of his life. His public career was a collection of comic squabbles and fierce disputes; therefore his life in exile must become the same admixture of farce and fury. The relations between Chernyshevsky and his eldest son Sasha are adduced as evidence: 'With a kind of sadistic obstinacy, with pedantic callousness matching that of any prosperous bourgeois in Dickens or Balzac, he called his son in his letters "a big ludicrous freak" and an "eccentric pauper" and accused him of a desire "to remain a beggar"' (pp. 331/282). In the letter Fyodor quotes from, Chernyshevsky adds that his impression of his son may be only a superficial one, because after talking to him (Chernyshevsky had just returned from exile) he is convinced that Sasha has 'a good, honourable heart' (vol. XV, p. 410). Nabokov no doubt thinks that this stuff is fit only for some officially sanctioned, luridly sentimental account. But I think he lets Fyodor go to the other extreme with 'sadistic' and 'prosperous bourgeois'. The subject of Sasha's finding a job comes up often in the letters, not because Chernyshevsky wants to extol the glories of wealth, but because he knows how desperate his own financial situation is and feels guilty about not having provided for his family. Even at the end of his life he was still sending his thirty-five-year-old son fifty roubles a month. The dozens of letters he wrote him are almost always solicitous and loving: in one he says that the only thing that interests him about whatever country Sasha lives in is Sasha (vol. XV, p. 483); in another he jokingly calls his son *starina*, 'old man', marvels at the fact that he is already thirty and his brother twenty-five, and adds: 'I can't think of these figures without bitterness' (vol. XV, p. 425). If Fyodor were really after Chernyshevsky's human story, here it is. His biography is a great improvement on uncritical adulation, but it does not always tell the kind of truth its defenders have claimed for it.

All this imaginative sleight-of-hand, it could be argued, may reveal some of the limitations of Fyodor's approach to characterization, but Chernyshevsky merits only a limited humanity from an art form which he was never willing to grant independent life. And anyway, this question of character development is only of secondary importance in *The Gift*. Nabokov is much more interested in the critical judgments and theoretical pronouncements that Chernyshevsky and radical critics like him made. He says as much when he claims in the Foreword that the novel's heroine 'is not Zina, but Russian Literature' (p. 8). There is no shortage of critics who endorse this position – Field,[14] Appel,[15] and Donald Morton[16] all make passing comments about Nabokov's novel's being a study of Russian literature – but because of the predominant interest in the formal aspects of his work, no one has examined this subject in any detail. I want to analyze how Nabokov goes about making his case against Chernyshevsky's ideas on literature and his thought generally, and assess how convincingly he makes it.

First a word of explanation. Up to this point, because I have been dealing only with Chapter Four, I have mostly confined myself to talking about the views of Fyodor, Nabokov's fictional character. But Nabokov makes no sustained attempt at maintaining a fixed distance between himself and his creation, and we need not pretend that he has done. True, he says in the Foreword: 'I am not, and never was Fyodor Godunov-Cherdyntsev' (p. 7), but that is not at issue. What is important for the reader to know is that most of the time, unless there is specific evidence to the contrary, he can safely assume that Fyodor speaks for his creator. This at least is the consensus among a variety of critics. Stanley Edgar Hyman argues that Nabokov's disclaimers in the Foreword should be enough to alert us to the fact that the opposite of what he says is true.[17] Karlinsky notes that Fyodor's literary opinions are 'clearly Nabokov's',[18] a view generally borne out by an examination of Nabokov's critical writings on individual authors. Fowler claims that 'Fyodor's voice is almost perfectly equivalent to Nabokov's own.'[19] And two émigré writers who were friends with Nabokov in the thirties have some interesting things to say on this subject: Nina Berberova, who writes in her memoirs that she was 'present at least once at a conversation between Godunov-Cherdyntsev and Koncheev',[20] that is, between Nabokov and Khodasevich, the poet and critic with whom she lived for some time; and Zinaida Shakhovskaya, who calls *The Gift* one of Nabokov's autobiographies, 'in many respects more frank' than the other three.[21] For all these reasons I talk about 'the Nabokov view' of various matters in what follows.

Nabokov sets out to prove that any critic who is passionately involved in contemporary affairs, and interested in literature only in so far as it is a commentary on those affairs must be completely incapable of recognizing true art when he sees it. To prove that this was the case with Chernyshevsky and the other radical critics he concentrates on their intemperate and unsubstantiated literary evaluations, leaving the reader to draw his own conclusions about the methods which could produce such judgments. For example, he notes, that 'during fifty years of utilitarian ['progressive' in *Dar*] criticism, from Belinski to Mihailovski, there was not a single moulder of opinion who did not take the opportunity to jeer at the poems of Fet' (pp. 225/192). This does not quite mean what Nabokov wants it to mean, i.e., all the radical critics naturally detested a pure artist like Fet. Belinsky for instance actually admired Fet, welcomed his debut as a poet, and predicted a great future for him. The 'jeer' that Nabokov must be referring to comes in a letter to a friend written in 1843. In it Belinsky says that in his present mood he can read only Lermontov, that he is 'sinking deeper and deeper into the bottomless ocean of his poetry, and when I happen to skim through a poem by Fet or Ogarev, I say: "It's good, but isn't it shameful to waste time and ink on such trifles?" '[22] Readers much less interested in the social function of literature than Belinsky was have been known to experience such moods. But Chernyshevsky certainly did jeer, and Fyodor quotes the letter in which he calls Fet an 'idiot' for attempting to write verse without verbs (pp. 269/229). The long years of intellectual solitude made Chernyshevsky more prone than ever to this kind of cantankerous outburst, but that is no excuse. Yet it is at least worth pointing out that he included the poems of Fet on the list of books to be sent to him in Siberia. And in a letter to Nekrasov he defends the right of a poet like Fet to obey the demands of his own muse: 'The freedom of poetry', he observes, 'does not consist in just writing trifles like black magicians or Fet (who is, however, a good poet), but in not inhibiting one's gift by arbitrary constraints and writing about what one has a liking for. Fet would not be free if he took it into his head to write about social questions, and if he did the result would be rubbish' (vol. XIV, p. 314). I am not going to argue on the basis of this single pronouncement that Chernyshevsky was a closet aesthete

or a determined champion of the writer's independence, but I think
the letter points to a conflict between what his aesthetic sense told
him and what his public conscience demanded. And this conflict is
demonstrably there in various forms in many of the radical critics.
For that reason Nabokov's example of Fet, although it isolates an
important characteristic of their criticism, turns out to be less clear
cut than it first appears.

The comments in *The Gift* on Chernyshevsky's attitude to
Tolstoy give an even better example of Nabokov's problems in
making his case against Chernyshevsky and those who viewed
literature as he did. Fyodor stresses his subject's hatred for
Tolstoy, quotes some very nasty remarks about him in a sycoph-
antic letter Chernyshevsky wrote to Turgenev, and adds near the
end of the biography a preposterous depreciation of Tolstoy made
by Chernyshevsky when he was in exile. The clear implication is
that the radical critic's extra-literary interests so blinded him to the
aesthetic qualities of good literature that the greatest of Russian
novelists received only contemptuous insults from him. The
problem here is that one of Chernyshevsky's most famous essays on
literature is an 1856 review of Tolstoy's *Childhood*, *Boyhood* and
War Stories, and it is filled with the most glowing praise for him as a
writer. Nabokov must have known about this review, but no doubt
he assumed that it was written only to flatter Tolstoy, whom
Chernyshevsky wanted, along with Turgenev, to publish exclusively in *The Contemporary* in 1857. Chernyshevsky himself admits
in a letter to Nekrasov that his article was written to please Tolstoy,
'without at the same time too much infringing on the truth'
(vol. XIV, pp. 329–30). Yet what is so interesting about this review
is not why he wrote it but what he says in it. He defines the
distinguishing characteristic of Tolstoy's fiction as an interest in
observing

how a feeling immediately arising from a given situation or impression,
being subjected to the influence of memory and to the power of the
associations produced by the imagination, changes into another feeling,
once more returns to its former point of departure and wanders again and
again, changing along the whole chain of memory; how a thought, born of
a first sensation, leads to other thoughts, is carried farther and farther
away, blends reveries and real sensations, dreams of the future with
reflections of the present. . . . Count Tolstoy is above all interested in the
psychic process itself, its forms, its laws, to express it in terms of a
definition – in the dialectic of the soul.   (vol. III, pp. 422–3)

He then coins the term 'interior monologue' (vol. III, p. 424) for this kind of representation; and notes in passing that literature seldom makes us aware of this complex process of association of thoughts and feelings, because even monologues, which one might think would serve admirably as an expression of that process, 'almost always express the conflict of feelings, and the noise of that conflict distracts our attention from the laws and transitions by which the associations of ideas are accomplished' (vol. III, p. 425). I submit that anyone who could write like this about literature had at least some of the gifts of a first-rate literary critic. By adopting the polemical tone often favoured by his opponents, and opting for the big generalization rather than the detailed argument, Nabokov leaves himself open to some important objections. Since Chernyshevsky had less talent as a critic than some of his fellow radicals, we might conclude at least provisionally that Nabokov's contention that such critics were necessarily literary nincompoops seems extremely tenuous.[23]

It would be tedious to take up author after author in this way, so I propose to concentrate on what Nabokov says about Chernyshevsky's approach to one author in particular, the one he singles out as the crucial test of a Russian literary critic's abilities: Pushkin. The four pages devoted to him in the Chernyshevsky biography provide some fascinating examples of how Nabokov deals with his opponents' views on Russia's greatest poet, and suggest just how much is at stake in this battle over how Russian literature is to be discussed.

Fyodor begins by defining the autonomy of the aesthetic artefact in the most uncompromising terms possible. Any critic interested in Pushkin, he insists, must concentrate only on things like metrical blemishes or careless repetitions, the technical side of his art, and refrain at all costs from judging him according to criteria borrowed from 'sociological, religious, philosophical and other textbooks'. All the rest is 'irrelevant chitchat' (pp. 285/243). Notice how this polarizes the issues right from the outset. The rather large middle ground in which most critics function is supposed not to exist. In theory that is – in actual practice Fyodor is engagingly, humanly inconsistent. In his comments on Chernyshevsky's *What to Do?*, for example, he uses the very approach he rejects here. He condemns not only Chernyshevsky's aesthetic incompetence but also his naïveté, his simplistic solutions to complex social problems, his sentimentality – in short, the view of human life presented by his novel. Nabokov's own studies of Pushkin feature the same combination of austere theoretical *ukaze* with a rich and multifaceted practical criticism. In the *Eugene Onegin* commentary, he describes as foolish any attempt to discuss Onegin as a real person or a social type, and dismisses the literature on this subject as 'one of the most boring masses of comments known to civilized man'. But inevitably Nabokov's own ideas about what social set Onegin might have belonged to are soon added to this mass.[24]

Then Fyodor proceeds to group Chernyshevski with the other radical critics. This is of course only natural, but it is particularly important for him to do it at this point because it enables him to write: 'When Chernyshevski or Pisarev called Pushkin's poetry "rubbish and luxury" . . .' (pp. 285/243). That is, the vituperative harangue was a regular feature of these people's discussions of Pushkin. Writing some seventy-five years after the events being described for a readership composed at least in part of émigrés who would not remember the specific views of the various critics of the time, Nabokov could get away with linking the two men in this way. But Chernyshevsky and Pisarev differed in some important respects on Pushkin. Chernyshevsky never called his poems 'rubbish and luxury'; both the tone and the sentiments are quite unlike him when he was discussing Pushkin. For him, Pushkin was the cornerstone on which he hoped Russian literature would continue to build. Here is a typical remark:

> In discussing the importance of Pushkin in the history of the development of our literature and society, one must not examine to what extent various strivings met with in other stages of the development of society are expressed in his works, but take into consideration the most urgent needs both of the past and even of the present – the needs of literature and human interests generally. In this respect the importance of Pushkin is immeasurably great.   (vol. II, p. 475)

And another: 'the artistic genius of Pushkin was so great and excellent, that, although the era of absolute satisfaction with pure form has passed for us, we still cannot not be carried away by the marvellous artistic beauty of his works' (vol. II, p. 516). Slightly vacuous praise perhaps, with a certain automatic quality about it, but praise none the less.[25] Pisarev's position was quite different. He set out, in an essay called 'Pushkin and Belinsky', to demolish the links that Belinsky (and Chernyshevsky after him: in the first of his two long studies of Pushkin he often quotes Belinsky, always approvingly) had posited between great art and the progressive evolution of society. As Victor Terras points out in *Belinskij and Russian Literary Criticism*, Pisarev believed that 'Pushkin's poetry was purely "imaginary", that it had none but aesthetic value, and that its relevance to the reality of Russian life was negligible'.[26] Chernyshevsky would have been appalled by Nabokov's claims about the utter irrelevance of Pushkin's work to contemporary issues, or by his limiting legitimate criticism to metrical matters. Pisarev, on hearing the same claims, would have smiled, nodded, and agreed that Nabokov was right. 'So what if these minor differences existed?', someone is bound to object. 'These critics believed in committed art, Nabokov didn't.' But these differences are essential if Nabokov's argument is going to convince those who need convincing. He doesn't help his cause by using colourful details to disguise judicious omissions.

The section on Pushkin continues with the charge that Chernyshevsky dismissed Pushkin as 'only a poor imitator of Byron' (pp. 286/243). The trick here is to report a very specific comment about an aspect of one of Pushkin's early poems as if it were a casual, dismissive summary of a whole *oeuvre*. Critics don't normally devote hundreds of pages to the works of an author they consider to be a 'poor imitator' of someone else, and Chernyshevsky was no exception. What Nabokov must have in mind is the discussion of 'The Caucasian Captive' in Chernyshevsky's 1856 study of Pushkin. This poem, he says, was written when the young poet was under the influence of (1) the sublime beauty of the mountains in the Caucasus, hence its 'magnificent and vivid pictures' of that region and (2) Byron, whose melancholy Pushkin reproduced in a much weaker form, because such a mood ran counter to his 'natural disposition' (vol. III, p. 332). What Chernyshevsky means is explained in one of his stories in which the character who speaks for the author says of the same poem: 'If we study Byron's heroes we see why they are suffering ... If they reject life and despise people we know why they do it: life and people do not correspond to their demands; but they obviously are conscious of what those demands are.' The hero of 'The Caucasian Captive' curses life and people 'simply because he gets it into his head to play the fool for himself and for others with his fine-sounding phrases; I think that all these are purely fantastical whims that give him a great deal of secret pleasure, and that he simply drapes himself in suffering' (vol. XI, pp. 668–9). In other words, Chernyshevsky's comments on early Pushkin were as perceptive as the next man's. (Here at least part of his assessment is supported by no less an authority than Nabokov himself who, in his Pushkin commentary, describes 'The Caucasian Captive' as 'a Byronic search for inner "liberty" '.)[27] In fact, the whole notion of Pushkin as an imitator of Byron is one that Chernyshevsky regularly argued against. In one place he notes that by 1824 Byron's influence on Pushkin had disappeared altogether (vol. III, p. 333); and in another he insists that Pushkin was quite unlike Byron, and that his greatness lay in those qualities which made him fundamentally different from that English 'misanthrope' (vol. III, p. 146). So Chernyshevsky did not dismiss Pushkin in the way that Fyodor implies, and what he did say about the Byronic aspects of his work, regardless of the 'method' he was using, constitutes genuine criticism. As this kind of detail accumulates, we start to realize that Nabokov's 'all-or-nothing' thesis is putting him under considerable strain. He must keep on denouncing, while his opponents, at least some of the time, are actually talking about the texts. He cannot undertake a leisurely, detailed analysis of their work, because he is committed to the view that it doesn't merit that kind of examination. His wit and brilliance can distract us from these problems for a time, but he has difficulty sustaining the effect.

The rest of the section attacking Chernyshevsky's views on Pushkin involves Nabokov in similar problems. To avoid having to come to terms with what Chernyshevsky says about Pushkin's knowledge and education, he has Fyodor finesse with Dobrolyubov's slighting remark, 'Pushkin lacked a solid, deep education' (pp. 286/243), a shrewd tactical move, since Chernyshevsky was given to saying things such as: 'every one of his pages seethes with intelligence and the life of educated thought' (vol. II, p. 475); and: 'he was one of the best educated people of his time' (vol. III, p. 327). What about Pushkin's rough drafts, and Fyodor's portrayal of Chernyshevsky as someone so 'ridiculously alien to artistic creation' (pp. 286/243) that he criticized Pushkin for not writing out exactly what he wanted to say the first time? Once again, this is the kind of thing that Chernyshevsky should have said, given his theoretical views and his reputation generally, but things are not so simple. The discussion of Pushkin and his revisions occurs in the second of four long articles on him that Chernyshevsky wrote in

1855, and he devotes some twenty pages to the subject (vol. II, pp. 450–69). He begins by quoting Pushkin on the fate of Malherbe and Ronsard, two poets who according to Pushkin are now forgotten because they spent too much time polishing the form of their verse and not enough on its content. Very Chernyshevskian stuff this, but coming from a rather unexpected quarter. The radical critic goes on to praise Pushkin for spending such a long time planning his work and letting his ideas come to fruition. Chernyshevsky then admits that writers must proceed in these matters in a way that best suits their individual temperament, then apparently changes his mind and urges everyone to do it the way that obviously works for him, i.e., write without any constraints and save the revision until later. He then claims that the writer's most important task when revising is to cut out mercilessly any excess, spends two pages praising Pushkin for doing just that, advises contemporary writers to follow the example of the author of 'The Captain's Daughter', disagrees with those who assume that there is some necessary connection between blotted lines and great poetry, and concludes by explaining how Pushkin's temperament obliged him to spend a great deal of time reworking what he wrote. Neither here nor anywhere else does Chernyshevsky say that Pushkin's many revisions mean that he couldn't have been a genius. He may have believed, as Nabokov says, that common sense '*knows* what it wants to say' from the start (pp. 286/243), but the photographic reproductions of Chernyshevsky's own rough drafts (see vol. XI, pp. 449 and 641) suggest that his common sense did not 'know' what it wanted to say until copious revisions had been made.

Fyodor concludes his remarks on Chernyshevsky's Pushkin by noting that the radical critic thought that Russia's greatest poet was the author of 'vulgar drivel' (pp. 287/244). Surely this ill-considered remark will do mortal damage to Chernyshevsky's reputation. The poem which elicited it, 'Stamboul is by the giaours now lauded', is about the taking of Istanbul by Russian troops. The city is to be crushed, says Pushkin, like a 'sleeping snake' under the army's 'forged heel'.[28] Chernyshevsky, in his commentary on Alexander Kinglake's *Invasion of the Crimea*, links this poem to all the other expressions of bellicose nationalism in the 1820s, all the pledges to capture the Bosphorus and subdue the infidels with the power of Russia's armies. His views on these sentiments are indeed harsh: 'It was talk, reader, idle talk, just like the discussions of the Manilovs

[in *Dead Souls*] about building a bridge across the pond and
constructing shops on it; the vast chattering majority of the Russian
public and of Russian writers did not intend to sacrifice one drop of
its blood, not even a brass farthing for this affair' (vol. X, p. 330).
But they are certainly no harsher than Nabokov's own opinion of
Pushkin's poems about the way the Russian army had crushed a
rebellion in Poland, which he calls 'a torrent of lurid nationalism'.[29]
In its context, Chernyshevsky's remark bespeaks the same kind of
honesty and courage.

Why all these gaps between what Nabokov accuses Chernyshevsky of saying and what he actually wrote about Pushkin?
Maurice Couturier suggests one way out for the author of *The Gift*:

> The biography and portrait of Chernyshevsky are above all an exercise in
> writing: Fyodor was anxious to demonstrate that his writing was sufficiently
> strong and beautiful to silence the character, to supplant him on the stage of
> the book. For Nabokov, the novelist is not a historian, he is a learned
> practitioner of writing (just like the poet).

In another discussion of the novel he claims that Fyodor's task is to
'free writing from any referential obstacle'.[30] The temptation to see
The Gift in this way, in the retrospective glow of a novel like *Ada*, is
a real one, but I think it should be resisted. There is too much talk
about the importance of 'historical truth' (pp. 230/196) in the novel,
too much emphasis on the crucial nature of the issues at stake for the
biography to be only an 'exercise in writing'. And as late as 1969
Nabokov said that the Chernyshevsky biography was based on
'longer and deeper research' than his book on Gogol, and that 'the
plain truth of documents' was on his side.[31] I have already made
some suggestions about the ways in which Nabokov's novelistic and
satiric interests affect the truth-content of Fyodor's *Chernyshevsky*.
I think another part of the answer lies in the fact that Chernyshevsky
is a common reader and Nabokov an uncommon one. The radical
critic's Pushkin, the one who made poetry popular in Russia and
raised the general cultural level of the people, is not Nabokov's.
What makes Pushkin the 'gold reserve' (pp. 83/74) of Russian
literature for him is what the common reader doesn't like or doesn't
understand. When Edmund Wilson praised Lenin's taste in literature, Nabokov wrote him: 'When [Lenin] says "Pushkin" he is not
thinking of our (yours, mine, etc.) Pushkin, but an average-Russian
mixture of a) school manuals, b) Chaykovsky, c) hackneyed quot-
ations, d) a kind of safe feeling about Pushkin as being "simple" and

"classical".'[32] Pushkin belongs to the relatively few people who do not read him in this unimaginative, popular way. All these possessive pronouns suggest that this conflict between two ways of reading is a very personal one, and that in the end much more than alternative approaches to literature is at stake. A look at the discussion in *The Gift* of Chernyshevsky's thought in general – his philosophy, his erudition, his skill as a writer in putting his ideas across – will help to shed some light on these ideas of Nabokov's about the common reader and the uncommon one, and about the difference between the popularized version and the specialist's knowledge.

Chernyshevsky's brand of metaphysical materialism now ranks with phrenology and encounter groups as a serious intellectual subject. In espousing its doctrines, Chernyshevsky is at his most vulnerable, and Nabokov coolly demolishes his 'philosophy' by simply quoting a sample: 'We see a tree; another man looks at the same object. We see by the reflection in his eyes that his image of the tree looks exactly the same as our tree. Thus we all see objects as they really exist' (pp. 273/232).[33] Given the helpless quality of this kind of reasoning, it is not surprising that, as Nabokov points out, Chernyshevsky, when attacked by a philosopher, Professor Yurkevich, for his failure to account for 'the spatial motion of the nerves being transformed into nonspatial sensation' (pp. 276/235), could not even come up with a counter-argument. But he did write a couple of things about the criticisms made of him: the first was a page-long explanation of what had led Yurkevich astray, the second a long polemical article describing what he was trying to do in his philosophy. The first is a feeble thing. Chernyshevsky points out that his opponent is a seminarist, and that therefore his approach to metaphysics is derived from the same textbooks that Chernyshevsky used when he was in a seminary. If Yurkevich accepts Chernyshevsky's offer to send him some different books, he may escape the limits of his narrow education (vol. VII, pp. 725–6). The radical critic thought that his materialist philosophy had superseded idealism, that his approach was self-evidently the right one, that its truth did not have to be defended by logic. The other article is more interesting, because in it Chernyshevsky does say something about the way he sees his role that suggests that the logical muddles of his materialism are not finally what is most important in his intellectual position. He writes (addressing the editor of *Notes of the Father-*

land, the journal in which Yurkevich's article originally appeared): 'Is it necessary that I explain to you the difference between being widely read and being a specialist, between a specialist scholar who advances knowledge in one science or one branch of science and a journalist, for whom it is sufficient to be an educated man, who only popularizes the conclusions made by scholars, only ridicules crude prejudice and backwardness?' (vol. VII, pp. 764–5). A lousy philosopher but a good popularizing journalist, interested in all the problems that occupied the educated people of his day, who sometimes got in over his head? Perhaps Chernyshevsky should be judged by different standards.

This will definitely not get him off the hook as far as Nabokov is concerned. As if anticipating this very objection, he launches repeated attacks on the effects of Chernyshevsky's journalistic approach to knowledge. One of the most telling, because his own words are cited, is Chernyshevsky's dismissal of all kinds of specialized study as a waste of time: 'It was a love of generalities (encyclopedias) and a contemptuous hatred of particularities (monographs) which led him to reproach Darwin for being puerile and Wallace for being inept (". . . all these learned specialities, from the study of butterfly wings to the study of Kaffir dialects")' (pp. 270/229). The ellipsis here is strategic, for the phrases quoted are taken out of context in a most ingenious way. They occur in one of Chernyshevsky's letters from exile to his sons, in which he writes:

> How are your scholarly projects coming along? I once spent several years on Slavonic philology. In itself this specialization is estimable, like every other scholarly specialization, from the study of butterfly wings (e.g. that absurd Wallace) to the study of Kaffir dialects. But I think one should start immersing oneself in these trifling occupations only when one has mastered a general scientific education.   (vol. XV, pp. 324–5)

The whole passage admirably illustrates the conflicting tendencies in the man. On the one hand, he knows that his radical credo compels him to regard specialized subjects as 'trifling'; on the other, he finds some of these subjects so interesting that he spends years on them, and he hopes that they will one day take their proper place in the general curriculum. But more is at stake here than Fyodor's clever manipulation of his sources to serve his own polemical purposes.[34] His remarks fundamentally distort Chernyshevsky's real attitude to science itself. He did not dismiss the scientists with a contemptuous sneer. On the contrary, he took them very seriously indeed. He even wrote a long essay on Darwin near the end of his life, and a very revealing one it is. He begins by expressing his opinion of Darwin's abilities as a researcher: 'thanks to his conscientiousness, skill, industry and erudition, [his monographs] were outstanding. Because of his passion for scrutinizing everything his eye lighted on, he made during the expedition of the Beagle many subtle, beautiful observations. His diary account of them gained him the reputation of a great scientist. He fully merited it' (vol. X, p. 750).[35] Now of course there is a 'but' hovering over this account. Nabokov would have us believe it is something like: 'But who cares about these specialist studies when urgent social problems cry out to be analyzed and remedied? Out of your ivory tower, scientist', etc. Chernyshevsky actually goes on to make a very different point. He regrets that Darwin hurried the publication of *The Origin of Species*. He feels that Darwin's thesis was based on insufficient evidence, that he wandered outside his own special area in drawing his conclusions. And natural selection seems to make Chernyshevsky very nervous. Add to this the wistful references to the great naturalists whom Darwin should have known about, the ones who had spoken of the genealogical relations between the species, and the real Chernyshevsky reveals himself. He is an enlightenment man, a defender of Lamarck against the new beliefs, an uneasy observer of the paths now being taken by the science for which he so fervently propagandized all his life. Like a humanist faced with the implications of the conclusions of someone like Malthus, he stammers and hedges and digs in his heels. Mankind was progressing in leaps and bounds, not regressing to this savage, survival-of-the-fittest kind of existence. For a popularizer committed to the belief that knowledge, general and specialized, would rescue Russia from its benighted condition, these 'false' ideas were threatening, and so Chernyshevsky spoke out against them.

For a real understanding of his thought, the best procedure is to stand Nabokov's formula on its head: it is an interest in general ideas that is often conspicuously lacking in Chernyshevsky, and a fascination with details that redeems his work time after time. Nabokov never tired of telling his students to concentrate on the details when reading a novel; yet here, faced with a man who approached real life in precisely this way, he is so busy judging him that he forgets to look and see what he actually did. Nabokov is very stern, for example, with 'The Anthropological Principle in Philosophy', dismissing it as 'an infantile assessment of the most difficult moral questions' (pp. 276/234), i.e., lots of feeble general ideas. When we actually read the essay, we find something quite different. Chernyshevsky keeps promising the elaboration of moral philosophy that Nabokov accuses him of bungling, but he can't seem to get started. The pastimes of the idle rich, a comparison of the Yakuts and the people of London and Manchester, the physiological process by which Newton's brain arrived at the theory of the motion of celestial bodies, the difference between that process and what happens in a hen's nervous system when it is looking for food, the question of whether animals can think, including some speculations on how aged 'larks, swallows, moles and foxes spend the time of their decrepitude' – this is the sort of thing that occupies him (vol. VII, pp. 271–82). The whole effect is one of considerable erudition conveyed with a quasi-Gogolian offhandedness, and a shrewd journalistic sense of what people want to read. Three pages from the end he remembers that he has not explained the meaning of 'anthropological' in his title, hastily claims that those books which do not espouse the anthropological principle are junk (although there are some good things in them), and concludes that one general law will eventually be found to cover all the various laws in science, but until that happens there will be difficulties (vol. VII, pp. 293–5). But Chernyshevsky is interested in details for more than their educative or entertainment value. Far from being a materialist to whom theories were more important than things, as Nabokov's witty formula suggests, he had a great influence on the politics of the day precisely because he did know the details of things: the causes of student unrest, the economic consequences of the various plans for liberating the serfs, the reasons for the government's reluctance to push through genuine reforms. If this sounds like something out of a Soviet eulogy to 'The Great Predecessor', let me cite an unbiased observer on the same point:

[Chernyshevsky had] a capacity rare among Russians for concentration upon concrete detail. His deep, steady, lifelong hatred of slavery, injustice and irrationality did not express itself in large theoretical generalisations, or the creation of a sociological or metaphysical system, or violent action against authority. It took the form of a slow, uninspired, patient accumulation of facts and ideas – a crude, dull but powerful intellectual structure on which one might found a detailed policy of practical action appropriate to the specific Russian environment which he desired to alter.

Thus Isaiah Berlin in his book *Russian Thinkers*.[36] The Nabokov view of Chernyshevsky's knowledge and thought will not stand up to the evidence.

So why does he argue so vehemently for that view? What we are really listening to here is the debate about Pushkin all over again, transposed to a different key. Nabokov would contend that Cherny-shevsky, by using his knowledge to serve a certain set of social ideas, cheapened and adulterated it as surely as the 'school manuals' did Pushkin. Anyone interested in such ideas will sooner or later join forces with a mob and compel everyone else to accept his practical, popular, commonsense view of things. The levelling that inevitably results means the end of pure, abstract knowledge and the end of freedom for the researcher. This is what Nabokov means when he says that Chernyshevsky hated and sneered at specialists, even though in his particular case it doesn't happen to be true. The whole idea was not to be fully expressed until *Pale Fire*, where Gradus inherits the traits Nabokov gave to Chernyshevsky: 'He worshiped general ideas and did so with pedantic aplomb. The generality was godly, the specific diabolical ... People who knew too much, scientists, writers, mathematicians, crystalographers and so forth, were no better than kings or priests: they all held an unfair share of power of which others were cheated.'[37] But traces of it are there in *The Gift* as well. Fyodor's father tells of his encounter with a 'progressive schoolmistress' (pp. 124/107) who was shocked by the fact that he was engaged in hunting butterflies, that irresponsible indulgence of the upper class. And, in a passage that Nabokov cut from the novel when he revised its translation, the lepidopterist spots a howler in one of the books recommended by his son's geography teacher, and chuckles at the ignorance of the woman who compiled it (p. 122). The point is that those responsible for the humdrum process of general learning remain outsiders in the private world where only the expert belongs. Only private lessons, the ones that concentrate on details that are of no practical use to anyone, can communicate the really important knowledge. The problem is that Nabokov never does prove that there is a necessary link between an interest in democratizing education and the adul-teration of knowledge. Nor does he ever admit that in a great many disciplines the specialist studies of one generation are the general knowledge of the next. It is hard for us now to share the confidence in education that characterized the second half of the nineteenth

century, exemplified by a Chernyshevskian remark such as 'Erudite
literature saves people from ignorance, and the fine arts save them
from coarseness and banality; both are equally beneficial and
necessary for true enlightenment and the happiness of mankind'
(vol. III, p. 313). Yet this hardly makes an aristocracy of the
intellect a viable alternative. Surely any subject can be taught in a
way that stresses both its internal consistency and autonomy *and* the
modestly enriching contribution it can make to human life.
Nabokov did this with literature when he was a teacher, with great
sensitivity and acumen, and what he taught was not less true for
having been widely disseminated.

In the second part of this chapter I want to focus on one of the
principal issues raised in *The Gift*: the whole question of artistic
freedom in the 1850s and 60s, and the effect of the critical views
formulated in this period on the subsequent development of
Russian literature. Nabokov deals with this question in two different ways, comic and serious. The following excerpt from a
discussion of 'the epoch' is a good example of the first way:

At this point sparks flash from our pen. The liberation of the serfs! The era
of great reforms! No wonder that in a burst of vivid prescience the young
Chernyshevski noted in his diary in 1848 . . .: 'What if we are indeed living in
the times of Cicero and Caesar, when *seculorum novus nascitur ordo*, and
there comes a new Messiah, and a new religion, and a new world? . . .'
The fifties are now in full fan.[38] It is permitted to smoke on the streets.
One may wear a beard. The overture to *William Tell* is thundered out on
every musical occasion. . . . Under this cover Russia is busily gathering
material for Saltikov's primitive but juicy satire.   (pp. 277–8/236)

Here Nabokov sees the whole period as gathering material for his
purposes. His parodic version of newsreel history sets the hyperbolic tone, and the spirit of 1848, and the reforms, and the social
unrest, and the revolutions, all float away in the hot-air balloon he
has prepared for them. The epoch with all its important issues
becomes a mere simulacrum. The radical critics, the men who along
with Chernyshevsky played such an important role in the debate
about these issues, are treated just as irreverently. Think of the
images we are left with. Belinsky: 'that likeable ignoramus, who
loved lilies and oleanders, who decorated his window with cacti (as
did Emma Bovary)' (pp. 225/192); Dobrolyubov: wrestling with
Chernyshevsky, 'both of them limp, scrawny and sweaty – toppling

all over the floor, colliding with the furniture – all the time silent, all you could hear was their wheezing' (pp. 290/247); Pisarev: his 'perverted aestheticism', 'unbearable, bilious, teeth-clenching phrases about life being beautiful', and 'completely insane' letters (pp. 310/264). With the opposition in this kind of farcical disarray, Nabokov presses home his advantage by allowing them to put their case for committed literature in only its most unconvincing and exaggerated forms. The argument might almost be won by default.

It isn't, because the issues involved are so momentous that they cannot be mocked into non-existence. But before I take up the serious things Nabokov has to say about the status of literature at this crucial point in Russian history, I want to give someone else a chance to present his view of just what was at stake for Russia and its culture in the 1850s and 60s. I am thinking of Dostoevsky. He mistrusted the radical critics as much as Nabokov did, but he too thought their ideas about literature needed to be discussed. Of course he fares rather badly in *The Gift*. His work is dismissed in two delightful one-liners: 'Bedlam turned back into Bethlehem' (pp. 83/75), and 'a room in which a lamp burns during the day' (pp. 353/299). And he makes a personal appearance in Chapter Four as a panic-stricken supplicant, come to plead with Chernyshevsky to stop the St Petersburg fires. Nevertheless, concerning this question of the obligations of the literary artist in mid nineteenth-century Russia, his analysis is a model of clarity and good sense.

In 1861 Dostoevsky wrote an article called 'G. —bov i Vopros ob Iskusstve' ('Mr —bov and the Art Question'),[39] an overview of contemporary criticism (the figure alluded to in the title is Dobrolyubov), in which he discusses the debate between the advocates of pure and committed art. He asks the reader to imagine himself in eighteenth-century Lisbon just after the great earthquake. Half the city's population has been destroyed; its buildings lie in ruins; dazed survivors wander the streets. A newspaper appears, and, eager for information about the catastrophe that has befallen them, the people rush to see what it contains. What, asks Dostoevsky, are they to think if featured prominently on the front page they find the following poem by Fet?

> A whisper, timid breathing,
>   A nightingale's trills,
> The silver and flutter
>   Of a somnolent brook,

> Night's light, night's shadows,
>   Endless shadows.
> A series of magical changes
>   Of a dear face,
> In smoky clouds the purple of roses,
>   The reflection of amber,
> And kisses, and tears,
>   And the dawn, the dawn![40]

His answer is that the distraught citizens, outraged at the very idea of this kind of poetry's being written in the midst of their agony, would seize the author and summarily execute him in the public square for his inhuman and antisocial act. But he goes on to suggest that fifty years later they would erect a monument to the poor poet, for his wonderful verse in general and for 'the purple of roses' in particular. Dostoevsky concludes that it was not the subject matter of the poem that was at fault but the poet's insensitivity. Once the public issues that so occupied the people are forgotten, the value of the poet's work can be assessed at its true worth. The message for critics like Dobrolyubov is plain. Yet having made clear that the demand for literature which addresses itself to certain social problems can only encroach upon the writer's freedom, Dostoevsky is careful to point out that the writer's inspiration can come as easily from a political or social issue as from anything else. And he takes it for granted that when any nation finds itself on the edge of an abyss, every citizen, writers included, should work together for the common good. They cannot be coerced into doing it; but if literature is allowed to develop freely, it will become the powerful weapon the utilitarians want it to be.

The existence in Dostoevsky's Russia of a large body of literature that is related to the major social and political issues of the day suggests that Russian writers felt themselves to be caught up in events as potentially destructive as any earthquake, and that at this time, in this place, they had the most fundamental contribution to make to their country. Chernyshevsky asserted quite unequivocally that this was the Russian tradition: while great writers in other countries at other times had worked with the perfection of their art in mind and for the benefit of their country only indirectly (vol. III, p. 136), Russian society, because of its relative immaturity, intellectual history and (though this could not be said openly) its political history, had always relied on literature, and for some time to come must continue to do so, in a way that other nations did not.

Literature *was* Russia's political and social history. Most writers, more conscious of the problems created for their art by this tradition, and more aware of the contradictions inherent in their situation, wanted to write about social problems without producing the social tracts that Chernyshevsky often advocated. Yet even the 'aesthetes', whom Fyodor so roundly condemns (pp. 266–7/227), sound more than a little like their progressive enemies at times. Druzhinin argued that all art was linked to the moral development of society, extolled the merits of practical experience in the working world for the aspiring writer, and insisted that if poetry was 'the flower of life', it must be much more firmly rooted in the national soil than it was.[41] And Turgenev, classified as an aesthete in *The Gift* for his 'much too elegant "visions" and misuse of Italy' (pp. 267/227), wrote in one letter that 'There are epochs when literature cannot remain *merely* art, when there are interests higher than poetic interest'; and in another that a novel like *Fathers and Sons* had been written at the right moment, had been of some 'benefit' to the nation, and that this was the only thing that had any ultimate significance.[42]

Nabokov really has three answers for all this talk about a Russian writer's social obligations. The first involves him in a detailed and subtle parody of these very sentiments in *The Gift* itself. Both A. Y. Chernyshevsky and Vasilev make respectful noises about 'the epoch' and 'national life' in relation to Fyodor's book at the end of Chapter Three, but the main attack is saved for the reviews of the biography at the start of the last chapter. These show Nabokov at his best, brilliantly imitating a type of criticism that he knew well. The sentiments expressed above are brought up to date in the remarks of someone like Mortus, who combines civic concerns with a trendy apocalypticism in his denunciation of *Chernyshevsky*: 'The fact that it is precisely now, precisely today, that this tasteless operation is being performed is in itself an affront to that significant, bitter, palpitating something which is ripening in the catacombs of our era' (pp. 339–40/288). But this comedy is deadly serious. In the long review of the book by Professor Anuchin, Nabokov works at exposing the whole notion of an era or epoch as a concept that inevitably leads to all sorts of intellectual dishonesty. The critic argues:

What is important is that, whatever Chernyshevski's views may have been on art and science, they represented the *Weltanschauung* of the most progressive men of his era, and were moreover indissolubly linked with the development of social ideas, with their ardent, beneficial, activating force. It is in this aspect, in this sole true light, that Chernyshevski's system of thought acquires a significance which far transcends the sense of those groundless arguments – unconnected in any way with the epoch of the sixties – which Mr Godunov-Cherdyntsev uses in venomously ridiculing his hero.   (pp. 342/290–1).

Anuchin is not just a Nabokov straw man, to be knocked over with a casual backhand when he has served his purpose, but a Trojan Horse wired for sound, spouting all sorts of 'truths' that, if accepted, turn out to be absolutely fatal for the enemy camp. His argument that Chernyshevsky's ignorance of aesthetics is unimportant because it comes wrapped up with many nobler sentiments in a big progressive lump is the kind of reckless defence Nabokov wants his opponents to advance. The same goes for Anuchin's contention that there is only one humanitarian tradition in Russian literature, from which all 'non-progressive' writers are excluded. For it was critics like Chernyshevsky, with their arbitrary judgments about what kinds of literature were in step with the progressive movement, that made their own case so vulnerable to attack, and actually deflected attention from the genuinely radical arguments they had to put forward.

Nabokov's second answer is: 'Look what happened' – when the Chernyshevskys came to power in Russia, when their ideas about what literature should be became the only acceptable ones. When Vasilev's *Gazeta* refuses to publish Fyodor's book, Nabokov forces the reader to think about what kind of freedom-loving tradition would deny freedom of expression to those who happen to disagree with the traditional view. And several unobtrusive comparisons between Chernyshevsky and Lenin remind us of the consequences for literature in the Soviet Union of some of Chernyshevsky's ideas. Nabokov notes that, according to Lunarcharsky, Chernyshevsky shared with Lenin 'breadth and depth of judgment' and the same 'moral make-up' (pp. 275/234), and that he was the Russian leader's favourite novelist and critic, leaving the reader to draw his own conclusions. Here a distinction should be made between Chernyshevsky's aesthetic views, which do lead directly to socialist realism and the like if one adheres to them more strictly than he himself did, and his 'moral make-up'. Unlike Lenin, he would not have welcomed the starvation of peasants in the famine of 1891, or advocated the censorship of literature in 1921, because both events were in

keeping with the logic of history or helped 'the Cause'.[43] Nevertheless, the persecution of Soviet writers fills in the gaps in Nabokov's
argument about the importance of artistic freedom, and helps him
to point an accusing finger at anyone who sets out to limit it.

The third argument should be the clincher. What do we find,
Nabokov asks, when we look at the literary works of those who
believe that the writer's primary obligation is to his age and country,
as compared to the works of those who view their tasks as writers
differently? And what happens when we read the whole of Russian
literature as something other than a commentary on contemporary
affairs? His answers are found in the many passages devoted to
literary matters in *The Gift*. The remarks on the formal aspects of
literary art alone – Pushkin's prose style, narrative transitions in
different novelists, Bely's scansion of Russian verse, Chernyshevsky's attempted scansion of Russian verse, the extraordinarily
rich account of how a poem actually comes to be written – are
enough to justify the claims made for the novel as an important
study of Russian literature. The parodies and the evocative details
chosen from the works of various authors (and here Nabokov cuts
across party lines) show us what a sensitive reader its author was.
But it is the evaluations which effectively rewrite Russian literary
history and form the centre of the argument in *The Gift* about
committed and uncommitted art.

The most audacious and controversial of these evaluations occurs
in the first imaginary conversation between Fyodor and Koncheev.
In their discussion only four prose writers, Pushkin, Gogol, Tolstoy
and Chekhov, are admitted to the first rank. Their brilliant colloquy
on these figures raises certain questions: Why does Fyodor forbid
Koncheev to say anything negative about Pushkin? Why does he
follow up this admonition with an unqualified acceptance of Chekhov's work as well? Why are minor criticisms of the great Tolstoy
allowed? Why is Dostoevsky so pointedly excluded from this
group? A cogent and suggestive response to these questions is found
in Simon Karlinsky's 'Nabokov and Chekhov: the Lesser Russian
Tradition',[44] in which he argues that Nabokov's own art can be
traced back in a direct line that runs through Chekhov to Pushkin.
These three writers, unlike Dostoevsky or Tolstoy, refuse to subordinate their art to some social or ideological purpose, and yet each is
a committed writer in a different sense. Their approach involves a
cool diagnosis of social and human problems, biological as opposed

to social humanitarianism. A writer in this tradition uses 'precision of observation and restraint in evaluation'; he 'describes what he sees and refrains from sweeping conclusions or generalizations'.[45] This helps explain some of Nabokov's assessments, but if we move to the novelists he places in the second rank there is still a problem. Goncharov, we are told, is a poor writer because *Oblomov* is a committed novel. Fyodor calls its hero, who happens to share a patronymic with Lenin, 'that first "Ilyich" who was the ruin of Russia' (pp. 82/74). This is a witty dismissal that occurs during some rapid-fire repartee, but it does suggest the link in Nabokov's mind between writing 'useful' literature and decreeing that nothing but 'useful' literature can be written. Now any objective appraisal of Goncharov's novel would have to acknowledge that, although the author has chosen to represent certain aspects of contemporary Russian society, he has not subordinated his art to some social or ideological purpose, and that the 'Oblomovism' he describes was a more important factor in the 'ruin' of Russia than his description of it. Here we can see the problem with Karlinsky's formulation. Not because there is no room for Goncharov in his schema – he can easily be placed between the two tendencies outlined above – but because Nabokov, with this impetuous and undiscriminating condemnation of socially relevant literature, commits his own to all the things that are supposed to characterize the 'other' tradition, to 'sweeping conclusions', 'generalizations', even 'ideological purpose', if campaigning against those with an ideology is itself an ideological commitment. Throw out Goncharov's most important novel in this way, and you have to throw out Aksakov, Leskov, and a host of other novelists who have a variety of social and political views and use their fiction to discuss them, without becoming excessively dogmatic or didactic. Nabokov seems to be on the brink of doing just that, if we are to judge by the decidedly mixed reception given these authors in *The Gift*. Twenty years later he warned Edmund Wilson to steer clear in his Russian studies of the 'Goncharov–Aksakov–Saltïkov–Leskov porridgy mass'.[46] He had decided to throw them out. Unfortunately, he never convinces us that we should take such judgments seriously.

This kind of dismissal is misleading in another way. It threatens to obscure the very real resemblances between Nabokov and the writers he characterizes so arbitrarily. The Aksakov who wrote lengthy and detailed accounts of the pleasures of hunting butterflies, and who created a world in which memory and nostalgia are at the very centre of human experience, is more important to the Nabokov reader than the one dismissed as 'wretched' (p. 75)[47] by Fyodor for the blunders in his descriptions of nature. The pointed criticism of Turgenev can also distract us from more significant matters. Accusing the author of *Rudin* and *Smoke* of appeasing the radicals, or dismissing *Fathers and Sons* for its 'inept tête-à-têtes in acacia arbours' (pp. 84/75) – these claims are so unusual that they may have the desired effect and actually make us reconsider Turgenev's work. But when we hear his descriptions of nature being ridiculed for their 'howlers' (pp. 84/75), we may well begin to feel that the 'novelist's novelist' is being deliberately misrepresented by one of his old admirers, now overly anxious to assert his independence. Consider the following passage from Chapter Five of *The Gift* (Fyodor is lying on his back in a forest, looking upward):

And still higher above my upturned face, the summits and trunks of the trees participated in a complex exchange of shadows, and their leafage reminded me of algae swaying in transparent water. And if I tilted my head back even farther, so that the grass behind (inexpressibly, primevally green from this point of upturned vision) seemed to be growing downward into empty transparent light, I experienced something similar to what must strike a man who has flown to another planet. (pp. 372/314–15)

Now compare it with a passage from *A Sportsman's Sketches*:

It is an extremely agreeable occupation to lie on your back in the woods and look upwards! It seems that you are looking into a bottomless sea, that it is spreading itself out far and wide *beneath* you, that the trees are not rising from the ground, but, like the roots of huge plants, dropping perpendicularly down into those glass-clear waves; and the leaves on the trees are now transparent as emeralds, now condensed to a goldish, almost blackish green.[48]

A coincidence perhaps, but a more promising field of inquiry for someone interested in Nabokov and his relations with Russian novelists of the mid nineteenth century than the territory so zealously fenced off in *The Gift*.

Nabokov anticipates and forestalls some of this criticism by including his own auto-critique in the second dialogue imagined by his hero, when Koncheev tells Fyodor that he sometimes says things in *Chernyshevsky* 'chiefly calculated to prick your contemporaries' (pp. 381/322). Another possibility is that the novel's iconoclastic excesses are the mark of Fyodor's immaturity, something he must

leave behind him if he is to become a full-fledged novelist like his
creator. But this desire to 'prick' contemporaries becomes more
prevalent in Nabokov as he gets older; and even if we agree to accept
these judgments as mere youthful exuberance, the main point
remains unchanged: Nabokov's insistence on the necessity of the
literary artist's freedom is eloquent and persuasive, but the view of
literature that results when this single criterion is applied in an
idiosyncratic and dogmatic way is not very convincing. He has not
dealt successfully with the special problems of the writer in the
Russia of the 1850s and 60s, and he is so determined to ridicule what
he imagines to be the opposition that he misrepresents the epoch
and the literature he knew so well.

Of course Nabokov's discussion of nineteenth-century Russian
writers takes him beyond the arguments about committed and
uncommitted literature at a given period in the nation's history. In
the final part of this chapter, I want to explore in more detail his
search for his antecedents and his attempt to establish the exact
nature of his relationship with them. I am specifically interested in
why he calls Chapter Two 'a surge toward Pushkin' (p. 8), and why
he says at the end of that chapter that his hero is moving from
'Pushkin Avenue to Gogol Street' (pp. 164/141). The search for
some answers to these questions takes us to the heart of what being a
Russian writer means to Nabokov.

First Pushkin. It is clear from the commentary on Pushkin's art
that the lucidity of his prose and the precision of his observations are
what most impress Fyodor when he reads Pushkin to help him
prepare for his own literary tasks. Karlinsky's attempt to place
Nabokov in a tradition of Pushkinian objectivity is not confirmed by
the literary criticism in *The Gift*, but perhaps it is borne out by this
quality in other parts of the novel. One of the works Nabokov
singles out for special praise is *Journey to Arzrum*, Pushkin's
account of his experiences in the Caucasus in 1829. A comparison
between this short work and Nabokov's novel turns out to be
instructive.[49]

Pushkin's work is especially rich in simple allusions to small
details: the graffiti on a minaret, the special rites used by the
Georgians to open their casks of wine, the way the sky changes as a
storm approaches. Opening *The Gift* at random, we find something
like 'the sound of hooves had been heard on the bridge (a swift

wooden drumming which was immediately cut off)' (pp. 144/124), something as simple and real as these details in Pushkin, something which, although we have always known about it, becomes more clear to us because it has been recorded in this way. Pushkin's special kind of lucid objectivity takes other forms as well. Interested in seeing what a military engagement is actually like (he is with a Russian army which is in the Caucasus to fight against the Turks), he is sent by a Russian general 'to the left flank'. The poet rides on a little and then wonders to himself: 'What does left flank mean?'[50] This simple question and the descriptions of the disorderly skirmishes that follow are a perfect example of Shklovsky's famous *ostranenie*, the device that forces the reader to look at what is actually happening instead of merely putting it in a conventional frame of reference.[51] Nabokov's use of the device is different but the effect is the same. The branches of a poplar 'resembling the nervous system of a giant' (pp. 62/57), 'the radiance of a lawn-sprinkler that waltzed on one spot with the ghost of a rainbow in its dewy arms' (pp. 182/156), a caterpillar 'checking the number of inches' between two people (pp. 379/321) – Nabokov uses metaphors in this way to add strangeness to beauty, and to reveal that strangeness in phenomena that most people look at but never see. Few novels are as rich as *The Gift* in this kind of detail, and this is particularly true of Nabokov's act of homage to Pushkin in Chapter Two, Fyodor's biography of his father, with its splendid evocations of the natural world and its mysteries in the countries visited by the lepidopterist.

But these resemblances are not what is finally most important. As we read *Journey to Arzrum* we are struck by a fundamental difference between Pushkin and Nabokov in so far as a third kind of objectivity is concerned, the desire to describe what one sees and refrain from 'sweeping conclusions or generalizations'. Pushkin's account of an incident that occurred while he was stopped by the side of the road, waiting for a military convoy to go by, will help illustrate what I have in mind:

While the carriages were passing, the officer of the convoy informed us that he had a poet from the Persian court with him, and, at my request, presented me to Fazil-Khan. With the aid of an interpreter I began a bombastic eastern greeting, but how ashamed I was when Fazil-Khan answered my inappropriate intricacies with the simple, wise politeness of a decent human being! 'He hoped to see me in Petersburg; he regretted that our acquaintance would be short-lived,' and so on. Embarrassed, I was obliged to forgo my pompously humorous tone and to adopt ordinary European phrases. Here is a lesson for our Russian derisiveness [*nasmeshlivost'*]. In future I won't judge a man by his sheepskin cap and his painted fingernails.[52]

It is this kind of objectivity that is often quite foreign to Nabokov's art. He needs this 'Russian derisiveness' for satiric bite, and he doesn't shirk from making the peremptory judgments it gives rise to. The most obvious example in *The Gift* is the treatment of the Germans. Many passages highlight the traits of various individual Germans, but their national characteristics are summed up at the beginning of the 'surge toward Pushkin' chapter. Among other things, Fyodor hates them for their

love of fences, rows, mediocrity; for the cult of the office; for the fact that if you listen to his inner voice (or to any conversation on the street) you will inevitably hear figures, money; for the lavatory humour and crude laughter; for the fatness of the backsides of both sexes . . .; for taking pains with dirty tricks, for the abominable object stuck carefully on the railings of the public gardens; for someone else's live cat, pierced through with wire as revenge on a neighbour, and the wire cleverly twisted at one end; for cruelty in everything, self-satisfied, taken for granted.   (pp. 93–4/83)

But the man who prompts this outburst by bumping into Fyodor on a tram turns out to be a Russian, and Fyodor, who has 'seen' all these characteristics in the physical features of the man, is forced to face up to the dangers of generalizing about the moral character of national types. So it is tempting to see this, as some critics have done, as a first step in the process of Fyodor's maturation.[53] But what are we to make of the passage near the end of the book in which Nabokov describes a 'typical' group of German bathers?

Old men's grey legs covered with growths and swollen veins; flat feet; the tawny crust of corns; pink porcine paunches; . . . the pimply shoulder blades of bandy-legged girls; the sturdy necks and buttocks of muscular hooligans; the hopeless, godless vacancy of satisfied faces . . . And over all this, especially on Sundays when the crowding was vilest of all, there reigned an unforgettable smell, the smell of dust, of sweat, of aquatic slime, of unclean underwear, of aired and dried poverty, the smell of dried, smoked, potted souls a penny a piece.   (pp. 376–7/318–19)[54]

He thought this particular passage so important that, when he published excerpts from *Dar* in *Poslednie Novesti*, he added it to the end of the third one, 'A Walk in the Grunewald', omitting the eight paragraphs that join Fyodor's 'walk' and his discovery of the

Germans by the lake.[55] I do not want to wax morally indignant here. Nabokov often includes such passages because he knows how much readers enjoy reading lists of energetic insults, watching all the obnoxious details pile up like the bodies on the beach. But this was how he felt about Germans,[56] and the derisiveness Pushkin warns us about obviously does have some unfortunate effects. Here it speaks the language of snobbery and prejudice, and prevents the observer from seeing what he is supposed to be looking at. It can even lead to foolish ranting, as when Fyodor describes the Germany of the 1920s as a country 'where a novel about incest or some brash trash, some cloyingly rhetorical, pseudo-brutal tale about war is considered the crown of literature; where in fact there is no literature, and hasn't been for a long time' (pp. 393/331).[57] (*The Magic Mountain* was published in 1924, *Steppenwolf* in 1927, etc.) In the Foreword to *The Gift*, Nabokov does the noble thing and admits that there is something wrong with these anti-German diatribes. He attributes it to the influence of the Nazis: 'history shows through artistry' here, he says (pp. 7–8). I think it makes more sense to see it as art flouting history, savage comic caricature winning out over objective representation.

What Nabokov means by taking up residence on 'Gogol Street' has already been explained by G. M. Hyde. He notes that 'The style of the novel at once becomes more comic and devious, more fanciful and "metaphysical", yet at the same time more grotesquely involved with the minutiae of Berlin life', adding that 'the resources of baroque Gogolian wit will be stretched to the utmost by being applied to such an apparently unsuitable subject as Chernyshevsky'.[58] I think this is essentially true; but the relation between the two authors is more complex than this formula suggests. Berlin as seen through Nabokov's eyes and the Chernyshevsky biography often do remind us of Gogol, but great chunks of both these sections of *The Gift* also remind us that the two writers differ in a fundamental way. It is perhaps best summed up by saying that Nabokov is more personal than Gogol: he makes us conscious of his presence in a way that the author of *Dead Souls* does not. To read Gogol on *poshlost'* is to learn about the crude, the vulgar, the corny. To read Nabokov on the same subject is to learn about all that, and about him and the long list of things he loathes. Gogol is as merciless in his exposure of human absurdity, but he travels along the roads his heroes take; and when he eludes us, he does so by disappearing into the world he has created. When Nabokov ridicules someone or something, we feel the unbridgeable gap between him and the object of his contempt.[59]

We can see the difference clearly if we look at the portrayal of the Russian people in *The Gift*. In the retrospective sections of the novel, they appear as a collection of ignorant outsiders, mostly servants, who are totally out of place in the special world inhabited by the hero. Think of them gawking uncomprehendingly at the mysterious rites of the elite Entomological Society, whose members are huddled together studying a rare species in the woods. Fyodor describes the scene, and adds: 'to this day I am wondering what the coachmen waiting on the road made of all this' (pp. 123/107), a remark that constitutes at least a muted recognition of the gulf separating the classes. But instead of developing this insight, Nabokov proceeds to exploit the comic consequences of such a gap. An orderly borrows Fyodor's butterfly net and brings home to the young master all sorts of things that strike him as worth collecting in the countryside, only to have his offering rejected with disdain.[60] We get the distinct sense that we are reading about the self-satisfied snobbery of callow youth which the author is about to expose and condemn. But Nabokov's aims are quite different. He concludes with a sarcastic 'The Russian common people know and love their country's nature' (pp. 124/107). Gogol has a great deal of fun with the ignorance of his 'common people', but he never deals with them quite so sharply as this.

The point is that Nabokov's Russia, like his Germany and his Chernyshevsky and his history of Russian literature, is a very personal thing. Field tells us that the Nabokov family regarded itself as 'a little nation'.[61] Nabokov himself said in an interview that his Russia was 'very small': 'A road here, a few trees there, a sky. It is a treasure chest to which one returns again and again.'[62] For all the memorable portraits of Russian people that Nabokov created, what he remembers here is a Russia with no people in it.[63] Of course one can find similar musings in Gogol. In some of his letters he says practically identical things about a Russia seen from the vantage-point of exile.[64] But once again there are some important differences. Gogol worked in a country that had hailed him as a great Russian writer and criticized him for what it took to be his short-comings, a country that had linked its destiny with his. His exile was self-imposed; his works, despite the censorship, were published; he could say 'we Russians' in a way that Nabokov could not. Gogol actually says as much in *The Gift* itself: 'Longer, longer, and for as long as possible, shall I be in a strange country. And although my thoughts, my name, my works will belong to Russia, I myself, my mortal organism, will be removed from it' (pp. 202/173), quotes Fyodor in the 'Gogol Street' chapter. Although Nabokov is certain that he too will one day be thought of as one of the great Russian writers, he is not bound in the same way to his native land, and he is not so sure about where that recognition will come from.

He deals with this question in *The Gift* by means of a seemingly casual allusion to a poem by Pushkin which sets up associations that eventually include the entire Nabokov *oeuvre*. Fyodor and Koncheev are discussing the problem of a readership for the émigré writer. 'Who knows my poems?' asks Koncheev. The answer in *Dar* is: 'One hundred, one hundred and fifty, at most, at most, two hundred intelligent expatriates, of whom again ninety per cent don't understand them. That's provincial success, but not fame' (p. 383). These figures increase by a factor of ten in the English translation, and Nabokov adds the sentence: 'Two thousand out of three million refugees!' (p. 323). He regularly helps the English reader out with bits of information of this kind, but only very rarely changes actual points of detail in a translation that is not a substantial reworking of the original. No doubt he did so here because he thought the second set of figures more realistic. But the point about a paucity of receptive readers is essentially the same in both versions, and Koncheev makes it again when he says that only ten people (a dozen in *The Gift*) among the émigrés will be able to appreciate Fyodor's book (pp. 345/292). That is the situation as it stands, declares Koncheev, and 'a great deal of time will have to elapse before the Tungus and the Kalmuk of Pushkin's "*Exegi monumentum*" begin to tear out of each other's hands my "Communication", with the Finn looking enviously on' (pp. 383/323).[65] In that poem, Pushkin announces that his literary achievement is a monument more impressive than the Alexandrine Column in St Petersburg and more durable than flesh, and that his greatness will eventually be appreciated by all the Russian people, because he 'exalted freedom' in his 'cruel age' and 'called for mercy toward the downfallen'.[66] The arrogant sound of this is qualified by the fact that the four stanzas which contain these sentiments are actually a delicate parody of Derzhavin's 'I've set up to myself a monument', which is itself based on Lomonosov's translation of Horace. The fifth stanza adds more qualification:

> To God's command, O Muse, obedient be,
> offense not dreading, and no wreath demanding;
> accept indifferently praise and slander,
> and do not contradict a fool.[67]

When he wrote *The Gift*, knowing that he would not be going back to Russia, uncertain about the chances of being published there during his lifetime, and already contemplating abandoning Russian for English, Nabokov must have been wondering what kind of monument he had erected and how long it would last.[68] Presumably he alludes to Pushkin here because this poem gets the balance about right: it is written by a poet who really does care how he will be remembered but who knows that the expression of a desire to be immortalized by his own verse must be, at least in part, a conventional rhetorical exercise, and that he can't do anything about it anyway.

The analogy between Pushkin's situation and that of the émigré writer is picked up again in another allusion to '*Exegi monumentum*' in a Nabokov poem called 'Slava' ('Fame'), written in 1942, which turns out to have an important link with *The Gift*. The speaker of the poem has a debate with a nasty and pessimistic inner voice that insists he renounce any hope of an admiring posterity. Once again Pushkin's 'monument' is contrasted with the exile's lack of one:

> 'No, never will anyone in the great spaces
> make mention of even one page of your work;
> the now savage will dwell in his savage ignorance,
> friends of steppes won't forget their steppes for your sake.'

But the poet triumphs over such gloomy predictions because he has a 'secret' that makes him immune to this 'empty dream / about readers, and body, and glory'. He can't give it away but he can hint at what it is: 'A book's death can't affect me since even the break / between me and my land is a trifle'; and: 'I've read in myself how the self to transcend.'[69] In her introduction to *Stikhi*, a collection of Nabokov's verse published two years after her husband's death, Vera Nabokov suggests what the secret is. She defines it as *potustoronnost'*, 'the hereafter', the 'chief theme' of the Nabokov *oeuvre*, the one that all the critics missed. Knowing this secret gave Nabokov his 'imperturbable cheerfulness' and made him 'invulnerable to all

the very stupid or malicious attacks' made on him.[70] She directs
readers interested in learning more about this secret to a specific
passage in *The Gift*, the paragraph in Chapter Two where Nabokov
describes a mysterious, indefinable quality that Fyodor notices in his
father, a special, inviolable solitude, a knowledge that cannot be
shared with anyone else (pp. 130–1/113–14).

There is certainly no need to worry about posterity if you've got
the hereafter on your side, and W. W. Rowe's remarkable book,
Nabokov's Spectral Dimension, has convincingly demonstrated the
importance of spirits and the 'other world' in Nabokov's work;[71] but
I cannot help thinking that the Nabokov secret has little to do with
some mysterious knowledge of an ineffable beyond, that it is really
an open secret, lying there like the purloined letter in Poe face up on
the table. The intensely subjective view of Chernyshevsky, of
Russian literature, of the role that literature is to play in society, of
the writer's 'gift' as something the special individual is entrusted to
keep safe from the 'malicious hags and crooked hucksters' of the
general populace who would like to steal it from him (pp. 93/82) –
what are all these but versions of Nabokov's 'secret', the possession
of a creative imagination so powerful that it remakes every aspect of
the world it comes into contact with? This is why he doesn't have to
worry about his 'monument'. If Russia is lost, Fyodor will create a
new Russia, revisit his country 'with pen in hand' (pp. 32/31), look
up from his writing and 'see a Russian autumn' (pp. 197/169). The
country estate at Leshino? Re-created in the play of sun and shadow
in the isolated paths of Fyodor's private Grunewald. The romance
with a girl before the revolution? Fyodor even tries to create his new
love out of the shadows of the Berlin streets; and when he finally
meets her, he gives her the name of his muse, 'Mnemo*zina*',[72] and
decides to write a novel about how 'fate' has brought them together.
It is no good objecting that all this does not happen in real life.
Nabokov thought otherwise. Andrew Field once asked Nabokov's
wife what she thought her life would have been like had the
Revolution not occurred and she not emigrated and met a young
Russian writer in Berlin. Her husband interrupted her response
with: 'You would have met me in Petersburg, and we would have
married and been living more or less as we are now!'[73] A man born
on Shakespeare's birthday whose grandfather might have been the
son of a Tsar cannot help but feel that he was born to create his own
tradition and his own destiny.

When Nabokov published the English translation of *The Gift* in the early sixties, he had done just that. His books were being read; his reputation was made; his mastery had been acknowledged. Yet the Foreword to the novel is not full of the exultant self-assertion one might expect. The doubts expressed there are related, not to his own work, but to the communal enterprise of which they once formed a part: émigré literature, one of his links with Russia, is gone, and he feels its loss. Not the émigré literature so amusingly demolished in the novel: the frauds and schemers of the Writers' Union, spending all their time in endless wrangling and petty intrigues, the mediocrities who frequent the poetry readings, the critics fussing about ineffectually in a world circumscribed by their own ignorance and prejudice. Not this, but the other émigré literature, the one represented by the names Nabokov intones in the Foreword: Bunin, Aldanov, Remizov, Khodasevich. All but Aldanov are from the older generation of exiles; all have strong links with the Russian literature of the past. They and Russian intellectuals like them were the representatives of a whole world.[74] That world is now a 'phantasm', Nabokov tells us, and its history reads like 'the wanderings of some mythical tribe' (p. 8). Elsewhere he talks about the air of 'fragile unreality' in which the émigré writers found themselves, 'hardly palpable people' trying to hold on to Russian culture in order to pass it on to the next generation.[75] Nabokov does not seem entirely convinced of their success. Yet seen from another point of view, this ghostly wandering of Russian culture and its representatives may actually constitute a living link with the past, and some kind of hope for the future. Perhaps it was always thus. In 1841, Belinsky wrote to a friend: 'We are men without a country – no, worse than without a country, we are men whose country is a phantom – is it any wonder then that we ourselves are phantoms, that our friendship, our love, our aspirations, our activities are phantoms?'[76] This feeling may be the very essence of Russian literary culture and its history.

4

Lolita

In the last two chapters I have tried to make a case for reading Nabokov's novels as something other than 'stagings' of his 'inventions', and to show that their 'real plot' exists, not only in the 'gaps' and 'holes' of the narrative,[1] those places where Nabokov interrupts his story and shows us the actual workings of his novels, but also in their ostensible content. *Invitation to a Beheading* and *Bend Sinister* can be discussed in terms of their social and political ideas; *The Gift* is a commentary on Russian literature. These are novels which, after the image patterns have been traced and the devices explained, still make propositions about a human world and a human nature that we can isolate and examine, argue with and endorse. Nabokov, I have tried to suggest, is a committed novelist, intent on expressing certain views and dramatizing certain truths. Reading his novels we feel, not just that various precepts about the autonomy of the aesthetic artefact are being exemplified, but that a view of man is being advanced.

In the case of those novels, this kind of criticism was an attempt to fill a definite gap. With *Lolita*, the problem is a little different. For people began arguing about it almost as soon as it appeared, and the subject of their argument was the novel's content: 'view of man', 'human values', 'attitudes that inform the work' – the people who thought about literature in these terms were the ones who wrote the reviews and letters to the editor that the novel's publication provoked. Why spend a chapter going over ground already well trodden? The first critic in Frederick Crews's *The Pooh Perplex* remarks that 'our ideal in English studies is to amass as much commentary as possible upon the literary work, so as to let the world know how deeply we respect it'.[2] That is a reason of sorts, but it also seems important now, nearly thirty years after the controversy about *Lolita* began, to reaffirm that some useful 'new directions' in Nabokov criticism might be discovered by reconsidering some of the old directions that many critics now regard as dead-ends. The edition in which a generation of students has been reading the novel is Alfred Appel's *The Annotated Lolita*.[3] Wittily and provocatively, his long introduction and extremely detailed notes advance a view of Nabokov that now dominates critical discussions of his work, but which, as I have been arguing, needs substantial qualification. He insists that Humbert's desire for young girls is only the novel's 'ostensible subject' (p. lvii), that *Lolita* is only 'supposedly about perversion' (p. 434), and that what seems like a depiction of real life is revealed for what it is when the 'authorial voice' reminds us that 'the characters have "cotton-padded bodies" and are the author's puppets, that all is a fiction' (p. xxxi).[4] He is joined by critics such as Julia Bader, who calls *Lolita* 'a novel about literary originality', and claims that 'The questions tackled by *Lolita* are artistic, or aesthetic, and the "moral" dilemma is treated in aesthetic terms.'[5] Brenda Megerle asserts that '*Lolita* is about tantalization, specifically that tantalization which Nabokov finds in the aesthetic experience'.[6] Even Maurice Couturier, who has some insightful things to say about sexuality in the novel, contends that it is 'first of all a poetic work having to do with the very process of poetic creation'.[7] When the 'big' issues raised by the novel are perceived to be of strictly secondary importance, the attention of many Nabokov readers shifts to the smaller parts of the elaborate structure that constitutes *Lolita*. They wonder about details: does 'Will Brown, Dolores, Colo.' (p. 253), one of the signatures in a motel register that Humbert reads as Quilty's mockery, mean 'I will sodomize Dolores'?[8] They seek out hidden parallels: Lensky in *Eugene Onegin* is 'analogous' to Quilty, we are told, because both are murdered and both have 'murdered the artistic ideals each author cherishes'.[9] The process of annotation promises to be a long and complex one. Appel points out one of the areas still unexplored when he observes, only half-jokingly, that his Notes 'seldom comment on H. H.'s topographical observations; the field remains wide-open. A generous grant from the Guggenheim Foundation or the American Council of Learned Societies will no doubt one day enable some gentle don to retrace meticulously H. H.'s foul footsteps' (p. 384). The main directions of *Lolita* criticism seem to have been determined.

I hope to show in this chapter that there is still something to be gained from treating the 'ostensible subject' of *Lolita* as the real one, by looking for the author, not so much in the stage-effects he arranges, as in the human drama he depicts. And I want to argue that only by recognizing the primacy of the human problems in a book like *Lolita*, by admitting that its force as a work of fiction depends on our responses to these problems, can we understand just what the novel has to tell us about the creative task that Nabokov has set himself. What follows is divided into three sections: (1) Nabokov's treatment of his sexual subject matter; (2) the whole question of *Lolita*'s ambiguity and the dilemmas it creates for the reader; and (3) the relation between Nabokov's aesthetics and the content of his novel.

As everyone knows, *Lolita* began life as a *succès de scandale*. Many bought the latest novel from Paris's Olympia Press thinking it was pornographic. The British government debated its merits at cabinet level and asked the French to ban its sale. It even had a certain political impact: Nigel Nicolson narrowly lost his Bournemouth seat because he publicly supported its publication. The appearance of the book in England caused some particularly violent outbursts. Looking back from our vantage-point, we might well be reassured by the denunciations of *Lolita* in letters to various journals. They often express the genuine concern of people who cared about literature. Nabokov's novel is not the handbook for child molesters that some of them took it to be, but we can hardly be condescending about their anxieties. The source of them was the firm belief that the publication of a book was an important event, that a novel could actually affect people's lives.[10]

What was not generally known at the time was that the author of *Lolita* shared many of the conservative views of his attackers in so far as the literary representation of sexual relations was concerned. In a 1946 letter to Edmund Wilson, whose *Memoirs of Hecate County* had offended the law, Nabokov offered his friend some examples of real pornography for use in the campaign to keep the novel from being banned. One is a chapter from Thomas Heggan's *Mr Roberts*, in which there is a story 'about sailors looking through a telescope at nurses having showerbaths and the point of the story is a mole on one of the girls' fanny'. The other is an article in the *International Digest* 'about the way Eskimos copulate'. It includes pictures of children imitating the actions of their parents who, says the reporter, 'chuckle at their youngsters' realism'.[11] Nabokov deplored not just this kind of vulgarity but explicit sexual references in serious literature as well. Lawrence he calls 'a pornographer',[12]

and even the revered *Ulysses* is criticized for its 'obnoxious, over-
done preoccupation with sex organs' and for the 'sexual affairs'
which 'heap indecency upon indecency'.[13] But how is the bruise
on Lolita's thigh which so fascinates Humbert in his encounter
with her on the living-room sofa different from the mole that
interests Heggan's sailors? And isn't *Lolita* as preoccupied with
sexual affairs as *Lady Chatterley's Lover* or *Ulysses*? A comparison between Nabokov's approach to his highly charged
material and those of some of the authors he criticizes will help
clarify matters.

Here is a description of an orgasm, taken at random from *Lady
Chatterley*: 'And she quivered, and her own mind melted out.
Sharp soft waves of unspeakable pleasure washed over her as he
entered her, and started the curious molten thrilling that spread
and spread till she was carried away with the last, blind flash of
extremity.'[14] Lawrence's prose here is that of a writer who does
not really care about words as such. Sex is not mental; therefore
only an approximate language is available to describe it. The
occasional slovenliness of the style that results is uncomfortably
close to the kind of stuff that can be found in any sex shop, and
this makes Nabokov's 'pornographer' remark seem less absurd
than it at first appears. He thought this kind of sex in fiction was
crude and anti-artistic. Whatever else he does in *Lolita* Nabokov
never writes like this.

The contrast with Joyce is more complex. Here is a short
excerpt from *Ulysses* (Bloom is watching Gerty Macdowell):

And then a rocket sprang and bang shot blind and O! then the Roman
candle burst and it was like a sigh of O! and everyone cried O! O! in
raptures and it gushed out of it a stream of rain gold hair threads and
they shed and ah! they were all greeny dewy stars falling with golden, O
so lovely! O so soft, sweet, soft!
Then all melted away dewily in the grey air: all was silent. Ah![15]

Nabokov would never have written this either. In one of his
novels a character with Bloom's background and interests could
enjoy only a decidedly inferior kind of sexual pleasure, and there
would therefore be no linguistic fireworks to record it. His skilled
lovers are always aristocrats of some sort, and his commoners are
copulators. (In his Joyce lectures he says that Bloom 'indulges in
acts and dreams that are definitely subnormal in the zoological,
evolutional sense'.)[16] Besides, Nabokov could never allow lan-

guage to let go in this way. Consider Humbert's Bloom-like autoerotic arrangements:

all the while keeping a maniac's inner eye on my distant golden goal, I cautiously increased the magic friction that was doing away, in an illusional, if not factual, sense, with the physically irremovable, but psychologically very friable texture of the material divide (pajamas and robe) between the weight of two sunburnt legs, resting athwart my lap, and the hidden tumor of an unspeakable passion.   (p. 61)

Whereas Bloom's excitement is represented by the breakdown of normal sentence patterns, and the breathless association of interjections and epithets, run together with commas and co-ordinating conjunctions to create a prose analogue for his experience, Humbert's is a lexical adventure, in impeccable syntactic uniform. Joyce is intent on giving us the actual physical details of his two synchronized explosions. In Nabokov it all ends, not with an explosion, but with what Humbert later describes as a sort of muffled 'internal combustion' (p. 133). More importantly, Nabokov has his hero blend romantic hyperbole ('unspeakable passion') with a technical precision ('friable texture') that reinforces the contrast between what is happening and how it is being described. Humbert occasionally reminds us that at the time he slipped out of mental gear, as when he recalls how he recited the lyrics of a popular song to disguise his mounting excitement, but we are given only bits of what we would have heard had we been there. In the text, the nonsense verse of incipient orgasm is simply an indecorous interruption in what has become a formal rhetorical adventure. And decorum, sexual and syntactic, is what Humbert insists on: 'anxiety forced me to work', he says, 'for the first minute or so, more hastily than was consensual with deliberately modulated enjoyment' (p. 61). When ecstasy is finally imminent, he emphasizes not frenzied abandon but order and control. He has reached what he calls 'that state of absolute security, confidence and reliance not found elsewhere in conscious life' (p. 62). The elaborate formal apparatus makes all this carnal desire different in kind from the experiences conveyed by the authors Nabokov criticizes: even the passage from Joyce seems explicit by comparison. If sex must be dealt with in a novel, Nabokov seems to be saying, authors should proceed with Humbert's circumspection.

Here we seem to be on the verge of admitting that someone like Appel is right, that sex is only what *Lolita* appears to be about, and that the fictional form in which that subject is dealt with is what in the end should be the principal object of the reader's attention. But look at what happens in one of the last reported sexual encounters between Humbert and Lolita, the one at Beardsley School:

> At one of [the desks], my Lolita was reading the chapter on 'Dialogue' in Baker's *Dramatic Technique*, and all was very quiet, and there was another girl with a very naked, porcelain-white neck and wonderful platinum hair, who sat in front reading too, absolutely lost to the world and interminably winding a soft curl around one finger, and I sat beside Dolly just behind that neck and that hair, and unbuttoned my overcoat and for sixty-five cents plus the permission to participate in the school play, had Dolly put her inky, chalky, red-knuckled hand under the desk.   (p. 200)

There is more novelistic foregrounding here. Reading is represented as an activity that cuts people off from life, the equivalent of that 'intangible island of entranced time' (p. 19) which Humbert imagines his nymphets inhabiting. Borges remarks that this sense of *dédoublement*, becoming aware of other people in a dramatic presentation doing what we ourselves are doing, frightens us because it suggests that we may be the characters in someone else's story, that our point of view may be part of an infinite series.[17] Nabokov uses the same device here, but its primary effect is to involve the reader in what is being represented. By dropping a mirror in front of the scene, he does make us aware that we are reading a book, lost in a world that is now suddenly looking back at us. But he shows us two readers, an innocent and a not so innocent one. Lolita, reading a book about acting, is not so cut off from the world that the transaction cannot be agreed upon, a transaction whose sordidness is not obscured by the mirroring device. The scene's shock value is enhanced by the presence of a fourth person, a sort of spirit that presides over the action: the young girl in the reproduction of Reynolds's 'Age of Innocence' which hangs above the blackboard. If we consider the title alone this may seem like overly obvious irony. However, if we recall the actual details of that painting – the kneeling figure of a young girl in a white dress, the bare neck, the soft curls, the slightly tense, abstracted gaze directed toward some point outside the frame, the dark shape and the overcast sky in the background – we realize that Nabokov has modelled his innocently unaware reader on this girl. (These effects would have been appreciated by more of Nabokov's readers than one might think. Copies of Reynolds's painting must have decorated many middle-class North American homes in the fifties, if the small Canadian town in which I grew up is any indication.) Of particular interest are the girl's hands, folded on her breast, right in the middle of the picture. For Nabokov 'centres' the hands of his figures too, with the usual combination of closely observed detail and a prose rhythm which becomes a significant part of the description: 'interminably winding a soft curl around one finger' is appropriately sinuous, and 'inky, chalky, red-knuckled' a wonderful example of how a different set of consonants can help to re-create a very different hand. The result for the reader then is a complex double awareness: human life and fictional analogues, the consequences of desire along with the devices of the novelist, the defilement of a precious image which is magnified by a subtle allusion. The intricacies of the style do not conceal what is actually happening under cover of overcoats and ellipses, and Nabokov succeeds in showing us just how shocking subtlety and restraint can be. This then is a good example of how he brings his 'ostensible' subject to life, in a scene that is neither simple literary artifice nor pornography, but part of a study of pornography, of how power and desire instrumentalize people.

Yet even the effect of this scene is not unequivocal. Humbert is with Lolita here because he has just survived an interview with the rather horrible headmistress, Miss Pratt, during which he solicits our sympathy by calling himself 'a cornered old rat' (p. 198), and by toying with the idea of marrying and strangling his inquisitor. The classroom masturbation session is reported by someone we have just been siding with. Clearly the issue of how sex is portrayed by *Lolita* is part of a larger problem. The book cries out for a condemnation, a defence, a judgment, yet for various reasons it actively subverts the judgment-making capacity of the reader. Anyone committed to determining the author's position in regard to the events represented must sooner or later come to terms with the fact that a great deal of *Lolita* works at denying him the very certainty he is seeking. He may even start to wonder just why he is so sure that the novel's moral recommendations ought to be clearly and coherently manifest, why he is so eager to find out 'the truth' and pronounce sentence upon it.

One way out of the dilemma is to decide that *Lolita*'s ambiguities and the doubts they create are the product of a naïve reading which the novel itself challenges the reader to move beyond. Solemnly

discussing a playful writer's improvised creations as if they were
real people becomes, if he chooses this option, the kind of response
that recent critical advances have thoroughly discredited. Here is
Appel again (p. xix):

> If one responds to the author's 'false scents' and 'specious lines of play',
> best effected by parody, and believes, say, that Humbert's confession is
> 'sincere' and that he exorcises his guilt, . . . or that a Nabokov book is an
> illustration of a reality proceeding under the natural laws of our world –
> then one has not only lost the game to the author, but most likely is not
> faring too well in the 'game of worlds', one's own unscrambling of
> pictures.[18]

Yet this seemingly sophisticated response threatens to oversimplify
matters considerably. Why, we might ask, can't the naïve reader
and the critical reader inhabit the same body? And if the naïve
reader, with his assumptions about the embodiment of a world in
Lolita that is mediated by but not supplanted by language, has been
defeated by the author, where then are the novel's tension and
complexity, its power to disorient and disconcert? Lionel Trilling
confesses at the end of his article on *Lolita* that one of its chief
attractions is 'its ambiguity of tone . . . and its ambiguity of intention, its ability to arouse uneasiness, to throw the reader off
balance, to require him to change his stance and shift his position
and move on'.[19] But he could not have felt this unless he took *Lolita*
to be in some sense 'an illusion of a reality proceeding under the
natural laws of our world'. Instead of alerting us to the novel's
problematic nature, Appel's dismissal threatens to banish it at a
stroke. The literary self-consciousness that he stresses here is
crucially important, but only because it involves the reader in a
complex range of responses.

Let us consider some specific examples from the novel with a
view to defining how the problem posed by parody and irony in
Lolita might best be approached. Here is Humbert's account of his
reaction at the scene of Charlotte's fatal accident:

> The widower, a man of exceptional self-control, neither wept nor raved.
> He staggered a bit, that he did; but he opened his mouth only to impart such
> information or issue such directions as were strictly necessary in connection
> with the identification, examination and disposal of a dead woman, the top
> of her head a porridge of bone, brains, bronze hair and blood. (p. 100).

That is, faced with the task of summarizing his response to an
appalling spectacle and the violent death of someone he knew well,

Humbert parodies a newspaper account and 'identifies' the gory remains of his wife with a cadenza of repeated consonants. One of *Lolita*'s reviewers was not so much disconcerted by this passage as outraged by it. In his *Spectator* review, Kingsley Amis cites parallels between Humbert's confession and Nabokov's autobiography, comparing both their interest in young girls by the seaside and their stylistic predilections, and argues that Nabokov endorses the cruelty and insensitivity that he portrays in the novel. He then quotes the above passage and appends a sardonic: 'That's the boy, Humbert/Nabokov, alliterative to the last.'[20] Of course there is a sense in which this identification is correct. Nabokov dislikes the Charlottes of this world, and getting her out of the way is as important for him as it is for Humbert: narrative and libidinous interests here coincide. And although he doesn't say it explicitly, Amis alerts us to something even more important, something often overlooked by critics more sympathetic to what Nabokov is trying to do. His comment reminds us that there is something profoundly disintegrative in Nabokov's sensibility that makes him write novel after novel about the various ways in which human beings go about destroying themselves. Yet it is the combination of violence and contempt on the one hand and gentleness and compassion on the other that makes Nabokov and his heroes so interesting. Charlotte's death scene is no exception. For the most striking thing about the whole range of Humbert's responses to her timely demise is that the language he uses points, not just to itself by virtue of things like alliteration, but to all those emotions which exist beyond language and can only be hinted at, and yet are in this oblique way effectively conveyed.[21]

The main problem for the reader seems to be deciding how relevant a criterion like 'sincerity' is when one is dealing with an intensely self-conscious rhetorical style, and what kind of authority is given to a particular view by the context. Here is another example of the Humbert style in action: 'I had always thought that wringing one's hands was a fictional gesture – the outcome, perhaps, of some medieval ritual; but as I took to the woods, for a spell of despair and desperate meditation, this was the gesture ("look, Lord, at these chains!") that would have come nearest to the mute expression of my mood' (p. 85). This kind of passage reminds us how often Humbert indulges in just this kind of 'fictional' gesture. Ten minutes with the text reveals six variations of 'monster', plus 'ape'

(p. 50), 'bestial' (p. 57), 'brute' (p. 195), 'Mr Hyde' (p. 208), 'shameful vice' (p. 266) and 'foul lust' (p. 285). For most readers these sessions of passionate self-mortification are genuinely perplexing: so much talk about guilt now that it is too late for anything but talk, and yet it is precisely the Humbert 'talk', the marvellously intelligent discourse that devastatingly indicts not just himself but a whole society, that makes him so attractive and keeps us sympathetic and involved. This is of course not a new problem. In his penchant for culpatory effusion Humbert joins a long line of guilty heroes, a whole literary tradition in fact, forcefully though somewhat uncharitably summed up by Wyndham Lewis in some remarks about the nineteenth-century decadents from whom Nabokov's hero has inherited some of his tastes and affectations: Lewis notes 'the astonishing role played by *morals*' in what he calls 'this spectacle of calculated perversity' and adds:

Byron, Wilde, Huysmans (that is to say – incest, pederasty and homicide) – what is that, at bottom, but the good old melodrama of *The Girl who took the Wrong Turning*? ... Here surely is an object-lesson, if one were needed, in the disadvantages of an excessive development of the ethical will: for by the simple expedient of reversing it, it can be converted into a first-class instrument of farcical self-display, with all the army of false values that marches upon the heels of such an operation.[22]

Humbert's 'farcical self-display' certainly leaves him open to this kind of criticism, but the literary nature of his self-consciousness changes the game considerably. A hero who Byronizes is one thing; one who tries out the role of handsome, moody, ill-starred protagonist while keeping up a running commentary on the literary precedents, is quite another.[23] How are we to pin down such a well-read hero and refute the notion that *Lolita*'s readers are trapped in a world that is bounded on all sides by literature?

A look at some passages in which explicit literary parody is the vehicle for Humbert's self-conscious declamations may provide some tentative answers. Consider the scene in which he ponders the implications of Charlotte's marriage proposal and then does an impromptu imitation of Dostoevsky's Underground Man: 'After a while I destroyed the letter and went to my room, and ruminated, and rumpled my hair, and modeled my purple robe, and moaned through clenched teeth and suddenly – Suddenly, gentlemen of the jury, I felt a Dostoevskian grin dawning (through the very grimace that twisted my lips) like a distant and terrible sun' (p. 72). In this scene I think we are meant to feel that Humbert is still very much in control of the language and the parody, and the effect is primarily comic. 'That may be all very well for Dostoevsky', he is saying, 'but my emotional turmoil will not be expressed so glibly.' The conventional nature of Dostoevsky's torments and relevations is exposed, and the arbitrary nature of Humbert's task, the freedom he enjoys in deciding how he will report what has happened, is subtly conveyed to the reader. Yet we know, even if Nabokov doesn't want to admit it, that his hero is intimately related to Dostoevsky's heroes, who are in turn part of a long tradition of 'superfluous men' in nineteenth-century Russian literature.[24] Just below the passage Nabokov is alluding to in *Notes From Underground*, the one in which the Underground Man, in his bathrobe, confronts the woman who loves him, we find this:

And all at once I burst into tears. It was a real fit of hysteria. I was hot with shame, but I could not restrain my sobs . . . 'Water, give me some water – over there!' I muttered feebly, conscious, however, that I could quite well do without water, or feeble mutterings either. I was *putting on an act*, as they call it, to preserve the decencies, even though my hysteria was genuine enough.[25]

Like Humbert, the Underground Man knows that his hysteria is spurious in the sense that it is the result of his self-dramatizing propensities; but he has come to realize that the same could be said about everything he does – hence his 'genuine' hysteria. In other words, he is as self-aware as one of Nabokov's heroes. And standing behind him is someone like Stavrogin who, again like Humbert, is at one point confronted by the ghost of a little girl he has 'killed'. The emotional resonance of this kind of antecedent looms up as soon as Dostoevsky is mentioned in *Lolita*. Even when Nabokov rejects his predecessors, as he does Dostoevsky, for what he considers their false values and their melodrama, he ends up rewriting and extending their stories.

Literary figures haunt *Lolita* right to the end, and their effects are just as complex. The murder of Quilty is a good example. Humbert's approach to 'Pavor Manor' is an imitation of the opening of Poe's 'The Fall of the House of Usher', yet the parodic effect is only intermittent: Nabokov has other things on his mind. Besides, Poe's narrator suffers from an 'utter depression of soul' which he compares to 'the after-dream of the reveller upon opium – the bitter lapse into everyday life – the hideous dropping off of the veil . . . an iciness, a sinking, a sickening of the heart – an unredeemed dreariness of thought which no goading of the imagination could torture into aught of the sublime';[26] and you cannot say fairer than that. Obliged to sustain the dramatic interest of a crucial scene, reluctant to interrupt his narrative with a distracting *tour de force*, Nabokov settles for parodic echoes only, a few details about the house, a little phony 'atmosphere'. The other literary presence in this scene is T. S. Eliot: Quilty's versified death sentence is, in part, a comic version of 'Ash Wednesday'. The distinctive repetitions of the first section of the poem positively cry out for parodic imitation:

> Because you took advantage of a sinner
> because you took advantage
> because you took
> because you took advantage of my disadvantage . . .   (p. 301)

Nabokov has some fun with what he regards as Eliot's pomposities, yet even as comic imitation the lines retain a kind of force that simple burlesque would not. They are funny, but they ring true. Significantly, Nabokov leaves Eliot in the next lines and mocks his own hero:

> . . . Because you took advantage of a sin
> when I was helpless moulting moist and tender
> hoping for the best
> dreaming of marriage in a mountain state
> aye of a litter of Lolitas . . .   (p. 302)

Surely this is the sentimental Humbert, out of control, being mocked by his creator for his *Stuffed Owl* style. Emotion spills onto the page, not as emotion but as clichés. Eliot's rhythms and diction turn up only occasionally after this ('the awfulness of love and violets / remorse despair'); and the poem, after summarizing Humbert's patently self-serving views on Quilty's responsibility for everything that has happened, takes yet another turn near the end and actually manages to create some more pathos, in lines such as 'took a dull doll to pieces / and threw its head away' (p. 302). Why has a small part of Eliot's poem been grafted onto this hybrid? If we try to account for its presence by pointing out that *Lolita* is the story of a sinner at the hour of his death, or about the 'torment / Of love unsatisfied' and 'The greater torment / Of love satisfied',[27] then it seems that we must take credit for isolating these lines, since Nabokov has nothing specific to say about them. Still, they are there in the background, providing a kind of resonance that we cannot ignore. The passage sustains its effect by using its literary antecedents to go beyond the literary.[28]

So does Humbert 'exorcize his guilt'? Does Nabokov make clear how his hero is to be judged? Some critics insist that he never does reveal himself: e.g., Brenda Megerle: 'the novel offers no authorial judgment of Humbert's actions'.[29] Others work at identifying the various elements of the hero's highly self-conscious discourse, and then try to decide when the reader is right to take him straight. Thus Nomi Tamir-Ghez, at the end of an article describing the rhetorical devices Humbert uses to manipulate the reader and justify his own actions, claims: 'It is his self-castigation, his readiness to face and admit his guilt, and his suffering at the realization of the truth, that make us accept him. At the end of the narrative he at last gives up the cynicism underlying his rhetoric, and his tone becomes more sincere.'[30] I think she is essentially right, but those who share Lewis's suspicions about the self-indulgent aspects of all that confessing are still not answered. Nor are those who wonder why Humbert's cynicism should stop here: what allows us to assume that he has not arranged this 'sincerity' in one last attempt to dupe the unsuspecting reader?

My sense is that the best answer is provided by the least rhetorical parts of the novel: the dramatized scenes, in which the reader, less distracted than usual by Humbert's syntax and diction, can listen to words that were actually said, forgetting for a moment that even these can be manipulated by an unreliable narrator. Humbert's last meeting with Lolita is one such scene.[31] It is as close as the novel comes to what would be the moment of the hero's conversion in a tragedy, though perhaps 'conversion' is not exactly the right word. After all, Humbert leaves Coalmont just as intent on killing Quilty as he was when he came. But there is a real change, one that involves the reader's perceptions of him as much as anything else. For the scene opens with Humbert in his role as executioner, dressed in black, gun in hand, croaking 'Husband at home?' (p. 272), his first words for Lolita, whom he hasn't seen for three years. In other words, we are seeing him at his most vile, all ready for a gruesome slaughter while the wife of his victim looks on, and he makes no attempt to hide this from us. By the time he has finished narrating this scene, he is making an impassioned plea for his love and repudiating his 'sterile and selfish vice' (p. 280). The contrast could not be more complete. The whole episode loses much of its dramatic point if we do not finally believe in this love, but Nabokov does not make it easy for us. Appel remarks on 'the parodic echo of Billy Graham's exhortation' when Humbert pleads with Lolita to come away with him ('Make those twenty-five steps. Now.'), and the 'purposeful banality' of 'And we shall live happily ever after' (p. 280).[32] Even at its most lyrical, his prose can take some unexpectedly crude turns, as when he describes Lolita as 'the faint violet whiff and dead leaf echo of the nymphet I had rolled myself upon' (p. 279). Those who want to believe in a reformed Humbert can point to the compelling simplicity with which he describes his feelings, a sharp contrast to the fulsome quality of his earlier declarations. Faced with someone who is 'hopelessly worn at seventeen', i.e., long past nymphet age, he says 'I looked and looked at her, and knew as clearly as I know I am to die, that I loved her more than anything I had ever seen or imagined on earth, or hoped for anywhere else' (p. 279).

It is easier to believe this, and to see his love as somehow ennobling, if we are convinced that it is no longer being lavished on an illusory object. Here we have to forget about rhetorical devices and compounded ironies for a moment and ask whether Nabokov wants us to believe in a changed Lolita as well. I think he does, although he has only this one scene to show how the twelve-year-old girl so clearly established in our minds has changed into a more mature and more reflective young woman. The first part of their conversation makes that conviction seem rather sentimental. After all, how much older and wiser is someone who still thinks Quilty is 'a great guy in many respects' (p. 278)? Although this is admittedly grotesque, Nabokov's reluctance to violate psychological realism makes such sentiments both plausible and necessary. Because of her arrested emotional development, Lolita will always idolize Quilty. He still represents the possibility of escape for her. But even her life with him has an unreal quality for her now, and the rest of the conversation with Humbert suggests just how much she has learned from the past and how far she has put it behind her. He insists on knowing what went on at Quilty's ranch, but she is reluctant to reply, probably because she thinks he is up to his old voyeuristic tricks. But he isn't. Rather, he wants to suffer, and for that he needs explicit details. Besides, killing Quilty will be sweeter if Humbert knows exactly what he is taking revenge for. Lolita

mentions 'weird, filthy, fancy things', but this is not enough for him:
'What things exactly?'
'Oh, things . . . Oh, I – really I' – she uttered the 'I' as a subdued cry while she listened to the source of the ache, and for lack of words spread the five fingers of her angularly up-and-down-moving hand. No, she gave it up, she refused to go into particulars with that baby inside her.   (pp. 278–9)

This is one of the finest moments in the book. The movement of the hand (Nabokov is always watching the hands of his characters) captures the whole nature of Lolita's predicament. Her sense of right and wrong is all the more moving because it is not in her power to say why she cannot tell. This refusal, taken together with her refusal to go along with Quilty's demands or to agree to what she (mistakenly) thinks Humbert is offering her when he asks her to go with him, requires us to re-examine our assumptions about her. Nabokov has already subtly misdirected these assumptions. As Humbert watches Lolita smoke a cigarette, he is struck by a resemblance: 'Gracefully, in a blue mist, Charlotte Haze rose from her grave' (p. 277) The implication is that Lolita is in the process of becoming another Charlotte, another cipher in mindless America. The tawdriness of Coalmont, the photo of the in-laws, the radio 'singing of folly and fate' (p. 279) all help create this impression. But in the midst of all this Lolita stands out as somehow different. A young Charlotte would be more harsh and bitter, a jaded teenager, old and wise before her time. Her daughter's bemused reflectiveness ('It was so *strange*, so *strange*' (p. 279)) seems to hint at another future. During a first reading of the novel, this future is still very much at issue. By the time the reader learns that she is 'Mrs Richard Schiller', he has probably long since forgotten what Dr John Ray says in the Foreword about the 'Mrs Richard F. Schiller' who 'died in childbed, giving birth to a stillborn girl' (p. 6). Her rejection of Humbert's offer of an escape may condemn her to a life of drudgery, but in committing herself to a husband and a baby she is making the only human choice available to her. Humbert understands this. His love is devastatingly unrequited but he sees its object clearly. And Nabokov, in this one scene, shows us all the poignancy of Lolita's attempt to build a future for herself in a world that was not of her making.[33] Such a scene doesn't 'solve' the problem of *Lolita*; the issues raised by the novel are not the kind that anyone ever solves. But it does remind us why *Lolita* matters and why we go on talking about it.[34]

Any attempt to discuss a novel of Nabokov's in terms of 'human values' must inevitably come to terms with the fact that he usually insisted that a novel's aesthetic values were pre-eminent in his mind while writing it, and that in general as an author aesthetic values were all he ever cared about. To an interviewer who asked him about the function of his novels he said: 'I have no purpose at all when composing my stuff except to compose it. I work hard, I work long, on a body of words until it grants me complete possession and pleasure.'[35] His well-known remark in the Afterword to *Lolita* expresses the same sentiments: 'For me', he writes, 'a work of fiction exists only insofar as it affords me what I shall bluntly call aesthetic bliss, that is a sense of being somehow, somewhere, connected with other states of being where art (curiosity, tenderness, kindness, ecstasy) is the norm' (pp. 316–17). I want to suggest in this final section that the human drama in the novel is itself an extended commentary on this question of the aesthetics of the pure artist. This sounds suspiciously like the '*Lolita* as aesthetic allegory' criticism that I was quarrelling with earlier, but it differs in this sense: rather than exemplifying the truth of precepts like the ones just quoted, *Lolita*, I want to argue, offers a less doctrinaire and more complex view of the subject than Nabokov's own comments generally do.

Like his creator, Humbert is pre-eminently concerned with 'aesthetic bliss'. Here he is on the subject of Lolita's tennis:

I remember at the very first game I watched being drenched with an almost painful convulsion of beauty assimilation. My Lolita had a way of raising her bent left knee at the ample and springy start of the service cycle when there would develop and hang in the sun for a second a vital web of balance between toed foot, pristine armpit, burnished arm and far back-flung racket, as she smiled up with gleaming teeth at the small globe suspended so high in the zenith of the powerful and graceful cosmos she had created for the express purpose of falling upon it with a clean resounding crack of her golden whip.   (pp. 233–4)

'Gleaming teeth' sounds like a toothpaste commercial, and a tennis ball leaves the racket with a sound that is less thin and less cruel than the 'crack' of a whip, but otherwise, how brilliantly this account freezes and immortalizes its subject. Notice the way Nabokov, in the second sentence, delays the subject of the second clause and thus imitates in prose the suspension he is describing. The spondee-like 'so high' has a similar effect, and the phrases that release the tension created form a brisk combination of iambs and anapests. Even if Humbert had made home movies ('Idiot, triple idiot! I could have filmed her!' (p. 233)), they would have been superseded by these sentences which take Lolita frame by frame through her subtle and elegant ritual. Humbert's 'aesthetic bliss' is a lot like Nabokov's: he too claims that the contemplation of the aesthetic object creates in the observer a sense of 'other states of being', what he calls 'the teasing delirious feeling of teetering on the very brink of unearthly order and splendor' (p. 232). This idea of discovering a hidden harmony by contemplating the Beautiful is of course not original with Humbert. It was a favourite of the Symbolists, and in matters of aesthetics both he and Nabokov often sound like one of them. Nabokov's most intimate link with this movement was with the Russian Symbolists, whose work he knew well even as a youth. A poem like Blok's 'The Stranger' or some of the passages devoted to Lyudmila in Sologub's *The Petty Demon* could almost serve as sources for the hero's fascination in *Lolita* with the body of the woman he loves. Vaguely evil, frightening, tantalizing, inspiring, all the time hinting at other, more perfect realms – Lolita is very much a creation born of this tradition. I don't want to push the parallel between Humbert and Nabokov too far; yet if there is a correspondence between the general aesthetic views being expressed here, then *Lolita*, to the extent that it is a study of the effects of holding such views, should have something useful to tell us about Nabokov's own art and about the tradition he inherited.

The novel offers one explicit comment on this question. It takes the form of Humbert's summing up of his own quest for beauty, at the moment when the narrative pauses between his last meeting with Lolita and the encounter with Quilty. In a small 'dead-of-night' (p. 284) town, Humbert thinks about what he has done. Nabokov suggests the symbolic implications of the setting by having him remind us that he is between Coalmont and Ramsdale: that is, between a town that epitomizes the bleakness Lolita will have to fight against, a town so grey 'You can't see the morons for the smog' (p. 268), and a town that represents the comfortable banality of the past and the home that he has deprived her of. The nameless, silent place where Humbert stops is a piece of quintessential Americana for Nabokov. Not oppressive or alienating or inhuman, ideal for 'dark night of the soul' thoughts about isolation and death, but depressing because of its emptiness and vaguely unreal quality.

Besides, its insouciant vulgarity violates the aesthetic sense. From
his car Humbert can see a 'large thermometer with the name of a
laxative' on the front of a drugstore, a 'display of artificial
diamonds' reflected in the 'red mirror' of a jewelry store, and the
silent, comic, curiously disheartening repetition of an 'animated'
neon sign (p. 284). The social criticism is only there by implication,
but the scene does instill in the reader's mind the idea of an
American 'sense of beauty', a point that will be important for an
understanding of what Humbert is about to say. (For those
expecting some Old World nostalgia here, Nabokov has a characteristic feint, the unexpected adjective at the end of a conventional series: 'Nobody strolled and laughed on the sidewalks as
relaxing burghers would in sweet, mellow, rotting Europe'
(p. 283), says Humbert.) As he reviews the past he realizes that he
will always be tormented by his conscience, because he will always
be guilty of having robbed Lolita of her childhood, and concludes
(p. 285):

I see nothing for the treatment of my misery but the melancholy and very
local palliative of articulate art. To quote an old poet:

> The moral sense in mortals is the duty
> We have to pay on mortal sense of beauty.

What does this mean exactly? Martin Green offers a useful
paraphrase:

The consolations of religion and the rigors of morality are both derived
from the aesthetic sense. What is beautiful is so because it satisfies our
moral sense among other things, but the idea of beauty is the larger. The
moral sense is an obligation, which we pay resignedly as a part of the price
of beauty. This duty is not Kantianly near to religion; it is nearer to
Customs and Excise.[36]

But does this fit the facts? Is Humbert's sense of beauty responsible
for his pangs of conscience? We know that his aesthetic sensibility
was finely tuned when he had no moral sense at all, when he was still
the pure embodiment of selfishness and self-indulgence, when he
thought that a lecher was an 'artist' (p. 19) and sex offenders were
'poets' (p. 133). Humbert may want us to believe that the 'moral
sense' is a late stage in the life cycle of the aesthetic instinct, but his
own story seems to suggest that the two things develop independently of each other.

I think the situation is clarified if we realize that two different conceptions of art are involved. Humbert's 'sense of beauty' begins as pure aestheticism: he defines his problems in aesthetic terms; he yearns for a private world constructed according to exclusively aesthetic criteria. His story records the consequences of trying to live in such a world. For Nabokov too there is a dual conception at work. The novelist begins his task with certain technical problems in mind. His novel resembles, as Nabokov said about *Lolita*, a 'riddle' with an 'elegant solution'.[37] But the feeling it produces in the end is more than just the sense of satisfaction that results from having successfully negotiated various artistic difficulties. Take another look at his definition of 'aesthetic bliss', in particular his defining 'art' with nouns like 'curiosity, tenderness, ecstasy'. These words hint at the kind of emotional and moral commitment involved in what he regards as the ideal relation between the observer and the aesthetic object.[38] *Lolita* is more than an impersonal artefact which gave its creator a certain amount of pleasure in the making, because it dramatizes the potential inhumanity of the kind of aesthetic attitude to experience that fails to make this kind of commitment. But it doesn't simply express a preference for warm and vital human beings as opposed to cold and impersonal works of art. Humbert's description of Lolita at tennis is an exercise in the special art of seeing her as an object, an art that only aesthetic detachment makes possible. And his 'Confession', the product of that detachment, is at the same time a study of its limitations. As Michael Bell points out in '*Lolita* and Pure Art', it is not 'that the awareness of others as "objects" is in itself wrong, but that it has to find its proper place in our general sense of them'.[39]

The correspondence between what Humbert finds out about the pursuit of beauty and what *Lolita* tells us about Nabokov's own aesthetics can be taken a stage farther. No one can read the last part of the novel without feeling the hectic urgency of the narrative: the aimless pursuits, the dead-ends, the night journeys to nowhere, the increasingly oppressive sense of solitude. Trying to find and kill Quilty means trying to make a sinister 'second self' responsible for what has happened, to isolate evil in a fundamentally narcissistic and unreal way. The search for that self is a waste of time. Humbert achieves nothing during the three years that he is away from Lolita; and looking back on these years, he realizes that his entire life has been little more than a large-scale version of them. He is forty-two years old and has left no evidence of his existence, done nothing that is of any use to anyone. He undertakes his story as a search for a 'private self', that very literary exercise with all the gloomy metaphors about probing dark areas and illuminating hidden depths. But by the time he is finished, he is reconciled to the fact that it is his public self, the record of what he has contributed and accomplished, by which he will ultimately be judged. He will be whatever his readers, the collective body to whom he appeals at the end, finally decide that he is. For all his talk about the artistic abilities of the nympholept, Humbert never really creates anything until he understands that the artist requires an audience, however dimly projected, if the circuit of communication is to function properly. He has no exalted notions about the kind of immortality he will gain by writing *Lolita*. Art is not a miracle cure for mortality, a fact he wryly acknowledges in his penultimate sentence about 'aurochs and angels' and 'the refuge of art' (p. 311). Angels escaped extinction by taking refuge in literature; the aurochs, a species of wild ox that formerly inhabited Europe, has vanished forever. Humbert hopes that a part-time beast, and former inhabitant of Europe, can imitate the angels and escape into literature too.

What about the parallel with Nabokov? Despite all he said about the self-sufficiency of the author's 'aesthetic bliss', he too cared about how his work would be received. In letters to Edmund Wilson written when 'the *Lolita* affair' was beginning, he twice confesses to being 'depressed' by the fact that some readers cannot understand that his novel is clearly not pornographic.[40] And *Lolita* itself, despite its current reputation, constitutes his admission that the reader is not there only to be teased and tyrannized but is a vital part of a co-operative enterprise, and that aesthetic principles exist to be analyzed, tested, and refined in the product of that enterprise. Can a novel that has created such a variety of readers go on creating new ones? Will its future be gradual academic extinction, or immortality? There are, according to Borges, two kinds of classic. First there is 'The Classic', the one everybody knows about but nobody reads. In this way, a masterpiece like *Don Quixote* can become, because of men's complacency and neglect, 'the occasion of patriotic toasts, grammatical insolence and obscene de luxe editions'.[41] The other is the genuine classic, 'that book which a nation (or group of nations, or time itself) has taken the decision to read as if in its pages everything were predetermined, predestined, deep as the cosmos, and capable of endless interpretation'.[42] *Lolita* is surely the Nabokov novel that has the best chance of becoming a classic, but it will only be the second kind if we remember that its greatness depends primarily on the human situation it portrays and on the human world it creates for us.

5

Ada

Ada is the crucial test for my critical method. Can the critic who is as interested in the view of man that informs a novel as he is in its form really make sense of a book like this? Or is he, like some nostalgic physicist, performing tests to determine the properties of an 'ether' that new experimenters with the novel have, like Michelson and Morley, added to the collection of quaint superstitions that figure in the early history of any new science? Almost all of *Ada*'s critics have concentrated on formal matters, so an extended study with a different emphasis, if it can prove that the novel has a content that can be discussed like any other, may be a useful addition to the criticism devoted to it.[1] If the ideas about human nature, human relationships, and human culture generally found in other Nabokov novels do manifest themselves in this strange new form, they deserve to be studied. Of Nabokov's last four novels I propose to take up *Ada* first for two reasons: the sheer range of reference in it makes it an ideal introduction to the late fiction, and, for my purposes, it can be juxtaposed with *Lolita* in ways that its predecessor, *Pale Fire*, cannot. The chapter is divided into three sections. In the first I talk about love and sexuality, jealousy and incest, and the nature of the emotional relationships in general in the novel. In the second I try to defend my ideas about the consequences of the shift in emphasis in Nabokov's late fiction by contrasting *Ada* with *Lolita*. In the third I use the discursive sections of the novel to fill in the portrait of an author and his ideas that I have been developing. In speaking about *Ada*, I shall sometimes ascribe to Nabokov opinions that strictly speaking belong to his narrator, Van Veen. There are of course risks involved in doing this, but they seem to me to be less great than the ones involved in assuming that, just because Nabokov does make intermittent use of first-person narrative, he has chosen to maintain a controlled distance between himself and his narrator. It is no good pretending that the Van Veen and the Nabokov views of the world never coincide. They do; and when they do, we learn something important about our subject.

Ada has been called many things: a novel about language,[2] a portrait of the creative process,[3] not a novel but a puzzle,[4] 'the most unconventional commentary on the novel ever written',[5] and 'almost self-parody'.[6] Nabokov himself, interestingly enough, told an interviewer that *Ada* was about 'passionate, hopeless. rapturous sunset love, with swallows darting beyond the stained window and that radiant shiver . . . '[7] Let us consider it from this point of view. If it is a love story, it divides into two distinct phases. Or, to put it another way, it is a love story and a lust story, a study of the erotic as a fully conscious human activity and of the carnal appetites. If we think of these two themes as rival angels fighting for the soul of the book then it must be admitted that the 'evil' angel triumphs in the end. But at least the first third of the book is about love, adolescent love with all its torments and pleasures. Here is an excerpt from one of the first encounters between Van and Ada:

Her plump, stickily glistening lips smiled.
(When I kiss you *here*, he said to her years later, I always remember that blue morning on the balcony when you were eating a *tartine au miel*; so much better in French.)
The classical beauty of clover honey, smooth, pale, translucent, freely flowing from the spoon and soaking my love's bread and butter in liquid brass. The crumb steeped in nectar.[8]

Tactful alliteration and assonance, a prose rhythm that the imagination may subliminally relate to what is being described, the rightness of the metaphor, the sentence fragments that simply place the details there without saying anything about them – vintage Nabokov this, wonderfully direct and compelling. The erotic inheres in the sensuous details, but this is basically a quiet language for a richly significant silence. They are interrupted by a wasp: 'The wasp was investigating her plate. Its body was throbbing' (p. 75). This is what wasps do: search out sweet things, and throb. The truth of the scene is a function of the accuracy with which the physical detail has been observed. Why dwell on such obvious things, such simple effects? Because the same insect somewhere else in *Ada* might have been a 'palpitating Diploptera' or a '*Vespa vulgaris* Nabokov', and the whole scene a thematic 'anthemion' celebrating both incestuous love and 'how incestuously . . . art and science meet in an insect' (p. 436). Nabokov's restraint here reminds us that to be fully conscious of something doesn't necessarily mean exploring every corner of the consciousness to see what associations turn up when one looks for the words to describe it, nor does it preclude leaving some things unsaid. As the scene evolves, absolutely nothing 'happens':

> Her hair was well brushed that day and sheened darkly in contrast with the lusterless pallor of her neck and arms. She wore the striped tee shirt which in his lone fantasies he especially liked to peel off her twisting torso. The oilcloth was divided into blue and white squares. A smear of honey stained what remained of the butter in its cool crock ...
>
> She considered him. A fiery droplet in the wick of her mouth considered him. A three-colored velvet violet, of which she had done an aquarelle on the eve, considered him from its fluted crystal. She said nothing. She licked her spread fingers, still looking at him.　　　　　　　(pp. 75–6)

The extraordinary specificity (using 'sheen' as a verb is a positively Joycean touch), the repetition of key words, the simple sentence structure and the slow buildup of naturalistic detail combine to convey the human drama taking place, and to charge it with all kinds of potential energy.

It all comes to nothing on this particular occasion, but the tenderness is possible because consummation is impossible. The erotic in Nabokov is always to be found at that moment when unfulfilled desire creates a kind of poignant hyper-sensitivity, an acute sense of how quickly the almost perfect present will become the irretrievable past. He expresses this very movingly in a subsequent passage: 'Endlessly, steadily, delicately, Van would brush his lips against hers, teasing their burning bloom, back and forth, right, left, life, death, reveling in the contrast between the airy tenderness of the open idyll and the gross congestion of the hidden flesh' (p. 103). Those who think of Nabokov as 'the *Lolita* man' might be surprised to hear him talk about the flesh in this way, but this duality is one of the constants in his work. In fact, the Nabokovian ideal is not all that far from the 'Cold Pastoral' of the Grecian Urn that immortalizes the eternal 'almost' of Keats's 'Bold Lover'.[9] The advantage of this is that adolescent yearning is powerfully evoked in novel after novel. The disadvantage is that, with love so bound up with loss, Nabokov cannot really study it as a process and an unfolding, what Lawrence calls the 'long event of perpetual change, in which a man and a woman mutually build up their souls and make themselves whole'.[10] Most often he settles for this kind of either/or formulation, 'airy tenderness' or 'gross congestion'. And since the latter is more congenial for farce and ribald fantasy, this love story first alternates with a lust story and then is superseded by it. Only rarely in Nabokov, in novels like *Mary* and *The Gift*, is sexuality a vital but not all-encompassing part of a rich and full human life. Far more often, in *King, Queen, Knave, Laughter in the Dark, Bend Sinister, Lolita, Pale Fire, Transparent Things*, it is wild and uncontrollable, bigger than the characters it manipulates and torments. As a novelist, Nabokov is fascinated by lust for three reasons: firstly, he is a comic writer, and lust automatizes people, making them ridiculous and pathetic; secondly, he is a story writer, and lust leads to the powerful and distintegrative obsessions which help to organize the compulsion-plot which is a standard feature of Nabokovian narrative; and thirdly, he sees the world like this – for all his anti-Freudianism, Nabokov depicts man as a creature of violent desires which are in constant conflict with a society that seeks to repress them.

Even before 'making love' in *Ada* becomes a bravura demonstration of professional gymnastics, the love story creates problems for the reader:

With his entire being, the boiling and brimming lad relished her weight as he felt it responding to every bump of the road by softly parting in two and crushing beneath it the core of the longing which he knew he had to control lest a possible seep perplex her innocence. He would have yielded and melted in animal laxity had not the girl's governess saved the situation by addressing him. (p. 87)

Obviously Nabokov has shifted to an entirely different lexical register here. The aura is gone, and with it the peculiar charm of the encounters studied above. 'Boiling and brimming', 'the core of his longing', 'melted in animal laxity' – this could be genteel pornography, and yet irony-markers like 'lad' suggest that we are dealing with an author who is too self-aware for that. I'm not so sure about the satyric leer and the arch allusions in the following: 'He groped for and cupped her hot little slew from behind, then frantically scrambled into a boy's sandcastle-molding position; but she turned over, naively ready to embrace him the way Juliet is recommended to receive her Romeo' (p. 121). Yet in the next sentence but one we find: 'For the first time in their love story, the blessing, the genius of lyrical speech descended upon the rough lad', and Van cries out 'in three languages – the three greatest in all the world – pet words upon which a dictionary of secret diminutives was to be based and go through many revisions till the definitive edition of 1967' (p. 121). So this is a great romance after all: Van's languages and passions are viewed here with a tender if slightly ironic eye by an author who shares them. Next sentence: 'impatient young passion . . . did not survive the first few blind thrusts; it burst at the lip of the orchid, and a bluebird uttered a warning warble, and the lights were now stealing back under a rugged dawn', etc. Sexual description flawed by gooey sentimental excess? enlivened by purplish parody? humanized by delicate evocation? All this to suggest that monitoring tonal shifts from sentence to sentence in a single paragraph of *Ada* can be a full-time occupation.

Every reader has three options at this point. He can edit judiciously, arbitrarily establish ironic distance, and then use particular passages to support almost any thesis. He can retreat, define the whole issue as an aesthetic *datum*, and praise Nabokov for his energetic equivocation. Or he can, after confessing his own uncertainty, go on talking about these problems as if they were things that most of the novel's readers are puzzled by. I have chosen the third option, although the temptations of the first two are real enough.

In the first part of the novel, two people are discovering each other; enough obstacles still exist at Ardis Hall to make them exercise considerable ingenuity in order to fulfil their desires; the relationship still means something. But then the super-imperial coupling begins in earnest, and Nabokov surveys the entire field of sexual literature in the process of describing it. Van 'feast[s] fiercely on [Ada's] throat and nipples' (p. 392) – good old-fashioned porn. Soon after that we are told how 'he steadied her lovely lyre and next moment was at the suede-soft root, was gripped, was deep between the familiar, incomparable, crimson-lined lips' (p. 392) – John Cleland *redivivus*. The long 'Villa Venus' sequence is parodic pornography like Terry Southern's without the requisite wit. There are jeering allusions: 'Aleksey and Anna may have asterisked here' (p. 521). There is the puerile cuteness of Ada's denying her infidelities: 'I'm not hiding one stain of what rhymes with Perm' (p. 430). Lucette and Ada wile away the hours kissing each other's '*krestik*' except when they have 'the flow' (p. 375). Van strokes Lucette's hair, while Nabokov reminds the reader that 'one can't stroke (as he did now) the upper copper without imagining at once the lower fox cub and the paired embers' (p. 368). Women in general become a collection of pubic hair and fleshy lumps, 'chubs', 'cruppers', 'bursting shorts', and so on. The vast supporting cast shares the Veens' principal interest if not their capacity. In short, the game seems to have become a little gamey. No one can emit outraged noises à la Mary Woodhouse these days without feeling a certain embarrassment, but the burden of proof is presumably with the text: it has taken up our time, it must justify the inclusion of all this stuff.[11]

So why is it there? Various answers have been proposed. Jane Grayson notes the increased tolerance for sexual explicitness in the sixties and the possibility that Nabokov wanted to repeat his *Lolita* success. She also suggests that in the late novels he may have set out to bait all the critics who accused him of being a pornographer because of *Lolita*.[12] This is the kind of explanation that every admirer of Nabokov would like to believe. But there is a little parable in *The Gift* about a man who imitates someone else so beautifully and so often that he begins to look and sound like his victim in normal conversation. And even the parody explanation does not account for this new sniggering, anti-human attitude to sex, which is so markedly absent from *Lolita*, for example. Ellen Pifer argues that the 'inhuman ardor' is related to Nabokov's ideas about 'inhuman art': 'In *Ada*', she says, 'he demonstrates that the "wildest flights" of art, ardor, and science spring from the same vital source: inhuman desire and curiosity.'[13] I think Nabokov may have had something like this in mind, but has he actually demonstrated it? Although 'inhuman' has a compelling resonance in the context – 'beyond the merely human' is what Pifer wants it to convey to us – what was quoted above is more appropriately called 'sub-human', in that it gives us a debased view of man; or 'human, all too human', since the idea of peeking at pubic hair or bragging about sexual technique and prowess is man's distinctive contribution to these matters. We note too that the energetic couplers in earlier novels, Franz and Martha in *King, Queen, Knave*, Martha in *Invitation to a Beheading*, Hustav in *Bend Sinister*, are symbols of everything that is inhuman and anti-art for Nabokov, and are condemned to frantic copulation for that reason. Another problem involves a lurking presupposition about the value of what is intensely experienced. Nabokov seems to endorse such a view by suggesting that the sexual encounters are all moments of profound vision because of their intensity, that imaginative perception is somehow rooted in 'inhuman ardor'. Of Van's orgasms he says: 'For one spasm or two, he was safe. The new naked reality needed no tentacle or anchor; it lasted a moment, but could be repeated as often as he and she were physically able to make love' (p. 220). For the first part of *Ada* we may be willing to believe in this; but the attempt to pursue intensity, to turn orgasms into repeatable epiphanies in this self-conscious way is bound to fail, because what he calls here a 'new naked reality' turns out to be that 'nothing matters any more' feeling which lovers usually remember somewhat sheepishly when they come back down. This fulfillment sounds suspiciously like disguised frustration. The attempt to make a case for ineffable visions occasioned by the stimulation of certain membranes fails. So the sex in much of *Ada* refuses to be anything but what it is: an aesthetic flaw, an authorial indulgence, and a sign of that curious anti-human quality that creeps into late Nabokov. The aesthete's penchant for instrumentalizing the people he most admires, so acutely placed and judged in *Lolita*, hovers menacingly over these automatized lovers; and at least part of Nabokov's 'new novel' looks like the old decadence in contemporary guise.

Nabokov often uses emotional obsession and all the complications it inevitably causes as the motor for his plots. In this crucial way, the novels are always more or less verisimilar, committed to representing both the forces that bind people together and the obstacles, often created by those very forces, that usually drive them apart. In *Ada*, incest and jealousy are assigned the role of chief obstacles.

First incest. The liaison between Van and Ada is a comic copy of the doomed love which makes desired sisters retire to nunneries and frustrated brothers roam the world, and Nabokov drops a number of allusions to Chateaubriand and Byron to remind us of the literary parallels. Of course despite all their self-dramatizing, Van's guilty forebears generally manage to convince the reader that they do feel there is something ignoble about their relationships with their sisters, and this adds to the pathos of *René* or some of Byron's poems. Van obviously feels none of this, and phrases like Ada's '*cher, trop cher René*' (p. 131) are amusing because of the ironic contrast. The more appropriate incestuous ancestors are a couple like Wagner's Siegmund and Sieglinde, with Nabokov in the role of a forgiving Wotan looking on lovingly from his authorial

Valhalla. But none of this makes incest much of an obstacle. The illicit aspect of Van and Ada's love never really counts for much, because the novel provides only a simulacrum of a family or society within which this love might be significant (compare the constraints felt by Albinus or Humbert).[14] Incest without guilt turns out to be somewhat unreal, and many readers go through the whole book without ever getting the relation straight. Nabokov critics have pointed out the carelessness of those who have displayed such ignorance in print,[15] but the fact that one can think of Van and Ada as half-brother and -sister and still make sense of the novel suggests that the relationship the reviewers missed when they skipped a few pages, or tired of checking which Veen had made love to which twin sister, is not of supreme importance.

As befits a kind of academic or abstract incest, the most interesting thing about it is the theories it has provoked. George Steiner argues that incest is 'a trope through which Nabokov dramatizes his abiding devotion to Russian, the dazzling infidelities which exile has forced on him, and the unique intimacy he has achieved with his own writing as begetter, translator and re-translator'.[16] Roy Swanson claims that 'Nabokov's conspectus is that each human being is psychologically both male and female and is both physically human and spiritually divine; each human being is a Tiresian solipsism.'[17] And John Updike suggests that 'to love one's self under the guise of a sister is to feminize one's soul, to make it other than the masculine ego, to externalize it – to give oneself, then, a soul'.[18] But does the actual felt impact of the text compel us to make these or any other identifications? Not really. *Ada* seems rather to free the commentator to suggest almost any equation, even if it ignores what actually happens in the novel. Surely the whole point about Ada, once Van's adolescent love affair with her is over, is that she becomes a lively, witty, lascivious projection of the masculine ego that Nabokov sets out to feminize with a small set of 'macho' notions about what femininity actually is. 'To love oneself under the guise of a sister' may symbolize auto-translation or 'Tiresian solipsism', but in narrative terms it means only to make love a lot.[19] Nabokov seems to have been confident that the critics would fill in any dimensions that were lacking, and on the whole he was right.

The other obstacle that serves to keep the lovers apart is jealousy. It organizes the plots of some of Nabokov's most carefully structured novels, *Laughter in the Dark* and *Lolita*, and he uses it here in one of his most freewheeling. Jealousy makes Van leave Ada, and the novel grows from three hundred to six hundred pages because of it.[20] One is tempted to conclude that this jealousy is just a novelistic device, a mere pretext, but Nabokov devotes dozens of pages to it, and repeatedly draws the reader's attention to the way in which this feeling works on his hero. Here is a typical passage: 'He wondered what really kept him alive on terrible Antiterra, with Terra a myth and all art a game, when nothing mattered any more since the day he slapped Valerio's warm bristly cheek; and whence, from what deep well of hope, did he still scoop up a shivering star, when everything had an edge of agony and despair, when another man was in every bedroom with Ada' (p. 452). Of course we have another tone problem: gentle mockery of gushy popular romance? emotional seriousness underlying desperate playfulness? uneasy marriage of factitious desire and overblown rhetoric? Does Nabokov want the reader to register the 'agony and despair' caused by this jealousy as more than a form of words? If so, why didn't he give Van some rivals? These men 'in every bedroom' have no real status, and even fat Percy and the tubercular Rack fade away to nothing when put beside someone like Quilty, who is himself a somewhat chimerical menace for the jealous lover. I think Hyde gets closest to an explanation of the issues involved here when he says of Ada: 'As the embodiment of desire she is the progenitor of pain (longing, loss) as well as the creative drive.'[21] 'Progenitor' is the key word. Ada is sterile, she will have no children with Van; but her progeny will be a 'family chronicle', the words she inspires, the book to be written about her. She is unfaithful only because as a muse she is obliged to provide the artist's 'creative drive' with some material – agony, despair, lonely wanderings – which he can use for his book.

In novels like *Laughter in the Dark* and *Lolita*, the suspicion of infidelity plunges the jealous lover into a violent and chaotic world from which the only escape is the death of the person he holds responsible for what has happened. Like Othello, both Albinus and Humbert realize instantly that, once the harmonious, blissful realm they dream of inhabiting with the women they love is shattered, their 'occupation's gone'. As in Shakespeare, what shocks us is the suddenness with which the realization comes, the speed with which passion becomes brutality. Albinus tries to kill Margot but ends up killing himself, the last of a series of self-destructive acts. Humbert kills Quilty but his attempt at a symbolic act turns out to be a messy, bloody business. None of the jealous violence in *Ada* involves the reader to anything like the same extent. Van kills off Rack and Percy, but they die literary deaths not literal ones, disposed of in a couple of marvellous flights of Veen fancy. Like the hero and heroine, they die '*into* the finished book' (p. 587), and so do the 'agony and despair' they cause Van, once their literary task has been accomplished. Whether all the fantasized violence linked with these emotions is the projection of some Nabokovian inner self must remain a matter for speculation. We know what he would have thought of such speculation. But presumably his quarrel with Freud is based on the assumption which we find everywhere in his work that many aspects of adult life including the sexual are profoundly rooted, not in childhood experiences of which we are not fully aware, but in adolescent ones of which we could not be more aware, so violently do they intrude upon us. Of course this is more properly the subject of a biography which it appears now will never be written.

What about the intra-familial relationships which form the novel's main sub-plot? Nabokov clearly works at supplementing his love story by creating a kind of emotional resonance in the relationships between Van and his father and between Van and Lucette. Let us see if he succeeds.

We first become aware that father and son are even remotely interested in each other in the long chapter devoted to the dinner on Ada's sixteenth birthday. And a very strange moment it is. I need to quote a long passage to show just what Nabokov is trying to do:

He had seen little of his father that year. He loved him with light-hearted devotion, had worshipped him in boyhood, and respected him staunchly now in his tolerant but better informed youth. Still later a tinge of repulsion (the same repulsion he felt in regard to his own immorality) became admixed to the love and the esteem; but, on the other hand, the older he grew the more firmly he felt that he would give his life for his father, at a moment's notice, with pride and pleasure, in any circumstance imaginable ... No accursed generalizer, with a half-penny mind and dry-fig heart, would be able to explain (and this is my sweetest revenge for all the detractions my lifework has met with) the individual vagaries evolved in those and similar matters. No art and no genius would exist without such vagaries, and this is a final pronouncement, damning all clowns and clods.   (p. 237)

For a number of very personal reasons having to do with his own experiences as a son and a father, Nabokov includes this passage here. But the difference between what this announcement promises and what the novel actually does positively leaps out at us. What is there in it to put beside the intimate interactions between father and son in *The Gift*, *Bend Sinister*, and *Speak, Memory*? The conversation at dinner illustrates the ordinary level of the exchanges between Demon and son: bits of satiric Americana: 'How is the car situation, Van?' (p. 257); the banter of two cronies in a bar: 'Do you like the type, Van – the bowed little head, the bare neck, the high heels, the trot, the wiggle, you do, don't you?' (p. 244); and some rather laboured jokes: (Van) 'I suppose you have not been much in Manhattan lately – where did you get its last syllable?' (p. 239). The only shared interest that might justify this vehement affirmation of filial love is Ada herself: Van vicariously enjoys the sight of Demon's lips being applied to various parts of his daughter's anatomy. Their other significant encounter is the confrontation scene, occasioned by Demon's discovery of his children's relationship. Instead of maintaining the tedious superficiality and blithely asserting the richness and profundity of the understanding between father and son, Nabokov does a bravura tour of the emotional possibilities of such a scene. Demon scowls menacingly, emits dreary clichés, forces the conversation to take a terrible 'neutral turn' (p. 442), undercuts the gloomy atmosphere with flippant asides ('I'm not concerned with semantics – or semination' (p. 442)), and ends up bursting into sobs which Van hears 'with horror' but refuses to respond to, because of the absurdity of having 'a good cry with Father' (p. 444). In other words, the whole encounter is a study in self-consciousness. We get the stock responses associated with a typical, novelistic scene, the desire to resist the temptation to indulge in such ordinary behaviour, the derisive commentary that almost reduces everything to the level of verbal play, and an underlying seriousness in the discussion about 'wrecking' Ada's life. But Van's feelings for his father remain undramatized and unconvincing.

And that is it. The 'beloved', 'respected', 'admirable' father never gets a look-in. Theoreticians of the novel have replaced Percy Lubbock's distinction between showing and telling with more subtle and elaborate formulations. As Gérard Genette points out, even the terms themselves are misleading:

the very notion of showing, like that of imitation or of narrative representation (and even more because of its naïvely visual character) is perfectly
illusory: contrary to dramatic representation no narrative can 'show' or
'imitate' the story that it is telling. It can only relate it in a more detailed,
precise, lively manner and thus give more or less *the illusion of mimesis*
which is the only narrative mimesis, for this unique and sufficient reason
that narration, oral or written, is a fact of language, and that language
signifies without imitating.[22]

The 'illusion of showing' then. But whatever we call it, to compare
the 'detail', 'precision', and 'vividness' (all honorific words in
Nabokov's aesthetic vocabulary) of the early love scenes with the
imprecision and deadness of the scenes involving father and son is
to see how Nabokov has, deliberately but unwisely and unneces-
sarily, sabotaged his own enterprise. In saying this we are not
criticizing him for having failed to live up to the principles laid down
by the traditional novel or its defenders, but for having failed to live
up to his own principles. The claims made in the passage quoted
above about the 'vagaries' of personal relationships, about how 'no
art can exist without such vagaries', were forgotten. In Nabokov's
own mind, the details and the drama were there; in *Ada*, they are
not.

Lucette figures much more prominently in the novel, but her role
is also beset by limitations Nabokov has imposed on himself.
Consider the following excerpt:

'But Van! Don't you dare think I "relanced" you to reiterate that I'm
madly and miserably in love with you and that you can do anything you
want with me. If I didn't simply press the button and slip that note into the
burning slit and cataract away, it was because I *had* to see you, because
there is something you must know, even if it makes you detest and despise
Ada and me. *Otvratitel'no trudno* (it is disgustingly hard) to explain,
especially for a virgin – well, technically, a virgin, a *kokotische* virgin, half
poule, half *puella*. I realize the privacy of the subject, mysterious matters
that one should not discuss even with a vaginal brother – mysterious, not
merely in their moral and mystical aspect – '
Uterine – but close enough. It certainly came from Lucette's sister. He
knew that shade and that shape. 'That shade of blue, that shape of you'
(corny song on the Sonorola). Blue in the face from pleading RSVP.
' – but also in a direct physical sense. Because, darling Van, in that direct
physical sense I know as much about our Ada as you.'   (p. 372)

There are pages and pages of this kind of writing in the novel. It is
amusing and imaginative but, for me at least, ultimately tedious,

because it is all so arbitrary. The delight of indulging in alliteration for its own sake frees Nabokov to team up 'mysterious' and 'moral' and 'mystical', but his freedom is our constraint, because the words don't mean anything. The rest of the speech is almost equally cut off from a world in which words mean certain things. It is not 'disgustingly hard' to explain: Lucette is actually looking forward to confessing her Sapphic indulgences and goes on to do it with obvious relish. There is no risk whatever in telling Van about them, since all sultans are titillated by lesbian fumblings in an off-duty harem. Readers who argue that all this superficiality is being used to characterize Lucette will have trouble accounting for the almost breathless admiration with which she is always presented to us. It may seem churlish to complain about superficiality, given the verbal felicities, the stylistic brilliance, and the imaginative flights in this and the long scene that follows. But stylistic brilliance is the norm in Nabokov, and in the earlier novels he puts it to better use.

The main defence against this kind of criticism would be to sweep it away as too solemn, too earthbound, too antiquated. It all presupposes an idea about novelistic character, someone might argue, that Nabokov has clearly dispensed with. In *Ada* we are not dealing with autonomous figures or representations of human personalities. The lusty French maid, the butler who is 'Quite the old comedy retainer' (p. 157), the evil blackmailer, the unrequited lover – these are not characters in any realistic sense, but simply 'nodes in the verbal structure of the work whose identity is relatively precarious'.[23] By giving his hero a variety of roles, making him 'a portrait of the artist as stud, philosopher, physical *and* verbal acrobat',[24] and the subject of a *Bildungsroman* who has nothing to do and nothing to learn, Nabokov challenges our conventional notions of character, and shows us the arbitrariness of deriving the conception of a personality from a set of described actions. Van fights a duel, not because some plausible sequence of events makes it necessary, but because the duel is one of Russian literature's obligatory rites; and Nabokov creates a small comic drama with his version of that traditional confrontation.[25] Because of his Mascodagama performances, Van cannot shrug his shoulders in later years, which prompts the authorial voice to wonder: 'Was Van's adult incapacity to "shrug" things off only physical or did it "correspond" to some archetypal character of his "undersoul"?' (p. 83), and one of criticism's obligatory rites suddenly looks a little silly. Or take the splendid passage that begins: 'How did the scuffle start? Did all three cross the brook stepping on slimy stones? Did Percy push Greg? Did Van jog Percy? Was there something – a stick? Twisted out of a fist? A wrist gripped and freed?' (p. 274). These burly brutes grapple 'on the brink of a brook' (p. 275) for a couple of pages. Just who is imitating what here? Perhaps the 'real-life' confrontation is just as artificial and literary as the prose that describes it. Richard Lanham, in his excellent book on style, argues precisely this when he suggests that for a writer like Nabokov life seems 'as stylized as literature. Ordinary experience seems fundamentally dramatic, a game of roles in which the self is not so much felt and possessed as presented and reenacted. For such an experience, the most faithful reflection will be a prose style equally contrived, literary, and self-conscious.'[26] But how 'ordinary' is the kind of experience which *Ada* presents us with? And how will this kind of Nabokovian experimentation force us to judge the principal characters of *Ada* by criteria totally different from the ones we normally use for family chronicles and their imitations?

The answers to these questions depend to a considerable extent on the view one takes of the history of the novel. If one believes that 'By placing his characters in a purely (and self-consciously) imaginative realm, Nabokov alerts the reader to the bankruptcy of realism as a literary device',[27] then one will probably welcome anything he does in this vein as a salutary challenge to a collection of unexamined assumptions about the nature of character in particular and about the human personality in general. If, on the other hand, one believes that the whole programme of the traditional novel involves humanizing the characters of fable and romance, so that the melodramatic villain of popular literature becomes the much more interesting Lovelace in *Clarissa*,[28] and the simpleton of Russian folklore is re-created in Dostoevsky's Prince Myshkin,[29] one might well conclude that Nabokov hasn't really forced us to re-examine our assumptions about lifelike characters, but simply resurrected the prototypes that novelists once found to be inadequate. To dispense, at times, with notions of psychological essence and coherence does not constitute a convincing case against such notions. It may be relevant to point out here that attempts to use Propp's study of the Russian folktale in analyses of character in the novel have had only limited success, because 'lifelikeness' has proved to be more than a simple set of conventions or an ideological prejudice. Greimas points out that 'a limited number of actantial terms is sufficient to account for the organization of a micro-universe', but warns against defining an entire genre by such a limited criterion.[30] To remake the novel in the image of the folktale by transforming it into a world in which one character seeks something, finds it or fails to find it, and is either helped or hindered by the characters he meets on his quest, is to look for that 'micro-universe' where it may not belong. Armed with his schema, the critic finds himself in the same position as the anthropologist who must explain all human behaviour in terms of the aggressive and territorial instincts of a hairy biped.

My own sense is that Nabokov's conflict with traditional notions of character was a battle that he fought against himself. He was the kind of novelist who could hardly put pen to paper without first imagining someone, in some ways like himself, doing something that inevitably involved other characters in a series of events which he as the author was responsible for unravelling. And the more intricate and detailed the map of that character's consciousness, the more all Nabokov's many talents were called into play.

We saw how in *Lolita* the parodic and the self-referential work at extending the force of the novel's human drama, how the novel's complexities involve us because they convince us that the truth is a complex thing, and how Nabokov skilfully uses his own material to argue against himself. What about the relations between parody and the human drama in *Ada*? Its complexities? Nabokov's arguments with himself? In this section, I want to try to answer these questions by focusing on two aspects of the novel which have explicit parallels in *Lolita*: the use of a dramatic concluding scene to 'point a moral', and the references to other literary works to give depth and emotional resonance to the novel.

First a look at one of the climactic scenes in *Ada*, Lucette's death by drowning. An interesting mixture of emotion admitted and emotion denied, it divides into two parts. First comes a very effective buildup, dramatic, laconic, inexorable, punctuated by startlingly appropriate metaphors such as 'she had planned everything except [her suicide] note, so she tore her blank life in two and disposed of the pieces in the W.C.' (p. 492). Then suddenly, just as Lucette jumps into the water, the world being told about is elbowed out of the way by the world of the teller. We hear Van chatting with his secretary, who struggles with his diction while Lucette fights the waves. He corrects a transcription error, spells out a neologism, misreads a word, interpolates various irrelevancies. This brief flurry subsides as quickly as it begins, and two more paragraphs, self-consciously 'written' in a deliberately precious way, take Lucette to the bottom and the reader to the end of the chapter. What is the effect of this kind of literary distancing? Perhaps Nabokov is using black humour here, the device that André Breton calls 'l'ennemi mortel de la sentimentalité',[31] to avoid the kind of death scene that Lucette's status in the novel would seem to require. Or perhaps he wants to mount a more sweeping attack on conventional ideas about reading. Here is Jonathan Culler on a passage in Stephen Crane's 'The Open Boat' which makes use of the same effect:

> ... unable to arrest the play of meaning and compose the text, or even its fragments, as spoken from an identifiable position by someone with identifiable attitudes, one is forced to recognize that the act of writing, of moving out of the communicative circuit of speech, has been successful, and that the level of *vraisemblance* at which the story becomes coherent is that of irony itself as project. Narrative dislocation, we might say, displays language as a kind of indifferent fate, which can put everything to the test with a distance and detachment that is unjustifiably cruel.[32]

His preconceptions assaulted, his expectations confounded, his responses devalued, the reader must come to terms with this new relation the author has posited between language and experience. But is this how we respond to *Ada*? The novel's critics have praised Nabokov for avoiding sentimentality here, but at the same time credited him with creating something very moving; and it seems clear that they are not being moved by the idea of language as an 'indifferent fate'. Some suggest that Van is manfully disguising his grief, and that the scene is the tragic *dénouement* of a cautionary tale. Van and Ada have been guilty of 'using' Lucette; therefore, they are in part responsible for her self-destruction: 'her suicide movingly records the high price their freedom exacts', as one critic puts it;[33] Ada's 'we *teased* her to death!' (p. 586) is 'the most painfully exposed nerve in the book: the cry of realization at the point of death', remarks another.[34] These critics seem to be arguing that traditional habits of reading are more deeply engrained than we are sometimes willing to admit, that we attach ourselves to a 'something' that is 'happening' no matter how it is being described. This may well be the case, but we cannot help being aware of the arbitrariness involved in whatever decision we finally make. The whole idea of calmly opting for one reading or another suggests how free *Ada*'s readers are compared to *Lolita*'s, but this freedom is bought at a certain price.

The other comparison I want to make between the two novels involves parody. In *Lolita*, Eliot and Dostoevsky, the diary and the confession, are the objects of Nabokov's parody, but he uses the authors and forms he refers to in a way that goes far beyond what we normally mean by that word. In *Ada* too he uses parody to comment on a variety of writers and their methods. What is he trying to do, and how well does he succeed? Two claims in particular have been made for this technique in *Ada*: (1) that it offers some important formalistic criticism of the nineteenth-century novel, and (2) that it forces us to revise our view of the reality represented in that novel. Let us see if these are justified.

Van Veen himself makes the first claim when he notes that 'Old storytelling devices may be parodied only by very great and inhuman artists' (p. 246). He is echoed by Alfred Appel, who asserts that 'Nabokov uses parody to re-investigate the fundamental problems of his art.' For example, he 'parodies the realist's efforts to limn "reality". On his first tour of Ardis Hall, Van announces "The Attic. This is the attic. Welcome to the attic", thus undermining the possibility that an examination of old novelistic furniture could reveal very much (p. 44), though he does catalog a goodly number of antiques before Part One is over.'[35] Of course for Nabokov the 'old novelistic furniture' actually reveals a great deal. The parodist in *Ada* is also the critic who believes: 'we must visualize the rooms, the clothes, the manners of an author's people. The color of Fanny Price's eyes in *Mansfield Park* and the furnishing of her cold little room are important.'[36] True, this was probably written in the 1940s, but all the physical detail of this kind in *Ada* reminds us that we are dealing with a writer who finds new uses for the conventions of the novel even while he mocks them. Yet the bulk of *Ada*'s commentary on formal matters in the nineteenth-century novel is restricted to interesting but minor details. Despite the numerous allusions to the technical idiosyncrasies of various authors, Nabokov's parody of storytelling devices, when compared to something like *Northanger Abbey*, for example, seems more entertaining than illuminating. Have we really learned very much when we are told that Austen uses the

'You recall Brown, don't you, Smith?' device for the sake of 'rapid narrative information?' (p. 8). Of the dozens of allusions to Pushkin and Chekhov, how many tell us something about these authors that we will remember when we go back to reread them?[37] Of course Nabokov does work in more devious and complex ways to comment on the novelist's art. At one point the reader finds himself wandering through a particularly involute and sententious passage about Lucette: 'Long ago she had made up her mind that by forcing the man whom she absurdly but irrevocably loved to have intercourse with her, even once, she would, somehow, with the help of some prodigious act of nature, transform a brief tactile event into an eternal spiritual tie.' This goes on for a while longer; the reader grows more puzzled; and then Nabokov gleefully springs the trap: 'He understood her condition or at least believed, in despair, that he *had* understood it, retrospectively, by the time no remedy except Dr Henry's oil of Atlantic prose could be found in the medicine chest of the past with its banging door and toppling toothbrush' (p. 485). This says to the reader: You thought you were finally getting the profound emotional account you wanted, but it was just a bunch of words. Conditioned by all the novels you've read, you were fooled into believing it. If you go back to James now, perhaps you'll see the artificiality of some of his effects.[38] But when we reread James we find that, as good as Nabokov's joke is, it has no serious point. He got the commas right, but that is about all.

The claim made for *Ada*'s insights into the kind of life depicted in nineteenth-century novels is vulnerable to the same kind of criticism. When Fred Kaplan calls *Ada* and *The French Lieutenant's Woman* 'Two of the most exhilarating explorations of the Victorian consciousness in recent years'[39] (this was written in 1973), he simply reminds us that Fowles's painstaking reconstruction of an entire society, including its ways of writing about itself, is different in kind from Nabokov's fantastic tour of a world that can only be called 'Victorian' by doing some violence to conventional usage. *Ada*'s subtitle, 'A Family Chronicle', is distinctly misleading in this regard. Kaplan goes on to argue: 'As for the major Victorian novelists, particularly English and Russian, for Nabokov the chronicle absorbs everything: it is the full tale of all our lives and arts, an absorptive and encyclopedic device in which what is sought is the permanence that lies behind and transcends the generational change.'[40] 'The full tale of all our lives'? With no society in which those lives unfold, no constraints on any desire? Nabokov has chosen to liberate himself from these aspects of the world of the nineteenth-century novel, not write a commentary on them. *Ada*'s range is narrower than some critics have supposed.[41]

Nabokov wrote his novel when the very idea that the novel had ever been 'the full tale of all our lives' was beginning to come under attack from various quarters. The parody in *Ada* is usually seen as part of that attack. A Nabokov critic writes of Antiterra's unusual geography and history:

> These strange phenomena call into question the status of the novelistic discourse; they relieve it of many constraints with which our traditional representations burden it and evoke, in our imagination, powerful fantasies. They disorient us, invite us to succumb to the fascination of the text, and thus, to get rid of the whole didactic or referential part which seems to rise to the surface all over the place.[42]

And we hear echoes of Barthes, a critic who has some sharp things to say about the conventional nature of the 'reality' in nineteenth-century fiction, and who insists that 'the pleasure of the text' can 'hamper the return of the text to morality, to truth, to the morality of truth'.[43] I have tried to explain in the preceding chapters how this kind of critical emphasis misrepresents Nabokov's novels; with the late fiction things are not so clear cut. Used discriminately, *Ada* can be a powerful weapon in the battle over what kind of fiction is appropriate for an epoch bemused by the artificiality of its own creations. But it must also be a source of considerable embarrassment. For Nabokov refuses to perform his role in 'the death of the author' rites that criticism has arranged for modern writers. Barthes reserves his highest praise for the author who arranges things so that 'one never knows whether he is responsible for what he writes (if there is a subject *behind* his language); for the essence of writing (the sense of the work which constitutes it) is to prevent one from ever answering the question: "Who is speaking?" '[44] Although he might be willing to leave us there, the author of *Ada* is quite definitely not. For all the places in the novel in which he undermines communication, exploiting the gaps between language and experience, author and reader, there are as many in which he wants to say very clearly something to someone. Is this the implied author or the narrative overvoice or the real Nabokov, or, as he liked to put it, the person he most often impersonates? One can quarrel with all these definitions. But it seems obvious, if we use his non-fictional utterances as our guide, that he made his novel into a 'farce' in the etymological sense, stuffing it full of his own ideas and distributing them to various characters.[45] It would be wrong to dismiss this voice as an amusing but irrelevant idiosyncrasy, or to condemn it as an unwarranted intrusion: its pronouncements are relevant to our inquiry. In what follows, I want to concentrate on Nabokov's forays into science, psychology, metaphysics, and art, with a view to discovering whether some sort of coherent picture emerges.

I begin with the discussion in *Ada* of a concept that has revolutionized twentieth-century physics:

At this point, I suspect, I should say something about my attitude to 'Relativity'. It is not sympathetic. What many cosmogonists tend to accept as an objective truth is really the flaw inherent in mathematics which parades as truth. The body of the astonished person moving in Space is shortened in the direction of motion and shrinks catastrophically as the velocity nears the speed beyond which, by the fiat of a fishy formula, no speed can be. That is his bad luck, not mine – but I sweep away the business of his clock's slowing down. Time, which requires the utmost purity of consciousness to be properly apprehended, is the most rational element of life, and my reason feels insulted by those flights of Technology Fiction. One especially grotesque inference, drawn (I think by Engelwein) from Relativity Theory – and destroying it, if drawn correctly – is that the galactonaut and his domestic animals, after touring the speed spas of Space, would return younger than if they had stayed at home all the time. Imagine them filing out of their airark – rather like those 'Lions', juvenilified by romp suits, exuding from one of those huge chartered buses that stop, horribly blinking, in front of a man's impatient sedan just where the highway wizens to squeeze through the narrows of a mountain village. (p. 543)

This is Van Veen in his *Texture of Time*; but his ruminations on time sound a lot like Nabokov's,[46] and besides, Einstein is an old target. Nabokov mentions him in the book on Gogol, where the lack of understanding is just as pronounced and the assertions just as rambunctious. He compares Gogol to the Russian mathematician Lobachevsky, who, he says, 'blasted Euclid and discovered a century ago many of the theories which Einstein later developed'.[47] Whoever is speaking in the passage quoted above, it is he who is insulting reason, not Einstein. The appeal to common sense is actually a defence of Newtonian mechanics, which simply doesn't explain the 'time dilation' of, for example, a particle like the cosmic ray, which moves at speeds approaching that of light and behaves as Einstein's theory predicts.[48] Why this risky venture into alien territory? The artist's mistrust of the scientist for one thing. The whole approach implies that this particular hypothesis and the facts which support it make up a kind of credo to which he doesn't happen to subscribe. Yet Nabokov was a scientist himself, which perhaps ought to have made him more circumspect. It didn't, because he was essentially a different kind of scientist. There are, in any discipline, the rigorous observers and classifiers, on the one hand, and those who search out secret laws, on the other. Nabokov was a lepidopterist, one of the former, and he regularly expressed his contempt for the latter, in all sorts of disciplines. The first group always has tangible evidence immediately at hand, in order to refute those who might want to argue, for instance, that they don't happen to hold with all that caterpillar/cocoon stuff. The second group often does not have such evidence, but they obviously are not less scientific for that. Of course there is more to say about Nabokov's account of relativity. He may have got his facts wrong, but he did get his images wonderfully right: those Lions 'exuding' from their bus are a typical example of the kind of vivid absurdity that always attracted his gaze. The temptation is to concentrate on such detail, attribute an easygoing whimsicality to the rest, and leave it at that. But Nabokov wants to be taken seriously, and such claims, both inside and outside the fiction, tell us a great deal about his world. It is one in which the individual's mind is at the centre, trusting its own rational processes but mistrusting the generalizer, uneasy about nature's strangenesses (Nabokov once assured Andrew Field that we still know nothing about electricity),[49] and audaciously asserting its right to defend the humanly comprehensible against the abstract truth.

Freud is another of those people who discovered that the true sense of certain things is hidden. Nabokov knows a good deal about the area in which Freud made his investigations, and thus he is on surer ground when he goes to the attack. The results are sometimes very funny. That delightful literalism of the imagination that he uses to refute Einstein is invoked again, as when Van argues that Greek myths can occur only in the dreams of 'a Greek or a mythicist' (p. 363). Nabokov's acute eye sees instantly where Freud is most vulnerable: 'I become a de*flower*er because I failed to pass my botany examination' (p. 577), quotes Van, and the image of a gloomy fatalist with a penchant for outrageous oversimplification is firmly established in the reader's mind. In Van's lectures on Freud, his students respond with 'laughter and applause' (p. 364) to some of his best sallies: the whole attack is clearly one of Nabokov's bravura comic performances. But once again he does want us to listen to the arguments and take him seriously. Nabokov's critics tend to come down on his side in this matter, usually by contrasting a Nabokovian 'individualism' with Freud's murky collectivist schema.[50] There is something to be said for this view, but it leaves certain things unsaid. First, Nabokov's basic disagreement with Freud about latent meaning always makes him overstate his case. Dreams, we are told in *Ada*, are characterized by 'mental mediocrity and bumble' and 'a dismal weakening of the intellectual faculties of the dreamer' (pp. 362–3); therefore, no moral, symbolic, or allegoric interpretation of them is possible. Because the active, conscious mind is either not responsible for dreams or only ineptly participates in their creation, no sustained analysis of them will elicit anything particularly revealing about the dreamer. In attacking not just crude or amateurish interpretation of dreams, but the whole idea of interpreting them, Nabokov is telling us that Freudian psychology, like Einsteinian physics, 'offends' his reason. What he is actually proposing is a retreat from knowledge. Why did Ruskin, for example, have recurrent dreams of serpents which he either showed to female companions or watched while they swelled up in his hand? No doubt Nabokov's answer to this would have been amusing, but I doubt if it would have convinced those who want to interpret this kind of dream, making use of Freud's insights in the process. Second, Nabokov's commonsense view does not really have the popular support he wants us to think it has. Although many people do think of Freud as Nabokov does, as the man who spent his whole life grimly reducing everything to sex, their attitudes to dreams in particular and to their unconscious lives in general are essentially Freudian. As Frank Kermode points out: 'Freud knew, when he wrote *The Interpretation of Dreams*, that the hypothesis of latent sense was one he shared, not with his colleagues and the authors of the scientific literature on dreams to which he alludes so patiently, but with most of the remainder of mankind through the centuries.'[51] Third, a jeering nastiness creeps into some of the humour, particularly in the obsessive repetition of that 'Signy Mondieu' joke, and the attempt to link psychiatry and fascism in 'Dr Sig Heiler'. Finally, the very real similarities between Nabokov's view of the world and the one he is attacking get lost in the rhetoric. In novel after novel he gives us something that distinctly resembles a Freudian view, in which the creative power struggles to find a form for its wish-fulfillment fantasies and to believe in the illusions that help to ward off death.[52]

The idea of the human mind as a lone crusader for its particular brand of truth gets more support in *Ada*'s 'philosophical' adventures. The inverted commas are there because, as everyone admits, Van's *Texture of Time* works, not as philosophy, but as part of the novel. It is worth asking why this is the case. First there is the tendency to see the humorous rather than the logical implications of a given proposition. Like Dr Johnson's friend Mr Edwards, Nabokov tries to be a philosopher, but 'cheerfulness [is] always breaking in'.[53] Then there is the feisty combativeness of the loner, expressed in ideas such as the one about the 'history of thought' being a collection of 'clichés' that the original thinker must somehow 'surmount' (p. 471). The third reason is the most important: Nabokov's metaphoric habit of mind. Most often he uses a visual image, not just to illustrate an idea, but also to organize its discussion. *Ada* is full of examples of this, many of them quite remarkable displays of his imaginative powers. When he talks about the 'birth' of Van's book, Nabokov uses this trick of letting the image direct the idea to reanimate a dead metaphor: 'Van had only reached the bridal stage; then, to develop the metaphor, would come the sleeping car of messy defloration; then the first balcony of honeymoon breakfasts, with the first wasp' (p. 324). And of course the *Texture of Time* is a sustained example of this technique. The result is a frenzy of strange identifications and marvellous metaphors, but it doesn't get us very far if we are interested in finding out something about time. For Nabokov is doomed to pure subjectivity from the start. He wants to study 'Pure Time, Perceptual Time, Tangible Time, Time free of content, context and running commentary' (p. 539); but instead of simplifying his task, this actually commits him to an impossible one. As Richard Webster, in a discussion of 'time' in Kermode's *The Sense of an Ending*, points out: 'although the word "time" is a substantive, one of its essential properties is that it does not refer to a substance – it is a word whose meaning is determined by its context'.[54] The very personal truth that results may be a philosophic weakness; but it is also a novelistic strength, because Nabokov's quest in search of this phantom 'time' gives us so many glimpses into the workings of his imagination that we feel as if we are listening in on the creative process itself.

Lastly we have Nabokov's views on art. The Veens are his spokesmen: they endorse his view of art as enchantment, and condemn the vulgarity and sham of so-called modern art with Nabokovian directness. Here is a typical passage: 'Andrey, or rather his sister on his behalf, he was too stupid even for that, collected progressive philistine Art, bootblack blotches and excremental smears on canvas, imitations of an imbecile's doodles, primitive idols, aboriginal masks, *objets trouvés*, or rather *troués*, the polished log with its polished hole à la Heinrich Heideland' (p. 462).[55] Nabokov was a master of invective and 'good copy' for the interviewers because he knew that vilification is always more fun than eulogy. But I confess to a certain unease when I read these passages. The word 'philistine' here creates an unintended irony, since there is nothing more typically philistine than reducing modern art to 'an imbecile's doodles'. If we heard Henry Moore (*Heide* is 'moor' in German)[56] being denounced in these terms at one of his exhibitions, we would presumably feel a mixture of scorn and pity for the ignorance being displayed. The humour militates against that reaction here, but the reader must wonder about the fallibility of such aesthetic judgments, particularly when they come to him so highly recommended. Perhaps it is best to interpret these outbursts, along with the railings against 'the *fokus-pocus* of a social theme' (p. 426) and the bellicose defences of pure art, as a kind of signature, like the crescendo finale in Rossini, reassuring the reader about where he is and reaffirming the author's identity. This sounds dismissive; but Nabokov is almost always more amusing as a polemicist than he is convincing, especially when he is trying to make a case for his estimations of other writers. Our century has been a good one for the outspoken artist, the Eliot or the Boulez who writes an article that explodes like a bomb in the camp of the enemy, spreading chaos and preparing the way for a successful advance. Nabokov's attacks produce the same sound effects but never inflict the same damage. *Ada* shows us why this is so. He groups together Thomas Wolfe, Thomas Mann, and T[homas]. S. Eliot for condemnation (p. 403) because they share a first name and an interest in 'general ideas', that hold-all phrase

Nabokov favours because its authoritative ring disguises its lack of meaningful content. Turgenev, he assures us, wrote only one memorable lyric (p. 412). Borges writes 'pretentious fairy tales' (p. 344). Translators come in two kinds: 'the well-meaning mediocrity' and the inept 'paraphrast' (p. 578). And so it goes. All this is served up with the serenity of someone who is unconcerned if his novel becomes a document in the history of one man's idiosyncratic taste. The last fifteen years of his life was a time for 'strong opinions', a time to make use of the public forum that was finally available to him.[57]

An intensely personal science, psychology and philosophy; a theory of art that puts a premium on the reactions of certain specially gifted individuals – is this galloping egocentricity and shameless elitism? I conclude with some thoughts on the various answers to these questions that the reader will find in *Ada*.

The novel actually involves us with three elites, one inside and one outside and one hovering above the text. Inside we have the 'super-imperial couple' (p. 71) and the aristocratic family: their brilliance, their genius, their good breeding, their general sophistication. Is this all as laudable as the self-congratulatory references to it would have us believe, this world of genteel patricians who comport themselves impeccably, and murmur devastating witticisms to one another while the servants look on admiringly? Its members tend to reassure themselves about their superiority by doing a lot of sneering: at the local peasants, at 'criminals, cripples and madmen' (p. 307), even at the occasional 'Chinaman' and the mentally retarded (p. 586). There is a lot of talk about 'honour', but it is the honour of boys' fiction: challenges flung out at the drop of an insult, scoundrels and cads dismissed with a good drubbing. There is a lot of talk about 'beauty', but it is the beauty of adolescent fantasy, of Eric Veen's girls: 'good teeth, a flawless epiderm, undyed hair, impeccable buttocks and breasts' (p. 351). And then there is the fabulous intelligence which manifests itself in 'the Veen wit', which too often sounds like only a slightly improved version of what can be heard at any pretentious cocktail party. If Nabokov seemed more aware of this, if it were satirized with the same zest that he reserves for philistinism and vulgarity, we would not feel so obliged to point out how phony it all is.

The elite outside the novel is less conceited and takes itself much less seriously. It is created by those aspects of *Ada* that separate those who 'belong' from those who do not. For example, only those who attentively followed the great translation debate in 1964–5 will know that Dr Alexander Gerschenkron wrote a review of Nabokov's *Onegin*, in which he criticized the translator for being unfair to D. I. Chizhevsky, a great Pushkin scholar; and only they will understand why a dictionary used for the scrabble games in *Ada* is described as 'a small but chippy Edmundson in Dr. Gerschizhevsky's reverent version' (p. 225). 'Yellow-blue Vass' (p. 187) frocks may be the latest in fashion on Antiterra, but they date from Nabokov's days at Wellesley, when he used this kind of phrase as a teaching aid for students trying to learn how to pronounce 'Ya lyublyu vas', 'I love you' in Russian. There must be hundreds of these in *Ada*, and only the publication of a definitive annotated edition will bring all us outsiders into the charmed circle occupied by those who have followed up the allusions, agonized over the puzzles, and got all the bonuses they deserve.

But in the end we are left with the most elite group of Nabokov's readers, the one he invoked in comments to interviewers about the author who writes for the person he sees in the mirror, for his multiplicate selves, for 'a room full of people wearing his own mask'.[58] *Ada* reminds us constantly that Nabokov is this kind of writer. Isn't that always the case in his fiction? What's the difference between the omnipresence of Nabokov in a novel like *Ada* and the very personal views that take over *The Gift*, for example? I think there is a difference, which can best be summed up by saying that the self-involvement of the younger man has become the self-admiration of the master. This does not make for a very attractive self-portrait, and bespeaks a certain narrowing of vision that has its detrimental effects on the fiction. At the end of the second chapter, I quoted Nabokov's comments on Chekhov's idealists; he talks about the 'pureness of spirit' and 'moral elevation' they represented, about the Russia of the future they tried to build but could not. It is hard not to see *Ada* in the context of these remarks as an antithetical vision, a retreat into an imaginary Russia inhabited by arrogant, amoral dreamers who insist that the private fantasy of the extraordinary individual is the only world left to create. In *Ada*, the creative imagination asserts its sovereign power, but at the same time it announces its own abdication.

6

Pale Fire, *Transparent Things*, and *Look at the Harlequins!*

It seems likely that the nineteen eighties will be a decade of increasing self-consciousness for literary criticism: more attempts to define first principles, more doubts about the whole enterprise, more arguments about the amount of 'science' involved in it, more extra-literary models proposed for its organization. Recent discussions of narrative have made us aware of the problems involved in saying how stories get told and what they mean, and cautioned us about the limitations of critical commentary and the problematic character of interpretation. Frank Kermode's *The Genesis of Secrecy* is a good example: for every insight into narrative he offers, he asks questions about what it means to interpret; and despite all the confidence with which he defends his approach, he ends on a resigned note: 'whether one thinks that one's purpose is to recognize the original meaning, or to fall headlong into a text that is a treacherous network rather than a continuous and systematic sequence, one may be sure of one thing, and that is disappointment'.[1] And Cary Nelson, in an article in *PMLA*, suggests that this disappointment, along with other subjective responses, may well be the critic's subject after all: 'Part of the pleasure of reading criticism is experiencing the subtle ways in which the biases, hopes, and frustrations of the critic are woven into the texture of his language and even into the language of the texts he examines. This dialectic between self and other, embedded in the critic's language and method, is really what criticism is "about".'[2] Nabokov's highly self-conscious late novels seem ideally suited to this kind of criticism; and of course most discussions of them explicate their 'treacherous networks', and explore the ways in which the author toys with both the form he has chosen and with the reader who must try to find his way through it. Such an approach may well be the most fruitful, but I want to see in this last chapter if the critic who is intent on analyzing the ostensible subjects of these novels as a kind of content, to see them as representations of a human world, is doomed to disappointment. My approach is basically the same as in the previous chapter. How does Nabokov experiment with his normal procedures for depicting character and event? What problems does this create for him? Does the increased emphasis on self-reflexiveness prevent the novels from being commentaries on things as they are? Has the author in these works become a fleeting image in a hall of mirrors? These are the questions that I want to try to answer.

First, *Pale Fire*; I propose to begin by cutting some critical knots in order to simplify my task. That there is no solid textual evidence to support claims for either Shade or Kinbote as single author; that 'Foreword' + 'Poem' + 'Commentary' + 'Index' = 'Novel'; that, as one critic puts it, 'there is no reason to doubt the existence of the basic fictional data'[3] – all these are assumed in what follows. My discussion consists of three sections. The first is an examination of what happens if we approach the novel as a study in human relations such as *Lolita* or *Ada*. In the second I say something about some other kinds of content in *Pale Fire* that have been the subject of considerable speculation. The third focuses on what the novel has to tell us about interpretation and critical self-consciousness.

What happens if we use the procedure that has been consistently utilized to this point and read *Pale Fire* as an account of a set of relationships between characters whose fates the author wants to involve us in? Even someone as concerned with the 'Jack-in-the-box', 'Fabergé gem', 'clockwork toy', 'chess problem' aspects of the novel as Mary McCarthy claims that 'Love is the burden of *Pale Fire*, love and loss.'[4] She is seconded by Robert Alter who argues that part of 'the serious imaginative business of the novel' is 'the inner life of the protagonists, the existential quandaries in which they are caught, the shimmering interplay of art and life generated by the events and the language of the narrative'.[5] And some hints from Nabokov suggest that this may be the correct approach: in one interview he spoke of John Shade's 'intense inner existence';[6] and he told Alfred Appel that 'Yeslove', the penultimate entry in the Index, was the simple message of the novel.[7] This suggests that the relationship between Shade and his wife is a good place to start our investigation. His evocation of her in Canto Two is a catalogue of Nabokovian 'positives': the minute detail of the description ('The glistening teeth / Biting the careful lip; the shade beneath / The eye from the long lashes'), the list of all the trivial things that become special because lovers bring them to each other's attention, the shared hush of respect for the past and the dead. He goes on to call her 'My dark Vanessa, crimson-barred, my blest, / My Admirable butterfly!',[8] and this kind of specialized reference too is always very important in Nabokov. The Red Admirable was a personal favourite, and its presence is a sort of seal of approval for the character it is associated with. In these lines it is only a beautiful natural thing that the poet alludes to; but if we obey Kinbote's injunction, 'see, see now, my note to lines 993–995' (p. 172), and follow it through the novel, we realize that it is actually a hovering emblem of the love between husband and wife. Kinbote describes how it lands on Shade's sleeve and flits off just before he is killed. Like the moth associated with Krug's wife at the end of *Bend Sinister*, its last appearance marks not just the end of a story and the end of a life, but also the promise of something ephemeral that endures. In these ways then their relationship is quietly and movingly presented for our approval, but if it is the key to the entire work there is surprisingly little of it. Shade's facetious disquisition on the twice-married man's problems in eternity is hardly calculated to tell us much about this love; it even threatens to trivialize it. And the glimpses of the Shades that Kinbote's commentary provides are on the whole not very helpful. Like V. in *The Real Life of Sebastian Knight*, he is permanently and comically excluded from the private life of his subject. So the relation is just presented to us as a given; it does not evolve or unfold; it is a positive and a constant, but an insubstantial one.

Perhaps the poet's love for his dead daughter is the key to *Pale Fire*. Many Nabokov characters die tragically young, and the death of a child provides the emotional focus of novels like *Laughter in the Dark* and *Bend Sinister*. But the case of Hazel Shade is somewhat different from these. Because of the structure he has chosen, Nabokov has only a few pages to tell the story of her life and death. The crucial event of the earlier novels takes on a more anecdotal status here. His attitude has changed as well. In the earlier novels he presents this kind of death by understating and yet emphasizing its pathos, bestows his compassion on those whose lives are ruined by what has happened, and reserves his irony for those too insensitive to understand the significance of suffering and disaster. The pain in Krug's howl of anguish at the death of his son is not so easily detected in Shade's disciplined couplets, and the sentimental aura surrounding little David is in sharp contrast to the intrusions of the ironical and the farcical in Hazel Shade's life and death. We hear a jaunty black humour in lines like 'Jim McVey / (The family oculist) will cure that slight / Squint in no time' (p. 43). The event that leads directly to her death is in one sense a gag – college boy, ugly blind date – that Nabokov includes for our amusement. And what inevitably comes to mind when we think about suicides and *Pale Fire* is not Hazel's stepping 'Into a crackling, gulping swamp' (p. 51) but Kinbote's annotation of that line, which includes the long note on a Zemblan Christian's ideas about taking his own life, one of the most sustained pieces of pure comic invention in the entire Nabokov *oeuvre*. By concentrating on this kind of material and confining himself to sketching in only a few details of the human tragedy, he deliberately minimizes our involvement. The real reason for this death begins to seem more like the author's need to set up a locus of symbolic sorrow and loss than anything else.

That leaves Kinbote and his interactions, if *Pale Fire* is to comment meaningfully on human relations in the way that so many of the novels do. Initially at least this seems promising. Kinbote has a lot to say on this very subject, particularly on one aspect of it: as Andrew Field points out, *Pale Fire* is much more concerned with sex than *Lolita* itself.[9] Surely this welter of sexual detail will lead us through the twists and turns of the psyche to some truth about the inner self or about how we define ourselves in relationships with others. Yet more disappointment awaits us here. Kinbote's *amours* only superficially resemble Humbert's. He ogles his quarry with the same breathy urgency, but this turns out to be just an elaborate arrangement of sound effects meant to disguise a quasi-total isolation. He is the equivalent of a Humbert permanently outside the schoolyard, secure in the splendid onanistic seclusion of the parked car. We saw in *Ada* how Nabokov's treatment of adolescent desire begins with a series of sensitive portrayals and ends in a sterile repetitiveness. In *Pale Fire*, Kinbote's sexual development is also arrested at the adolescent stage, but not so it can be delicately described or vulgarly exalted. Here Nabokov is more interested in the fact that obsessed people are funny. This makes for a joke at Kinbote's expense every time a male character is mentioned, a certain amount of repetition and a certain amount of tedium.

It might seem reasonable to most readers at this point to stop worrying the novel for something it doesn't have and to admit that the old critical notions simply do not work with it. But Nabokov is clearly unwilling to limit *Pale Fire* in this way. At some point he must have become conscious of the problem and realized that readers might tire of chuckling at his narcissistic invert. With a view to extending the range of Kinbote's interests, and involving the reader in a more meaningful way, he includes a detailed account of a meeting with Queen Disa on the Riviera and of the reflections occasioned by it. It is worth looking at the scene in some detail, because it is crucial for an understanding of how emotion works in the novel and of what Nabokov is trying to do. Kinbote reviews the history of their relations:

What had the sentiments he entertained in regard to Disa ever amounted to? Friendly indifference and bleak respect. Not even in the first bloom of their marriage had he felt any tenderness or any excitement. Of pity, of heartache, there could be no question. He was, had always been, casual and heartless. But the heart of his dreaming self, both before and after the rupture, made extraordinary amends.

He dreamed of her more often, and with incomparably more poignancy, than his surface-life feelings for her warranted; these dreams occurred when he least thought of her, and worries in no way connected with her assumed her image in the subliminal world as a battle or a reform becomes a bird of wonder in a tale for children.

He goes on to describe how she looked 'on the day he first told her he did not love her':

That happened during a hopeless trip to Italy, in a lakeside hotel garden – roses, black araucarias, rusty, greenish hydrangeas – one cloudless evening with the mountains of the far shore swimming in a sunset haze and the lake all peach syrup regularly rippled with pale blue, and the captions of a newspaper spread flat on the foul bottom near the stone bank perfectly readable through the shallow diaphanous filth, and because, upon hearing him out, she sank down on the lawn in an impossible posture, examining a grass culm and frowning, he had taken his words back at once; but the shock had fatally starred the mirror, and thenceforth in his dreams her image was infected with the memory of that confession as with some disease or the secret after-effects of a surgical operation too intimate to be mentioned.

The gist, rather than the actual plot of the dream, was a constant refutation of his not loving her. His dream-love for her exceeded in emotional tone, in spiritual passion and depth, anything he had experienced in his surface existence.   (pp. 209–10)

The whole passage is something of a set piece in its context. Here is the old Nabokov style and no mistake: the exotic rightness of the weird simile; the picturesque precision of a technical term like 'starred'; the erudition that sends us to the dictionary from which we come away wondering how that araucaria (a South American or Australian pine) got to northern Italy; that prose tint running not so much to royal purple as to pale mauve, calculated to upset the staid and make lovers of English nod their heads admiringly; the description that shocks by virtue of its strange audacities: 'can newsprint be deciphered through diaphanous filth?' we want to know (answer: yes, someone tells me he has done it through the scum of a tidal pool); and finally, the Nabokov signature, the list of nouns between dashes or parentheses that amplifies with the utmost economy, bespeaking both arrogant panache and weary laconicism: 'I don't really have to describe this garden in detail, do I?' he says, while he tosses out the phrases that fill it in exactly. Here are the old Nabokov themes as well: love as a permanently frustrated desire for a still unravished bride; the crudeness of contingency when compared to the fabulous attractions of the past; the difference between a desperate longing to take responsibility for one's actions and an ability to do so.

Of course it is no accident that the passage is a collection of Nabokov's best stylistic effects and of his thematic concerns. He wanted these issues crystallized in memorable prose so that his novel would have a clear emotional centre. Critics have responded accordingly. They invariably refer to the scene when discussing *Pale Fire*, and insist on its importance. Bader claims that 'Kinbote's is the agony which lies beneath all love relationships', and that his 'inability to "find" Disa [in another part of his dream] is an aspect of love's horror: the realization that the essence of the beloved is unattainable'.[10] Field argues that Disa represents 'the necessarily frustrating, inconclusive, and guilt-ridden emotions involved in actual love and in the more abstract and vague love we feel for our native land'.[11] And Alter says of Kinbote's farewell to Disa: 'The poignancy of this moment when the spell of the dream breaks illustrates how a fiction focused on the dynamic of fiction-making can address itself not merely to the paradoxes of the writer's craft but to the ambiguities of the human condition.'[12] But surely something is wrong here. Where in *Pale Fire* is 'the agony which lies beneath all love relationships'? How does the novel convince the reader that love is 'necessarily frustrating'? What are these 'ambiguities of the human condition'? Such claims have all the

disquieting effects of a dodged issue. After all, Kinbote's meditation is a short account of a 'real life' that has no substance, in a
novel almost completely devoted to the blissful release of the
imaginary. Disa exists, but only as an evanescent shimmer in these
dreamy regions. If the reader can guard against being seduced by
Nabokov's cadences, he will be left wondering just why he should
respond to Kinbote's soul-searching or to his self-condemnation. It
is all very well for Nabokov to have his protagonist talk about
'emotional tone' and 'spiritual passion and depth': in the novels
examined to this point he forces us to come to terms with these
things by representing them dramatically. Here we are being asked
to invent them ourselves. 'Oh, let me be mawkish for the nonce!',
says Humbert at one point, 'I am so tired of being cynical.'[13] And so
he moves between cruel detachment and pathetic involvement,
until he ultimately finds some way of making these two standpoints
one. Kinbote is allowed to sit on the sidelines and make dream
amends. In fact, he is so uninvolved, let off the hook so easily, that
we tend to forget him altogether in the above passage. The differences in style and tone from the rest of Kinbote's commentary make
the reader assume that he is listening to Nabokov himself, who is
sketching in the novel he might have written but chose not to.

Obviously he is counting on our getting luxuriously lost in trying
to puzzle out the truth and fiction involved in Kinbote's accounts of
his past. A certain amount of subjectivity inevitably enters the
argument at this stage. Some would argue, as for example John
Stark has done, that

one naturally treats the information about Shade as if it came from a
realistic novel (one that purports to tell the truth) and the information
about Kinbote as if it came from a nonrealistic novel (one that creates
patterns, some more manifest than others). To add an evaluation, the facts
of Shade's life are considerably less interesting than the discoveries one
makes trying to figure out Kinbote, which strengthens Nabokov's case
against the realistic novel.[14]

It would of course be just as plausible to claim that the search for
hidden meanings or patterns in Kinbote's notes, however diverting,
threatens to become very tedious every time it leads us into a
fantasy world which has relatively little to do with our own. Shade's
life, we might say, at least what we are allowed to see of it, simply
blows Kinbote's away. When, despite Sybil's objections, the
importunate neighbour attempts to visit 'his poet' in the bathroom,

Shade says: 'Let him in, Sybil, he won't rape me!' (p. 264). Precisely: the earthy humour and robust physical presence break the Kinbote spell and leave him and his paranoid patterns spinning in a self-contained void.

If *Pale Fire* is a trifle thin as a story about what Kinbote feels for people, it suffers from the same problem if we try to read it as a story about what he does not feel for them. Certainly he resembles a narcissistic artist-figure like Robert Horn, using other people for his own ends, but the theme has no real dramatic edge. The interactions between him and the writer who is to immortalize the exploits of King Charles are only brief interludes, and in most of their conversations Kinbote comes out a distinct second-best. He doesn't use or manipulate Shade; he is just oblivious to him. When he skulks about outside while his neighbours wipe away tears shed for their dead daughter, or brings out a glass of water for Shade's corpse after hiding his poem in the closet, we see traces of Nabokov's black humour, that depiction of a nasty inhumanity that makes us laugh and shudder. But the idea is not fully developed, and Kinbote remains a part-time, ineffectual villain. Fate, not Kinbote, is responsible for Shade's death, just as Fate will arrange for him to live on in his poems. Someone will rescue and republish 'Pale Fire', and the commentator, his design thwarted, will not get the last word after all.

Anyone interested in the novel's human world must in the end come to terms with the paucity of represented event, with the wedge that Nabokov has driven between fantasy and reality. The imaginary exploits of most of the Commentary, not only the fumblings with a young Duke whose 'bold virilia contrasted harshly with his girlish grace' (p. 123), but also the journeys down secret passages, and the daring escapes in cunning disguises by a noble leader and his trusty cohorts who always outwit the ferocious but ineffectual villains, identify the world of *Pale Fire* as another version of adolescent wish-fulfillment reconstructed by the over-ripe imagination. This is, in a sense, the world of *Lolita* and to a certain extent of *Ada* as well, but in those novels other links with the world of common experience give us a sense of solidity and depth that Kinbote's frolics, as funny as they often are, do not.[15]

If we turn now to some of the claims made for the aesthetic and philosophical implications of *Pale Fire*, some of the other consequences of this circumscription of the novel's world become apparent. Take Daniel Albright's imaginative reading of the novel as a commentary on the literary process:

> Kinbote's struggling against interruption – the whole poem and all the commentary on the poem constitute a vast interruption in the story of Zembla, making the novel a long tissue of interruption – is a faithful depiction of every novelist's struggle to keep attention focused on the text. Kinbote's novel, then, is a metaphor for the very process of reading and writing. Every reader reads in a constant tension of distractedness, holding erect the pseudo-reality evoked by the words while it is being penetrated by sewing machines, BB guns, random humming, amusement parks ... What I am reading becomes a thin veil, a scrim continuously violated by the more urgent but perhaps less interesting place in which I am sitting; and it is this sense, of the glittering unreality of the verbal and of its constant penetratedness, its transparency to the banal, that the Zembla fable embodies almost perfectly. These interruptions, these sudden breakthroughs of an earth with which the fiction has nothing to do, ... remind us of the dangerous inadequacies of art, or of a certain kind of art, to our present condition.[16]

This is subtly argued, but it raises certain problems. If Kinbotian art – fantasy and free association – is 'dangerously inadequate', why does *Pale Fire* depend so much on it? The plea that the fiction alerts us to its own inadequate nature neatly exempts it from the demands we want to make of it, but the same argument could be used to justify the shortcomings of any work at all. In addition, it is hard to escape the feeling that Nabokov, if this is what he wanted to say in *Pale Fire*, has not tested or explored or developed the idea in the fiction but simply repeated it. His novel is difficult to read, but it does not comment very illuminatingly on the difficult art of reading.

What about the novel's philosophic implications? This subject too has received considerable attention. Here, for example, is Robert Alter: '*Pale Fire* is, I would contend, finally a philosophic novel in the same sense that one can apply the term to Diderot and Sterne: its principal concern, moving through literature beyond literature, is with how each individual mind filters reality, recreates it, and with the moral quandaries generated by that problematic of epistemology.'[17] Now we know what it means to say that *Le Neveu de Rameau* and *Tristram Shandy* are philosophic novels: they force us to question received ideas; they remind us that the problems associated with any kind of human endeavour are seldom susceptible to straightforward solutions. And they present us with certain propositions: Rameau's nephew argues that man is an *enfant sauvage* who, left to himself, would strangle his father and copulate with his mother; Locke says that the thoughts of others are hidden from us, and Sterne obligingly puts his philosopher, Walter Shandy, in the isolated world that Locke invented for him.[18] These are ideas, in Diderot brought to life by the dialogue and conflict between his two speakers, in Sterne translated into characters and a plot. If *Pale Fire* is a philosophic novel, we should find something comparable in it, something like the anatomy of tyranny in *Invitation to a Beheading* and *Bend Sinister* or the critical history of Russian literature in *The Gift*, something we can interrogate and evaluate.

Of course both Shade and Kinbote are interested in specifically philosophic questions, and both study the world they live in in search of answers. Is it meaningful or not? they want to know, and in their different ways they arrive at the same answer. The astonishingly intricate series of coincidences that informs their world seems to hold the key. Kinbote points out the curious resemblances between Sybil Shade at thirty and Queen Disa, and adds: 'I trust the reader appreciates the strangeness of this, because if he does not, there is no sense in writing poems, or notes to poems, or anything at all' (p. 207). Literally hundreds of other links and intricate patterns serve to illustrate the same point about how human order can come out of seeming chaos. The poet's own investigations lead to an identical revelation, the moment when he perceives that the misprint, which led him to believe that a woman had seen the same mysterious object that he had seen in the 'other world' when he almost died, is itself the important thing, that coincidence and not communal vision is the key to understanding the nature of life after death:

> But all at once it dawned on me that *this*
> Was the real point, the contrapuntal theme;
> Just this: not text, but texture; not the dream
> But topsy-turvical coincidence,
> Not flimsy nonsense, but a web of sense.   (pp. 62–3)

He goes on to posit the existence of an unknown and unknowable 'they', who inhabit another realm and play games with our world. The crucial thing to note about these games is that they eliminate any notion of a distinction between the great event and the insignificant one. A king is assassinated, a farmer killed in an accident, a man's spectacles disappear – the whimsical masters of this pageant

just decide to arrange things like that. Thus there is no point in
trying to discover patterns of the conventional cause-and-effect sort
in history. One must content oneself with perceiving chance con-
nections and enjoying the patterns they form.

There are certain problems with this. For one thing, it is an
uncharacteristically fantastic conclusion for bluff, commonsensical
Shade to come to. We expect him to seize on the silly 'mountain/
fountain' confusion as proof that the whole search for an elegant
pattern or 'a game of worlds' is a fundamentally misguided one. For
another, there is nothing very elegant or patterned about a series of
coincidences. Precisely the opposite: things don't normally chime;
therefore we notice them when they do. Since coincidences are
remarkable only because of their relative infrequency, any organized pattern of them would end up being something else, like the
'similarities' that lead to the flattish generalities of the astrological
columns in newspapers, for example.[33] Finally, it seems a little
superficial. 'Is that all?' we want to ask, 'spending a life "Making
ornaments / Of accidents and possibilities" (p. 63), because history
has no other perceptible shape?' Accidents do radically alter the
course of people's lives but so do their own choices, and the society
or culture of which those lives form a part has a life of its own as well.
It comes into being and evolves and disappears in a relatively
orderly way, despite what Pascal says about history and the length of
Cleopatra's nose. Nabokov seems at least partly aware of the
problem, for he works at undercutting what his hero, who often
speaks with his master's voice, is proposing here. He takes pains to
point out that any attempt to build a theory on a system of accidents
and coincidences has its own self-destruct mechanism built in.
Shade says near the end of 'Pale Fire' that he is 'reasonably sure'
(p. 69) he will wake up on the morning of July 22nd, but the word
'reasonably' marks this assumption as one of those that Nabokov in
Pale Fire is eager to undermine. Critics have noted the similarities
between Shade's 'web of sense' and Pope's:

> All Nature is but Art, unknown to thee;
> All Chance, Direction, which thou canst not see;
> All Discord, Harmony, not understood:
> All partial Evil, universal Good . . .[20]

– but we see from Shade's fate that the resemblance is only a
superficial one. Pope's human history has a teleological shape;
Nabokov's is random. Pope's world makes moral sense; Nabokov's

is a personalized, farcical cosmology that is constantly surprising even those who think they have understood it.

I think all this does tell us something about the way the 'individual mind' filters reality, but the essential interest of *Pale Fire* seems to lie elsewhere. For it is constantly confronting us with the irrelevance of reality to someone like Kinbote, with the contrast between the furious activity of his imaginings and the material he is working on. Nabokov shows us how a labyrinthine phantasmagoria can be built almost out of nothing – a persecution mania, delusions of grandeur – and how the whole whirling structure can take on a life of its own, involving the reader in all the problems that ensue, just because they are so divorced from the world in which he is obliged to live.

Two objections might be raised at this point. First it could be argued that I have dismissed the verisimilar aspects of *Pale Fire*'s 'game of worlds' too summarily. There are many critics who would contend that the game metaphor has replaced an outdated way of looking at the world, and that a novel which conceives of reality as a sophisticated form of play is more realistic than a Victorian three-decker.[21] Here is a modern expert on game literature: 'play cannot be defined by isolating it on the basis of its relation to an *a priori* reality and culture. To define play is *at the same time* and *in the same moment* to define reality and to define culture ... The distinguishing character of reality is that it is played. Play, reality, culture are synonymous and interchangeable.'[22] One feels like a bit of an oaf making the obvious objection here, but it has to be made: although it makes sense to talk about playing by the rules when describing the conversational minuet of a genteel tea party, and it perhaps makes sense to say that changing a tyre or a nappy is a game, it doesn't seem very helpful to talk about choosing a wife or governing a country in the same terms, no matter how arbitrary or rule-determined such acts can be. Life is a complicated version of 'Monopoly' for some, but most of us act as if we believe that there are still more exalted ways of going about it. The implications of scrambling traditional notions of play and reality go far beyond literary theory. During the first Strategic Arms Limitation Talks we saw an example of what happens when those who take play too seriously end up by not taking reality seriously enough. The Americans who discussed nuclear holocaust in terms of 'zero-sum games' were greeted with blank incomprehension by their Soviet counterparts, whose policies had been formulated by old World War Two artillery experts who conceived their nuclear strategy in terms of explosions that kill people in increasingly devastating barrages. More may depend on sorting out these metaphors than we think.

The other possible objection concerns my methodology. To try to remake *Pale Fire* into a novel that asserts this, proves that, and dramatizes something else, someone might say at this juncture, is to miss the point entirely.[23] What Shade discovers about his world is not something Nabokov wants to relate to our own but a truth about the novel itself. Concentrating on texture and linear pattern, scorning the search for some profundity or depth – these are warnings about how to read the book we hold in our hands. They have nothing to do with 'reading' the world, and neither does *Pale Fire*. As Kinbote reminds us, ' "reality" is neither the subject nor the object of true art which creates its own special reality having nothing to do with the average "reality" perceived by the communal eye' (p. 130). The characters are forces alternately inhibiting and assisting the fulfillment of the novelist's task, and the whole complex structure they inhabit exists so that he can resolve certain formal problems. The critic's task is to puzzle out the answers to a series of mysteries and to discover ways in which all the details interrelate; the novelist's, to give the world another well-made artefact. It was this very argument that needed important qualification when it was used to describe what was happening in *Despair* or *Bend Sinister* or *Lolita*. Now those who advance it are on surer ground. They can find their way through Nabokov's marvellous labyrinth, while those who (like myself) keep insisting that literature is about something other than itself blunder along passageways which often turn out to be dead-ends.[24]

There is one other aspect of *Pale Fire* that is relevant to our inquiry: the fact that the whole crazy edifice is itself a model of that inquiry. Every commentator must keep a wary eye out for creeping Kinbotism in his own work; and since his remarks in the Foreword about providing a 'human reality' (p. 28) for Shade's text make Kinbote's method sound uncomfortably like my own, a word about how successfully Nabokov has arranged for the critic to see his own foolish face in one of *Pale Fire*'s mirrors would seem to be in order.

First, a short history of the criticism of the novel to establish a context for my remarks. As everyone knows, Mary McCarthy started it all with a truly extraordinary piece of explication, published in 1962, the same year that the novel was published. In fact, her article appeared in England before the novel itself, an interesting example of the process McLuhan calls the 'Reversal of the Overheated Medium':[25] saturated with literary texts, the audience is forced to accept the speeded-up world in which the dynamic process of criticism obviates the need for initial contact with the thing being criticized. This pre-emptive strike gave the McCarthy view of the novel a particular authority. Her account was widely read, and it set the tone for most of the discussion that followed. (Some thought that Nabokov had encouraged and approved the exegesis; some were even convinced that he had written it himself.)[26] Of crucial importance was her idea that *Pale Fire* was 'a do-it-yourself novel'[27] that invited the reader to become a co-creator, an idea which Andrew Field developed in his influential 1967 study:

Nabokov once said that his ideal readers consist of 'a lot of little Nabokovs', and *Pale Fire* is a structure whose general plan and pattern are so brilliant, so perfect, that the reader who follows after Nabokov long enough can . . . indeed continue on as a 'little Nabokov' without in any way destroying or distorting the pattern (the usual danger of academic overreading) or even the 'universal or ultimate truth' that seems to me to be present in this breathtakingly simple and endlessly complex novel. The realization that the anagram of Botkin [*nikto*, Russian for 'nobody'] is my own invention and discovery is a source of greater amazement to me than solving the most difficult of the author's own puzzles.[28]

We can see what has happened. Every reader has to begin by sorting out the basic fictional data for himself, with a little help, since *Pale Fire* is very much a critic's novel, from the readers who have been there before. After that, if it is not to be put back on the shelf with the other solved mystery stories, its hermeneutic back broken, the reader must breathe life into all the incipient codes and half-formed structures, and then find explanations for the new enigmas that he has helped create.

I can best illustrate what has happened since Field wrote this by quoting from four different studies of *Pale Fire*:

'Gradus' in Latin means 'step, *degree*'. A *Gradus ad Parnassum* is a dictionary used as an aid in writing poetry, and literaly [*sic*] means 'a step to the place where the Muses live'. 'Shade' is defined by the dictionary as 'shadow, degree of darkness; a disembodied spirit; to undergo and exhibit difference or variation'. There is thus a specific connection between Gradus and Shade, and the suggestion that the two characters are aspects of a single consciousness – that Gradus is a creation of the poet, a degree of Shade, or a step in the structure. Gradus, who is repeatedly identified with the inevitable ending of the poem – indeed, he arrives at the very last line – may be the final tool used by the poet to complete his work and arrive at Parnassus.[29]

... the enchanted kingdom conjured up by Pnin's sense of homelessness (a land, perhaps, beyond the frontier of death – off the edge of the page) foreshadows Zembla. Victor is of course the link: the crystal bowl he gives to Pnin and the 'portable world' Pnin's gestures evoke in the sports shop (he is trying to describe a football) point to both the glass factory and endless mirrors of Onhava, and Aunt Maud's paperweight:

> the paperweight
> Of convex glass enclosing a lagoon.

These stand for the autonomous and private world of art which does not reflect reality (is not a mirror held up to nature) but encapsulates it.[30]

Gradus, considered for the original Latin meaning of his name, 'steps', and for the automatic, uninspired, 'plodding' aspects of endeavour he symbolizes, may represent a notion that has deep roots in Nabokov's imagination. Nabokov says he wrote his first poem while on the toilet. As a smaller child, he had been led upstairs to use a potty, on the way playing a game of feeling out the risers with closed eyes while his adult guide chanted 'Step, step, step'. Once on the pot, he rested his head on the open door of his room and looked out to the real bathroom with its stained-glass window. Rocking his forehead back and forth, 'A dreamy rhythm would permeate my being. The recent "step, step, step" would be taken up by a dripping faucet.' ... Perhaps in suggesting Gradus as the 'step-by-step' approach to poetry in *Pale Fire*, even giving Gradus a bad case of the runs (p. 198), and associating him with stained glass . . . Nabokov is unconsciously giving testimony that all poetry is completely sublimated and transcended when the mature poet begins gesturing toward the empyrean.[31]

Though a 'heterosexual man of fashion' (p. 311), Count Otar's name is Russian for 'a flock of sheep' ('*otara*'), suggesting the man's actual (as Kinbote sees it) mundaneness, herd instinct, and perhaps even bestiality ... When [Kinbote] describes a drunk who 'started to sing a ribald ballad about "Karlie-Garlie" and fell into a demilune ditch' (p. 106), he juxtaposes 'dwarf' ('*karlik*'): homosexuality; 'smell of burning' ('*gar''*'): fear of damnation; and a 'demilune ditch': 'the fall, debasement' which his 'art' ('demilune': half-inspired, half-loony) cannot prevent.[32]

These are representative examples, taken from many that might have been chosen. The first two suggest ways in which the details of

Pale Fire should be used to compose variations on Nabokov's themes and images. Here are two kinds of 'do-it-yourself' novel that can be written according to his blueprint, with a view to enriching the experience of future readers. The third and fourth remind us that the creative critic is bound by the same rules that govern the novelist, and that he ignores tact and common sense at his peril. Nabokov may have wanted a lot of 'little Nabokovs', but he got a few little Kinbotes too. In this sense *Pale Fire* is a sort of anticipatory parody, since it vindicates its claim as a credible parody of the scholar-critic by some of the responses it generated.

From these examples it should be clear that, although it is certainly possible to become Nabokov's butt in writing about the novel, it is not inevitable. *Pale Fire* warns us against binding any text into an alien structure, but it hardly constitutes some final, damning comment on criticism in general. Nabokov's opinions on these matters have often been misunderstood. Although he tended to speak derisively of critics, this did not prevent him from devoting years of his life to Pushkin's *Eugene Onegin*, working on his translation and what eventually became a 1088-page commentary, in which he sometimes ridicules the misreadings of fellow Pushkinists and offers a definitive account of all sorts of problems related to the poet's life and work. Now the wary critic might point out here that Nabokov's *Eugene Onegin* is *Pale Fire*'s coeval, and that wheels within wheels are involved: perhaps Nabokov is to Pushkin as Kinbote is to Shade, and the two thick volumes of commentary a sly exercise in self-parody.[33] But is it? A very personal account, laced with some surprisingly unscholarly references to Nabokov's loves and hates and lost life in Russia – yes; but there are too many stern invocations to Truth, too many indignant defences of critical standards to give the self-parody thesis much credence. Consider what he says in one of his notes about the 'real life' of a historical figure and the general status of the facts in any critical inquiry. He begins by defending 'the reality of art' against 'the unreality of history', and it sounds as if we are on the way down the road that eventually leads to Zembla. But in the very next sentence we read: 'The whole trouble is that memoirists and historians (no matter how honest they are) are either artists who fantastically re-create observed life or mediocrities (the more frequent case) who unconsciously distort the factual by bringing it into contact with their commonplace and simple minds.'[34] So the facts are the proper object of investigation, and the critic, fully conscious of the many difficulties involved in sorting them out, can avoid some of the bias of his predecessors by sifting through their distortions to get at the truth. In Pushkin and in *Pale Fire*, there is a truth that exists independently of its fantastic re-creations, and the figure of the poet is its embodiment. Bad translation and insensitive criticism may murder the spirit of Pushkin, but for Nabokov there has been no momentous 'death of the author', and no consequent 'freedom' for the critic. Later on in the same note he talks about adding to 'our understanding of Pushkin's mind by the examination of an incidental character'.[35] The man who wrote that was not quite the enemy of literary criticism, with its interest in authors and their minds, that he is sometimes taken to be.

I turn now to *Transparent Things*, approaching it first, as I did *Pale Fire*, as a commentary on various human actions and emotions. In a second section, I try to define its content, not as the self-regarding artifice of Nabokov the master craftsman, but as a series of portraits of the artist as an old man.

Transparent Things is a tricky novel to come to terms with. Nabokov has written something new and different, but kept many of the surface features of the old. Compare the following passages:

Her very wide-set sea-green eyes had a funny way of traveling all over you, carefully avoiding your own eyes. Her smile was but a quizzical jerk of one eyebrow; and uncoiling herself from the sofa as she talked, she kept making spasmodic dashes at three ashtrays and the near fender (where lay the brown core of an apple); whereupon she would sink back again, one leg folded under her.[36]

Her unwieldy corpulence could be moved only by means of one precise little wiggle; in order to make it she had to concentrate upon the idea of trying to fool gravity until something clicked inwardly and the right jerk happened like the miracle of a sneeze. Meantime she lay in her chair motionless, and as it were ambushed, with brave sweat glistening on her chest and above the purple arches of her pastel eyebrows.[37]

The first is Humbert on Charlotte Haze, the second, a description of the Charlotte Haze equivalent – mother of the object of the hero's desire – in *Transparent Things*, Madame Chamar. The details in *Lolita* are part of an attempt to create an imagined life; the equally vivid ones in Nabokov's penultimate novel are there to remind us of the lively imagination that conjured them up. The first introduction is important for our understanding of Charlotte and what she goes on to do; whereas, in a metaphorical sense, Madame Chamar never does get out of her chair but remains fixed in place, the unmoved mover of Nabokov's satirical wit.

The novel's reviewers dismissed the characters as 'cursory squiggles' and 'ciphers',[38] and not just the minor ones but the hero as well. Can anyone be expected to believe in or care about someone called 'Hugh Person', someone whose life is almost as featureless and absurd as his name? Henry James, it will be remembered, objected to this kind of thing in Trollope: 'A Mr Quiverful with fourteen children . . . is too difficult to believe in. We can believe in the name and we can believe in the children; but we cannot manage the combination.'[39] And yet 'Person' is just possible as a name, and its owner is not just a collection of epithets, but a character with thoughts and feelings who falls in love, kills his wife, and goes through agonies of remorse. His story is clear enough in outline; and although we may feel rather foolish to take it as a story on this level, such a reading is inevitably part of our experience. Nabokov disarms the traditional critic by refusing to accept his terms as relevant, by challenging him to condemn the novel as a thin love story written by a psychological novelist who is a bit lost without a psychology to occupy him, but there is some truth in such a judgment, however partial it might be. In this regard, I was struck by a passing remark made by G. M. Hyde about Nabokov's being 'written by' this novel.[40] This seems a strange thing to say about an author who called his characters 'galley slaves',[41] and who insisted that any novelist who let his story take control of him in some unpredictable way was either 'very minor or insane'.[42] But Hyde is, I think, on to something important. Let us look more closely at how Nabokov, compelled by the exigencies of his chosen form and by the nature of his gifts, goes to work on his old material once again.

Whatever else he is, Hugh Person is certainly the vehicle for what gradually became *the* Nabokov theme: sexual desire is something very powerful that usually goes wrong, sometimes violently wrong. As that vehicle, he is more or less obliged to do what Kretschmar and Humbert and Kinbote and Van Veen do. Nabokov loves to turn the reader into a voyeur, to play on his reluctant sympathies and erotic interests, to make him aware of his complicity in the acts he feels obliged to condemn. Desire, he argues, turns people into things and makes them treat other people as things. Oblivious to what *is* happening, they develop an obsessive interest in what *will* happen; they dream of a moment when all will be unveiled, and the marriage of intense curiosity and the well-kept secret will be consummated. Various analogies between obsessed character and eager reader suggest themselves. How does this work in *Transparent Things*? In one sense, much as usual. Hugh pursues, obtains, but remains unsatisfied. He loses his way, commits a dreadful blunder, tries to understand what is happening to him. The violent climax occurs in the last chapter, in which the hero waits for his dead love to reappear: 'Person, *this* person, was on the imagined brink of imagined bliss when Armande's footfalls approached – striking out both "imagined" in the proof's margin (never too wide for corrections and queries!). This is where the orgasm of art courses through the whole spine with incomparably more force than sexual ecstasy or metaphysical panic' (p. 102).

But what makes this novel different from others in which Nabokov has used this identification as a conclusion relates to what I have discussed above: its 'dehumanized' condition changes the game considerably. The reader watches the characters being manipulated not by desire but by the author, and with only a limited human conflict to involve him, tends to register all the talk about the 'orgasm of art' as an interesting metaphor. Nothing wrong with that, but look at what happens when Nabokov tries to enlist him as a voyeuristic collaborator:

[Hugh] returned several times to the pictures of little Armande in her bath, pressing a proboscidate rubber toy to her shiny stomach or standing up, dimple-bottomed, to be lathered. Another revelation of impuberal softness (its middle line just distinguishable from the less vertical grass-blade next to it) was afforded by a photo of her in which she sat in the buff on the grass, combing her sun-shot hair and spreading wide, in false perspective, the lovely legs of a giantess. (p. 41)

Why spend so much time on this? A defence based on the way in which Nabokov has narrated events as seen through the eyes of Hugh Person might redeem it. The significant placing of the phrase 'false perspective' and the first sentence of the next paragraph, which begins 'He heard a toilet flush', suggest that the author has gone to some trouble to distance himself from his hero's response. And yet, invited to stare at this crotch, we think not about subtle ironies but about dangerous areas that the author of *Lolita* should avoid at all costs.

The passage raises two other important problems. First, because it turns the female body into an impersonal collection of private parts, it reminds us how often Nabokov's mature women exist only as repositories for various desires. Too often, when dealing with his female characters, we feel that, having made certain libidinous allowances, he would have agreed with Chesterfield's definition of women as 'children of a larger growth'.[43] Second, the erotic force of what is disguised in artistic ways just happens to be the essence of the sexual ethos that he satirizes in the novel. Hugh and Armande make love 'around teatime, in the living room, as upon an imaginary stage, to the steady accompaniment of casual small talk, with both performers decently clothed' (p. 65). In effect, the 'best business suit' that Hugh wears for these sessions performs the same function as Nabokov's 'impuberal softness': both turn the physical into a covert allusion. The euphemistic gentility of the adjective gives the whole passage the glossy sheen of the photographs being looked at, and the author implicates himself in the superficiality he is mocking.[44]

The sexual theme, as in many other Nabokov novels, is associated with violence, but here too the thinness of the flesh on the verisimilar bones makes for problems. Hugh insists that his system is 'poisoned' by Armande and that he will 'perish' if he cannot have her (p. 42), just as Kretschmar does in *Kamera Obskura*. In the early novel we both laugh at such foolishness and watch with a sort of horrified awe as Nabokov, using farce and satire as a comic counterpoint to the cruel machinations he is describing, plots the destruction that Kretschmar has chosen for himself. The same desires are theoretically there in *Transparent Things*, but what was arresting is now anaesthetized by a hyperbolic and facetious tone (Hugh is talking to Mr R.):

'I assure you that he [the publisher] is waiting for the manuscript with utmost impatience. By the way –'
By the way indeed! There ought to exist some rhetorical term for that twist of nonlogic. A unique view through a black weave ran by the way. By the way, I shall lose my mind if I do not get her. (pp. 31–2)

The 'black weave' is Armande's dress, seen by Hugh in the train, but these sentences, although they do report an event and describe a mood, mainly exist to inform on each other, to illustrate that everything is now 'by the way' except the pattern of clues that is working itself out. The mechanism of a conjunctive phrase is as worthy of attention as a sexual conjunction.[45]

It might be objected that 'transparent things' are by definition insubstantial; and that any story of 'a tangle of random destinies', Nabokov's own description of the novel's subject, told from the point of view of a disembodied Mr R., whose ghost, again according to Nabokov, keeps intruding on the plot,[46] is bound to make these 'things' seem even more impalpable to mere mortals. Nevertheless, a 'ghost story' like *The Eye* shows how much less narrow Nabokov can be when he retains some tension between the observer who sees only transparencies and the material world which mocks his transcendental profundities. By settling for the simple assertion of formulae such as 'every cause-and-effect sequence is always a hit-and-miss affair' (p. 92), skimping on human motivation, and asserting authorial omnipotence at every opportunity ('if it were necessary we could trace the complicated fate of ...' (p. 7)), Nabokov ends up confined by an illusory freedom to making endless assertions of the arbitrary.

Should the highly self-conscious, partly self-parodic aspects of the novel lead us to conclude that, as William Pritchard puts it, this book is 'too transparently a fiction, all made up',[47] that there is no human dimension left for the reader to care about? It is tempting. Critical analyses have appeared, showing how *Transparent Things* is really about itself, how it consists of 'a restless replication of fictional images that illustrate the protean shaping power of consciousness and art',[48] and how it reminds us that 'The text and the world which the Nabokovian hero "reads" are rich because they afford so many opportunities to make patterns out of what would otherwise be mere contingencies.'[49] The advance of the exegetical industry will cover our sheepish retreat. Yet this would mean ignoring one of the novel's most important qualities, what can only be called its highly personal nature. I want to conclude with some remarks about this aspect of it.

Everybody has noticed that in *Transparent Things* Nabokov gives us a slightly distorted version of himself in Mr R. The arrogance, the poses adopted to deal with fame, the exile safe in Switzerland – this is the public Nabokov of the sixties, a version of the personality he projected for the interviewers. Critics have been reluctant to take the identification any farther: it seems such an obvious trap, and Nabokov accused those who saw Mr N. in Mr R. of 'mere flippancy of thought'.[50] But, as we saw in relation to *The Gift,* such warnings can themselves be attempts to put readers off the track. The seemingly pointless allusions to an importunate literary agent named Tamworth are more understandable when we recall Nabokov's own anxieties about his literary affairs. Field was compiling material for his biography while *Transparent Things* was being written, and the violent family indignation caused by its publication shows how unwelcome even the best-intentioned 'intruders' sometimes were.[51] Sifting through other passages relating to Mr R., we get a sense of a private Nabokov: an old man, a little afraid of death and silence, forced to go on talking. Here is Mr R.'s 'last testament':

> It is comic – but I used to believe that dying persons saw the vanity of things, the futility of fame, passion, art, and so forth. I believed that treasured memories in a dying man's mind dwindled to rainbow wisps; but now I feel just the contrary: my most trivial sentiments and those of all men have acquired gigantic proportions. The entire solar system is but a reflection in the crystal of my (or your) wrist watch. The more I shrivel the bigger I grow. I suppose this is an uncommon phenomenon.   (p. 84)

It is hard to ignore the autobiographical elements in this. A mind big enough to encompass and reconstitute reality – Nabokov always believed he was uniquely gifted in this respect, but, as the passage implies, the relative importance of the two elements in the equation changed as he got older. Broadly speaking, it is true to say that before *Pale Fire,* Nabokov tended to say: 'How extraordinary this thing is in its unique thingness'; or: 'How strange that life should imitate art in this grotesque/beautiful/enchanting way'; and then: 'Only a rare epithet, an elegant turn of phrase, a *style châtié* can adequately convey this quality.' In the late novels he often seems to be saying: 'How extraordinary this thing is, because it touches off *n* associations in the *N* brain as it reads reality to find material for its novel.' It is not a question of a heightened level of craftsmanship – just the opposite in a way. As this mind becomes more assertive about its centrality, the idea of the novel as a form becomes less important. Reading *Transparent Things,* we are less likely to say: 'What an impersonal, glittering, made thing this is', than: 'Here is another chunk of Nabokov, and this is what it tells us about him.' (Compare Chesterton on Dickens's novels: 'They are simply lengths cut from the flowing and mixed substance called Dickens – a substance of which any given length will be certain to contain a given proportion of brilliant and of bad stuff.')[52]

Even its formal aspects cry out, not *nouveau romancier* or American fabulator, but 'Nabokov'. Think of the narrative devices of the classic novel of the nineteenth century, forsworn by the new novelists. (I take my examples from Gérard Genette's useful study of such devices in *Figures III*.) There is the *prolepse complétive*,[53] for example. With it the author takes time out to refer to the future of one of his characters, thus enforcing the reader's sense of a real-life continuum: 'I was never to see her again', that kind of thing. A novelist with enough confidence to speak about time in this way would be a bizarre anachronism in *avant-garde* circles these days. Compare Nabokov: 'On the morning of the widower's last day in so-called Switzerland (i.e., very shortly before the event that for him would cause everything to become "so-called")' (p. 10); or this passage about the hotel that is about to burn down: 'The hotel restaurant . . . was far from full, but one expected two large families on the next day, and there was to be, or would have been (the folds of tenses are badly disarranged in regard to the building under examination) quite a nice little stream of Germans in the second, and cheaper, half of August' (p. 100). Here Nabokov has, as it were, pitched his own camp between the opposing forces: the use of such techniques links him to the classical novelist; the self-conscious fun he has with them allies him with those who have rejected them. Consider another of these devices, the *analepse hétérodiégétique*,[54] a flashback about a newly introduced character, for example. Nabokov interrupts some love-making in Hugh's flat with these remarks: 'Now it so happened that those rooms were the same in which Julia had visited one of her best young males a couple of years before. She had the good taste to say nothing, but the image of that youth, whose death in a remote war had affected her greatly, kept coming out of the bathroom or fussing with things in the fridge' (p. 35). The emotional force of Julia's 'passionate memory' is zero; but Nabokov depends on this kind of information to move his story, such as it is, forward, and insists on his right to use it, whatever the current fashion. Or again, think of how the classic novel uses certain conventions to introduce its characters. Jonathan Culler points out that a sentence such as '[He was] one of those men whose eyes light up at the sight of a pretty woman' in Balzac reflects the author's serene confidence in both his reader and his world:[55]

the reader correctly decodes the message and the novel's world is filled in by a sort of quick reference. But Nabokov does it all the time: 'Julia liked tall men with strong hands and sad eyes' (p. 34), we read, and take this to signify superficial romantic yearning and more earthy desires, both of which, as it turns out, appear on the next page. Or: '[Armande] detested surrealistic novels of the poetic sort. She demanded hard realistic stuff reflecting our age' (p. 26). That is, she is not 'one of us': she would not read a Nabokov novel, and has only a subordinate role to play in its world. Presumably this kind of thing would raise a few critical eyebrows at the Cerisy colloquia, as would the garrulity of the narrator, the meaning that 'hides behind', the clarity of the narrative line, and so on. Nabokov always went his own way.

Then there is Nabokov the author-figure who watches over his creatures in a way that he acknowledges quite specifically in the penultimate chapter: 'All his life, we are glad to note, our Person had experienced the curious sensation . . . of there existing behind him – at his shoulder, as it were – a larger, incredibly wiser, calmer and stronger stranger, morally better than he' (p. 98). This figure occupies a prominent position in the late fiction, and often goes out of his way to draw attention to himself. Of course he has always been there, but in a novel like *Bend Sinister*, the hero's shadow is a *deus ex machina*, absent for most of the action. Here he is a *sine qua non*: 'had he been without that transparent shadow', the author informs us, 'we would not have bothered to speak about our dear Person' (p. 98), and the difference is suggestive. That immanent benefactor removed, Krug would still exist; and his story of madness and death would have a different, verisimilar ending instead of the non-ending that Nabokov arranges, but that is all. In *Transparent Things*, the story is justified because the author is omnipresent.

Creators who hover solicitously near their creations, advising the audience about how the whole production should be admired ('you are thinking, and quite rightly so, of . . .' (p. 1)), may be just playing the role of the showman, but they are often anxious about something, and Nabokov is no exception. The most succinct expression of this anxiety comes at the beginning of the penultimate chapter: 'What had you expected of your pilgrimage, Person? A mere mirror rerun of hoary torments? Sympathy from an old stone? Enforced re-creation of irrecoverable trivia? A search for lost time in an utterly distinct sense from Goodgrief's dreadful "*Je me souviens, je me souviens de la maison où je suis né*" or, indeed, Proust's quest?' (p. 94). The mocking questions ward off sentimentality, and the French quotation exposes the artificiality of excessively 'sincere' emotion. But why the contrast with Proust, especially when he and Nabokov are so often associated with each other because they share an interest in 'lost time'? Memory for Nabokov is a prodigious intellectual feat that distinguishes a very few people in a world of forgetters, and it is his chief weapon in a battle against time. Although he wins scores of victories with it in his autobiography, *Transparent Things* records considerable doubts about the whole enterprise. In Proust, memory is not so much a special gift as a means that one man uses, first to make sense of his life, and then to make that possibility available to everyone, to his prospective readers. Proportion, perspective, meaning – in Proust's novel these mark the end of the search, that moment when the shape of the past can be perceived and the act of creation can begin again. Nabokov is not so sure. Obviously, he is asking himself some questions as he gets older: What has all this remembering finally got me? Do my collected works, with dates in parentheses after each title, represent anything more than the ultimate victory of linear time? What do I do next?

At the heart of it all is the idea of 'mastery'. Before *Transparent Things*, *Ada* had been hailed as another 'masterpiece', and Nabokov was 'a master of language' and 'a complete master of technique'.[56] One of the unfortunate effects of this kind of praise was that it made him feel obliged to play a certain kind of role, to present the conquering hero image to the public at every opportunity. Notice, in the passage quoted above, that the 'stranger' at Person's elbow is 'incredibly wiser'. Nabokov said in an interview that he was 'an incomparably better artist' than Mr R.[57] When there were no more masterpieces to be written, he still had to be 'the master', ordering words about, menacing his 'galley slaves', enforcing import controls on dubious commodities like 'human interest'. But all this has to be expressed in words, and in regard to language no one, not even Nabokov, is master. Perhaps this is acknowledged, if only obliquely, in a wry aside near the end of *Transparent Things*, after a discussion of what language can be made to express: 'Raining in Wittenberg', writes Mr R., 'but not in Wittgenstein' (p. 91). I don't know about Wittenberg, but I think the Wittgenstein allusion is to the *Philosophical Investigations*, the passage in which he asks: 'Can I say "bububu" and mean "If it doesn't rain I shall go for a walk"'? – It is only in a language I can mean something by something. This shows clearly that the grammar of "to mean" is not like that of the expression "to imagine" and the like.'[58] Maybe it is not raining in Wittgenstein because his idea has not been expressed in a common language, in words whose meaning is determined by other people. Whether I have the allusion right or not, the general point remains the same: the master always has trouble admitting that what he creates depends for its meaning on how it is understood; he would rather issue authorized readings or be interpreted only by a privileged inner circle. Forces beyond his control seem to figure now at every stage of the aesthetic process. *Transparent Things* is the record of Nabokov's struggle with them.

The purpose of this chapter has been to examine whether it makes sense to talk about a distinct content in Nabokov's late novels, about characters and conflicts and authorial commentary. The answer thus far seems to be a qualified affirmative, a 'yes' followed by a lot of 'buts'. Has the balance shifted with his last novel, *Look at the Harlequins!*? Do the 'buts' have it? Does the search for the representation of a human world end with this novel, in which, as Maurice Couturier puts it, Nabokov 'has taught us to remain at the surface level of the text, to play the textual game without succumbing to the realist illusion or to the myth of depths', and has arranged things so that his novel 'does not speak, ... holds no discourse'?[59] Let us consider our last text with these questions in mind.

In one sense this kind of description is quite obviously misleading. The first thing about the novel that is bound to strike the reader is the resemblance between the protagonist, Vadim, and his forebears, with all that that implies about what this novel is 'about'. Once again, his creator works hard to create some emotional intensity, this time by involving him in a love triangle. Desire is sufficient to start events turning over, and jealousy keeps them going. The love scenes are handled with great skill, and the impatient machinations of unsatisfied passion are, as always, brilliantly portrayed. When Vadim finally does arrange his first tryst with Iris, Nabokov as usual avoids the bathos of a messy consummation, here by having his narrator telescope time at the moment of possession. Vadim evokes simultaneously his love-making and his memories of eavesdropping on a newlywed couple in his youth:

I must have been eleven or twelve when the nephew of my grand-uncle visited the Moscow country house where I was spending that hot and hideous summer. He had brought his passionate bride with him – straight from the wedding feast. Next day at the siesta hour, in a frenzy of curiosity and fancy, I crept to a secret spot under the second-floor guest-room window where a gardener's ladder stood rooted in a jungle of jasmin. It reached only to the top of the closed first-floor shutters, and though I found a foothold above them, on an ornamental projection, I could only just grip the sill of a half-open window from which confused sounds issued. I recognized the jangle of bedsprings and the rhythmic tinkle of a fruit knife on a plate near the bed, one post of which I could make out by stretching my neck to the utmost; but what fascinated me most were the manly moans coming from the invisible part of the bed. A superhuman effort afforded me the sight of a salmon-pink shirt over the back of a chair. He, the enraptured beast, doomed to die one day as so many are, was now repeating her name with ever increasing urgency, and by the time my foot slipped he was in full cry, thus drowning the noise of my sudden descent into a crackle of twigs and a snowstorm of petals.[60]

Admittedly, 'passionate bride', 'jangle of bedsprings', and 'manly moans' seem rather crude in this context, but the rest is superbly realized. Nabokov creates an erotic ambience by skilful elision, and the play of main events and subordinate clauses in the last sentence reveals him at his most adroit. Memory and desire blend in one archetypal event, endlessly repeated by the many, recalled and understood by only a few. An old Nabokov theme is invested with a new vitality. As usual, Death wins out over Love eventually: Iris is murdered by her lover, Starov, who then mortally wounds himself. In a kind of inversion of Vadim's recollection, Starov, dying, remembers not an adolescent paradise, the 'jungle of jasmin' on the country estate, but its demonic counterpart, a 'pleasure park' in which a miniature train runs round and round through 'a brambly picturesque nightmare grove whose dizzy flowers nodded continuous assent to all the horrors of childhood and hell' (p. 70). The peculiarly Nabokovian combination of humour, pathos, and meticulous patterning gives the whole first section which tells this story all the qualities of a good novella.

Again, like most of Nabokov's heroes, Vadim has an obsession that keeps threatening to twist his life out of shape. It can be summed up in a sentence: he can imagine walking to a certain point and back again, but he cannot imagine the scenery swivelling when he makes his about-face, and this preoccupies him constantly. I said that the obsession can be expressed in a sentence, but of course this is never how it happens in Nabokov, particularly when first-person narration is involved. Smurov and Hermann and Humbert and Kinbote love to hold forth on their 'theme', to rationalize and aestheticize their extraordinary conduct by turning it into a plausible story of which each of them is the hero. All this talking develops the idea of an obsession, complicates the issues involved, and invites the reader's sympathy or contempt or simply bewilderment. Insanity threatens them all; and Nabokov asks the reader to admire the flights of imaginative fancy that distinguish these characters from the mundane average, even while he makes clear that this doesn't exempt them from being judged by standards other than their own. *Look at the Harlequins!* fits the pattern, except for one thing. In it, obsession and madness are not integral parts of some essential human drama; they are just words, something to be talked about. The garrulous narrator's menaced sanity and his obsession with his obsession have become a rhetorical excuse for his creator: 'some kind of atrocious obstacle, which would drive me mad if I persevered, prevents me from imagining the twist which transforms one direction into another, directly opposite. I am crushed, I am carrying the whole world on my back' (p. 42) – says Vadim, and then forgets all about it for another fifty pages or so. In this crucial sense the usual Nabokovian mode of character portrayal has been abandoned. The increasingly elaborate descriptions of this supposedly terrifying space and the objects that refuse to move in it as the observer moves argue against their own content, since they demonstrate the speaker's serene confidence in the power of words over all that space. Even as a lexical experiment the descriptions of this obsession might be fun, but the mind-numbing repetition, the lack of development, the gusto with which the chunks of 'fine writing' are served up, and the unabashed silliness of it all finally take their toll. The ornateness of the Nabokov hieratic style – 'I must try, dear friend and assistant, to swing the entire length of the street, with the massive façades of its houses before and behind me, from one direction to another in the slow wrench of a half circle, which is like trying to turn the colossal tiller of a rusty recalcitrant rudder so as to transform oneself by conscious degrees from, say, an east-facing Vadim Vadimovich into a west-sun-blinded one' (p. 106) – makes it painfully inappropriate for something so trivial. As John Wain says about an over-written passage in *Speak, Memory*: 'to say it in such an over-elaborate manner is like touching off a firework display merely to look at one's watch in a dark street'.[61] We feel that Hermann's fastidious manner and Humbert's baroque prolixity are an inevitable consequence of who they are, and that the murderer's 'fancy prose style'[62] is an essential part of the process by which the facts become known. In *Look at the Harlequins!*, the language refuses to play any such role, and yet it constantly occupies stage centre, preening itself somewhat narcissistically. And so the facts of Vadim's case, his problems with conceived space, become, like some weekly visit to an old aunt that we put up with by speculating about the possibility of future rewards, a weary obligation and finally a deadly bore. The warnings of those who insist that the novel is not 'about' anything, that the act of writing is Nabokov's only subject, start to make more sense.

It is at this point that we are obliged to fall back on the kind of criticism that opened up *Transparent Things* for us. Let *Look at the Harlequins!* be a novel that teaches us to 'play the textual game without succumbing to the realistic illusion', we want to say, it can still be read as a 'discourse' whose subject is the plight of a novelist who is constantly mistaken for someone he is not, whose life and work now seem to him difficult to distinguish, who feels trapped by the reputation that has built up around him but does not know how to escape it. Hyde sums up this view of the novel succinctly: 'It is the work of a deeply isolated man, whose wealth and success have done little to temper this isolation. It is also the work of a man whose richest subject matter is himself, yet who feels estranged from his life's work – as if it were the work of someone else.'[63] The problem is that Nabokov is loath to admit that his subject is himself; he is self-conscious about his own self-consciousness. It is almost as if, anticipating this kind of reading, he sets out to forestall it so that the image of the old artificer confidently creating his self-sufficient structures remains intact. Let us look at two of the ways in which he obstructs our view of the self-portrait he wants, and does not want, to provide us with.

First, there is the use he makes of his own past and his *oeuvre*. To say something about what it is like to be forced to impersonate someone else, Nabokov collects some transmuted titles, scrambled plots, the bare outline of and many obscure details from his own life as an émigré, and uses them to prove, again and again, that Vadim is a sort of Antiterran Nabokov. It is very cleverly done, but it is somehow too easy. Vadim may have problems with his image, Nabokov often seems to be saying, but the 'incomparably greater, healthier, and crueler' (p. 89) writer who created him is above all that. And the point is made in language that often seems like a pale facsimile of the real thing. Having angered Vadim by confusing *Camera Lucida* and *Camera Obscura*, a publisher attempts to mollify him: ' "There, there", said Oks (really a very dear man and a gentleman), after a terrible pause during which all the remainders opened like fairy-tale flowers in a fancy film, "A slip of the tongue does not deserve such a harsh rebuke" ' (pp. 92–3). Note the repetition of 'man' in the parenthesis, the emptiness of an adjective like 'terrible', the simile that doesn't convince (all the remainders?), the stiffness of the dialogue. When Vadim inadvertently calls his daughter Bel 'Dolly', i.e., associates her with Lolita, the same kind of thing occurs, only with more purple prose and more emotional overkill (pp. 195–6). *Lolita* is, understandably enough, the novel that is haunting Nabokov, since it saddled him with the wrong reputation and yet brought him the success he so wanted. The scene in which Vadim revels à la Humbert in orgastic fantasy while stroking a young girl's legs is obviously a joke at the expense of those who speculated about the autobiographical elements in that novel; but when 'two cold-thighed, cheesy-necked girleens' try to sit on that side of Vadim's lap 'where the honey was' (p. 180), we may well feel that no writer should run this kind of risk just to exorcize a ghost.

In the end, the network of allusions to Nabokov's novels and to figures from his past creates a self-referential aesthetic of exclusion and becomes an exercise in self-flattery. Carl Proffer has performed a useful service by annotating all the Russian allusions; but he settled for that limited objective because, he explains, anyone who tries to decode all the allusions in *Look at the Harlequins!* could easily end up in a padded cell.[64] This may account for the fact that no more annotation has been attempted, but perhaps even the group of specialist Nabokov readers and critics I referred to at the end of the last chapter has decided that the work is too reclusive to reward even the most diligent search. The references to an *oeuvre* that few readers will know intimately and to Nabokov's literary acquaintances generally represent a rather large 'No Trespassing' sign for everybody else. Like all hermetic works, the novel ends up by seeming simple, because it never does compel us to attend to its complexities. I remember listening to Pierre Boulez in a television interview describing what it was like to be the conductor of the New York Philharmonic in the early 1970s. He talked about the great excitement with which the series of concerts devoted to contemporary music was awaited, and then went on to describe its actual reception: the critics' lack of enthusiasm and the public's growing bewilderment and disaffection. At one point he said something like: 'You can imagine how I felt seeing the number of empty seats increase week after week.' I was struck by that remark, and to this day I make a special effort to listen to any kind of new music that Boulez is involved in because he said what he did. He convinced me that he believed that the music he cared about had something to convey if only people would listen. When I criticize Nabokov for the hermetic aspects of a novel like *Look at the Harlequins!*, I do not mean that he should have aimed to accommodate lethargic readers or tried to write a bestseller; I mean that in this novel he never gives us the impression that he cares about the empty seats. No one could ever accuse Boulez of giving in to popular demand by making his music instantly accessible to those who like to hum along, but, as his example shows, keeping one's artistic integrity does not necessarily mean writing only for oneself.

The second obstacle that Nabokov erects for those who want to read the novel as some kind of personal statement about himself and his art is a 'No Trespassing' sign of a different sort. Think of some of the great novels written in the first half of this century: *Women in Love, Ulysses, À la Recherche du Temps Perdu, Dr Faustus*. One reason we think of them as modern is that their authors have made great art out of a rigorous process of self-examination. In these novels, characters who in some respects represent the author are placed and judged in a variety of ways. The men who wrote them are willing to speak about what is most important in their own lives. Compared to these novels, *Look at the Harlequins!* seems restrained and unadventurous, because it is the product of a writer who at this stage of his career is reluctant to probe too deeply or to give too much away. As Richard Poirier points out in his review of the book, it lacks 'the exploratory feeling that in Joyce and Proust . . . is a consequence of their wonderfully vital, vulnerable, intimidated (and not simply intimidating) relationship to fictional copies of themselves'.[65] Such comparisons set standards that may be excessively high, but they serve a useful purpose by forcing us to realize that in some ways this 'post-modern' novel is far more conservative than the fiction which antedates it by fifty years.

The best example of this reluctance on Nabokov's part comes near the end of the novel, in regard to the woman who is to become Vadim's fourth wife. Unlike Kretschmar or Hermann or Humbert, Vadim finds his 'island of entranced time',[66] in the person who solves his problems with space and reassures him about his identity. Because of her, desire turns out to be creative, not destructive; his love is a muse figure, not a *femme fatale*. She is the 'you' who is addressed in teasing asides throughout the book, the second person, feminine gender, Nabokov enlists to help his special heroes. Besides being a muse, she is a kind of adoring public secretary: she reads everything he writes; she is his staunchest admirer; she defends him against the world. In *Look at the Harlequins!*, this figure remains nameless and undescribed; but when she enters the room in which he is recovering from his illness, Vadim does refer to her as 'Reality' (p. 250): her appearance marks the end of the harlequinade. If this woman is so important, why not be more specific about the nature of her gifts or about the dynamics of their relationship? Vadim explains his reluctance to say anything about her this way: 'Reality would be only adulterated if I now started to narrate what you know, what I know, what nobody else knows, what shall never, never be ferreted out by a matter-of-fact, father-of-muck, mucking biograffitist' (p. 226). A surprising out-burst, considering how forthcoming he has been about all the other women in his life. To explain it we have to go outside the fiction. The same unpleasant tone was used to defend a jealously guarded private world when Nabokov protested so vehemently about critics' attempts to link Ada and his wife Vera.[67] What Vadim says here is actually Nabokov's private reassurance for the dedicatee of this and almost every other novel, and it announces that the writer has raised a barrier between himself and his readers. This then is the price of fame, that most fickle of muses: to be forced to write novels about oneself in which all the important things have been left out.

So what sort of conclusion for the Nabokov *oeuvre* does *Look at the Harlequins!* provide? Paul Valéry had some shrewd things to say about this kind of book: 'If one had to carve in hard stone', he once wrote, 'instead of writing on the wing [*au vol*], literature would be quite different.'[68] And the paperback explosion was still to come. We are the beneficiaries of this writing boom, so it seems ungrateful to complain about it. Still, some truth in advertising, some code of conduct for publishers in their blurbs would be of help to readers who can get through only a tiny fraction of all that literature written 'on the wing'. McGraw-Hill plugged the book with a quotation from a reviewer who compared *Look at the Harlequins!* and *The Tempest*. Someone at Penguin Books was even more resourceful. He read Martin Amis's very negative review in the *New Statesman* ('forlorn', 'ragged', 'boring', 'coarse'), and found in it this nostalgic reference to the greatness of earlier Nabokov novels: 'To read him in full flight is to experience stimulation that is at once intellectual, imaginative and aesthetic, the nearest thing to pure sensual pleasure that prose can offer.'[69] That sentence appeared on the back cover of the novel when it was published in Penguin in 1980, giving everyone the impression that this was vintage Nabokov in a brand new bottle. The author might have enjoyed the irony of seeing the kind of self-borrowing that goes on between the covers being mirrored on them. Dissatisfied customers should ask for their money back. But if they are interested in learning something about Nabokov and the way he saw the world, they should regard this book, not as a typically Nabokovian hall of mirrors, nor as a final statement on the man and his work, but as an invitation to go back to the novels that matter.

Notes

1. Introduction

1 *Speak, Memory: An Autobiography Revisited* (London: Weidenfeld and Nicholson, 1967), pp. 287–8. Nabokov published two other versions of his autobiography: *Conclusive Evidence* (later retitled *Speak, Memory: A Memoir*) (New York: Harper and Brothers, 1951); and *Drugie Berega* (New York: Izdatel'stvo Imeni Chekhova, 1954). References are to the revised English edition unless otherwise indicated. Significant alterations are mentioned in the notes.

2 *Speak, Memory*, p. 287. This is a change from *Conclusive Evidence*, where Nabokov calls Sirin 'the only major' Russian writer produced in exile (p. 216). The discussion of Sirin's work is omitted altogether in *Drugie Berega*.

3 Review of *Korol', Dama, Valet*, *Poslednie Novosti* (hereafter *PN*), 4 Oct. 1928, p. 3.

4 'Knigi i Lyudi', review of *Kamera Obskura*, *Vozrozhdenie*, 3 May 1934, p. 4.

5 '20 Let Evropeiskoi Literatury', *PN*, 10 Feb. 1939, p. 3.

6 Review of *Korol', Dama, Valet*, *Sovremennye Zapiski* (hereafter SZ), no. 37, 1928, pp. 536–7.

7 Review of *SZ*, no. 48 (containing a part of *Podvig*), *PN*, 11 Feb. 1932, p. 2.

8 'Perechityvaya *Otchayanie*', *PN*, 5 Mar. 1936, p. 3.

9 See, for example: Dabney Stuart, '*The Real Life of Sebastian Knight*: Angles of Perception', *Modern Language Quarterly*, 29 (1968), pp. 312–28; Geoffrey Wagner, 'Vladimir Nabokov and the Redemption of Reality', *Cimarron Review*, 10 (1970), pp. 16–23; and Richard Patteson, 'Nabokov's *Look at the Harlequins!*: Endless Re-Creation of the Self', *Russian Literature Triquarterly*, no. 14 (Winter 1976), pp. 84–98.

10 Helen Muchnic, 'Jeweler at Work', review of *Details of a Sunset and Other Stories*, *The New York Review of Books* (hereafter *NYRB*), 23, 27 May 1976, pp. 22–3.

11 'The Vault of Language: Self-Reflective Artifice in Contemporary American Fiction', *Modern Fiction Studies* (hereafter *MFS*), 20 (1974), p. 358.

12 'Upright Among Staring Fish', *Saturday Review*, NS 1, Jan. 1973, p. 36.

13 Introduction to *The Annotated Lolita*, ed. Alfred Appel, Jr (London: Weidenfeld and Nicholson, 1971), p. xxvi. See Robert Merrill, 'Nabokov and Fictional Artifice', *MFS*, 25 (1979), pp. 439–40, for another summary of critical attitudes to Nabokov's work.

14 Introduction to *Bend Sinister* (Harmondsworth: Penguin Books, 1974), p. 7.

15 Afterword to *Lolita*, p. 317.

16 *Nikolay Gogol* (London: Weidenfeld and Nicolson, 1973), p. 150.

17 *Lectures on Literature* (hereafter *LL*), ed. Fredson Bowers (London: Weidenfeld and Nicolson, 1980), p. 125. All subsequent references to this and the companion volume, *Lectures on Russian Literature* (hereafter *LRL*) (1982), are included in the text.

18 Interview conducted by James Mossman, included in *Strong Opinions* (hereafter *SO*) (London: Weidenfeld and Nicolson, 1974), p. 148.

19 Interview conducted by Nicholas Garnham, included in *SO*, p. 118.

20 *The Nabokov–Wilson Letters*, ed. Simon Karlinsky (London: Weidenfeld and Nicolson, 1979), pp. 212–13.

21 Interview conducted by Robert Hughes, included in *SO*, p. 57.

22 Afterword to *Lolita*, p. 317.

23 Review of *Sobranie Stikhov*, *Rul'*, 14 Dec. 1927, p. 5.

24 'Molodye Poety', review of *Chernoe i Goluboe*, and *Perekrestok 2*, an anthology of poems, *Rul'*, 28 Jan. 1931, p. 2.

25 See, for example, the review of A. Bulkin, *Stikhotvoreniya*, *Rul'*, 25 Aug. 1926, p. 5; and the comments on the poetry of P. Bobrinsky in 'Molodye Poety', p. 3.

26 Review of Boris Poplavsky, *Flagi*, *Rul'*, 11 Mar. 1931, p. 5.

27 'The enormous virtue of Pronin's poems is that in them the notorious revolution, the notorious changes for the better, are not felt at all' ('Novye Poety', *Rul'*, 31 Aug. 1927, p. 4).

28 'In [Arkadin's] poems there is an extremely obnoxious civic tint' ('Novye Poety', p. 4).

29 Review of Sergey Rafalovich, *Terpkiya Budni* and *Simon Volkhv*, *Rul'*, 19 Jan. 1927, p. 4.

30 'Novye Poety', p. 4. See also the review of Dimitry Kobyakov and Evgeny Shakh, *Rul'*, 11 May 1927, p. 4.

31 See, for example, John Hawkes's comments on the traditional novel, quoted in Robert Scholes, *Fabulation and Metafiction* (Urbana: Univ. of Illinois Press, 1979), p. 170.

32 Review of *Elan*, *Rul'*, 23 Oct. 1929, p. 5.

33 Discussing B. Sosinsky, 'Rasskazy o Nesushchestvuyushchem', review of *Volya Rossii*, no. 2, *Rul'*, 8 May 1929, p. 4.

34 Review of *Volya Rossii*, p. 4. He is speaking of Tsvetaeva's article 'Neskol'ko Pisem Rainer Maria Rilke'.

35 Review of *Zheny*, *Rul'*, 25 Sept. 1929, p. 5.

36 'Tri Knigi Stikhov', review of Boris Bozhnev, *Fontan*, Dovid Knut, *Vtoraya Kniga Stikhov, and Stikhotvorenie: Poeziya i Poeticheskaya Kritika, Rul'*, 23 May 1928, p. 4.

37 Review of *Poslednie i Pervye, Rul'*, 23 July 1931, p. 5.

38 Review of *Zvezda Nadzvezdaya, Rul'*, 14 Nov. 1928, p. 4.

39 'Molodye Poety', p. 3.

40 'Torzhestvo Dobrodeteli', *Rul'*, 5 Mar. 1930, p. 2.

41 *Ibid.* p. 2.

42 'Prof. Nabokov', review of *LL*, *Newsweek*, 20 Oct. 1980, p. 96.

43 Interview conducted by Andrey Sedykh, *PN*, 3 Nov. 1932, p. 2.

44 *Letters*, p. 96.

45 Interview conducted by Harvey Breit, *The New York Times Book Review* (hereafter *NYTBR*), 1 July 1951, p. 17.

46 Interview conducted by Mossman, included in *SO*, p. 147.

47 Interview conducted by Appel, included in *SO*, p. 66.

48 Interview conducted by Martha Duffy and Ron Sheppard, included in *SO*, p. 121.

49 Interview conducted by Alvin Toffler, included in *SO*, p. 41.

50 Interview conducted by Mossman, included in *SO*, p. 147.

51 Interview conducted by Garnham, included in *SO*, p. 117.

52 Interview conducted by Toffler, included in *SO*, p. 33.

53 Interview conducted by Garnham, included in *SO*, p. 117.

54 Afterword to *Lolita*, pp. 316–17.

55 'Under Cover of Decadence: Nabokov as Evangelist and Guide to the Russian Classics', in *Vladimir Nabokov*, ed. Peter Quennell (London: Weidenfeld and Nicolson, 1979), p. 49.

56 Interview conducted by Appel, included in *SO*, p. 77.

57 Interview conducted by Hughes, included in *SO*, p. 57.

58 See his 1972 article, 'Inspiration', written for the *Saturday Review*, included in *SO*, p. 313, for some comments on stories by both of them (and also on one by Barth). He mentions them again in a 1975 interview, e.g.: 'Salinger is another writer I admire tremendously. Beautiful stuff! He's a real writer' (Interview conducted by Gerald Clark, *Esquire*, 84, July 1975, p. 133).

59 Interview conducted by Appel, included in *SO*, p. 172.

60 'At first, Vera and I were delighted by reading him. We felt we were on a portico, but we have learned that there was no house' ('Prospero's Progress', article based on an interview conducted by Duffy and Sheppard, *Time*, 23 May 1969, p. 83).

61 Interview conducted by Appel, included in *SO*, p. 80.

62 Interview conducted by some New York journalists, included in *SO*, p. 4.

63 All references are to the Ardis reprints of the first editions: *Korol', Dama, Valet* (1928, Berlin; repr. Ann Arbor, Mich.: Ardis, 1979); *Kamera Obskura* (1933, Berlin; repr. Ann Arbor, Mich.: Ardis, 1978) – in *Nabokov: A Bibliography* (New York: McGraw-Hill, 1973), Andrew

Field says that the novel was first published in book form in 1932, but Michael Juliar argues convincingly for 1933 in 'Notes From a Descriptive Bibliography', *The Vladimir Nabokov Research Newsletter* (hereafter *VNRN*), no. 8 (Spring 1982), pp. 24–7; and *Otchayanie* (1936, Berlin; repr. Ann Arbor, Mich.: Ardis, 1978). Since the citation of the original texts in Cyrillic or transliterated form was not necessary for my purposes, I have quoted the translations Nabokov made or approved of. When the passage in the original is altered or omitted altogether from the English version, I have supplied my own literal translation. In the first case two page numbers are given in the text, the Russian preceding the English. In the case of alterations, I quote both versions and both page numbers. In addition, since all three novels were substantially revised in translation, I have sometimes quoted material that appears only in the English versions. The reader will find all this much easier to follow than my rather tortuous account implies. The translations referred to are *King, Queen, Knave*, trans. Dimitri Nabokov in collaboration with the author (London: Weidenfeld and Nicolson, 1968); *Laughter in the Dark*, trans. by the author (London: Weidenfeld and Nicolson, 1961); and *Despair*, trans. by the author (London: Weidenfeld and Nicolson, 1966).

64 *Nabokov: His Life in Art* (London: Hodder and Stoughton, 1967), p. 158.

65 *Nabokov's Dark Cinema* (New York: Oxford Univ. Press, 1974), pp. 34, 246.

66 *Vladimir Nabokov* (Boston: G. K. Hall and London: George Prior, 1976), p. 40.

67 He does say that the similarities between his novel and Dreiser's *An American Tragedy* are 'A coincidental resemblance, but a good one' (quoted in *Nabokov's Dark Cinema*, p. 109).

68 G. M. Hyde relates Franz to Musil's Moosbrugger and 'Nazism's exploitation of adolescence' (*Vladimir Nabokov* (London: Marion Boyars, 1977), p. 45). Nabokov himself makes indirect reference to the Nazis in a sentence added to the English translation in which he mentions the 'worse sins' (p. 138) Franz went on to commit when he got older, a remark he later explained by noting that 'a minute's thought should reveal to the reader what the activities of that type of man could have been' in Germany in the 1940s ('Anniversary Notes', in *SO*, p. 296).

69 Jane Grayson points out these parallels in *Nabokov Translated* (Oxford: Oxford Univ. Press, 1977), pp. 91–2. This is one of the most useful books published on Nabokov, and I am greatly indebted to it.

70 *Nabokov's Dark Cinema*, p. 109.

71 Reported in Andrew Field, *Nabokov: His Life in Part* (London: Hamish Hamilton, 1977), p. 182.

72 See Grayson, *Nabokov Translated*, p. 96.

73 The theme is adumbrated by Magda's automatic assumption that Horn is going to shoot her when he abandons her after their month together:

'"Don't move", he said, "and don't look at what I'm doing"'. "He's going to shoot me"', she thought for some reason, but stayed absolutely still. What was he doing? Silence. She moved her naked shoulder slightly. "Don't move"', he repeated. "He's aiming"', thought Magda, but without fear' (pp. 25–6). Nabokov left this out of *Laughter in the Dark*, probably because the business about the aiming did not ring true.

74 'Perechityvaya *Otchayanie*', p. 3.

75 Appel, *Nabokov's Dark Cinema*, p. 261.

76 Dabney Stuart, *Nabokov* (Baton Rouge: Louisiana State Univ. Press, 1978), p. 88.

77 Interview conducted by Peter Duval-Smith, *The Listener*, 68, 22 Nov. 1962, p. 858. This comment is omitted from the version of this interview included in *SO*.

78 *Nabokov's Dark Cinema*, p. 262.

79 The same contrast between a world of domestic joy and one of grotesque and powerful evil occurs in one of the Chekhov stories that Nabokov singles out for particularly high praise in the lectures, 'In the Ravine'. He stresses the fact that the young mother in that story is 'absolutely and divinely indifferent' to the evil that surrounds her (*LRL*, p. 272).

80 In his lectures on *Anna Karenin*, he calls Anna's adultery a 'filthy and soul-stunting sin' (*LRL*, p. 187).

81 *Rul'*, 24 June 1928, p. 2. Compare the idea expressed in the last stanza with this comment from the lectures: 'Literature must be taken and broken to bits, pulled apart, squashed – then its lovely reek will be smelt in the hollow of the palm, it will be munched and rolled upon the tongue with relish; then, and only then, its rare flavor will be appreciated at its true worth and the broken and crushed parts will again come together in your mind and disclose the beauty of a unity to which you have contributed something of your own blood' (*LRL*, p. 105). R. Milner-Gulland pointed out the similarity to me.

82 *Nabokov's Dark Cinema*, p. 262.

83 Stephen Suagee, 'An Artist's Memory Beats All Other Kinds', in *A Book of Things About Vladimir Nabokov*, ed. Carl R. Proffer (Ann Arbor, Mich.: Ardis, 1974), p. 61.

84 Stuart, *Nabokov*, p. 116n.

85 'Vladimir Nabokov: *La Méprise*', in *Situations I* (Paris: Gallimard, 1947), p. 59.

86 *Life in Art*, p. 231.

87 'An Artist's Memory', p. 62n.

88 *Life in Art*, p. 230.

89 *Lost in the Funhouse* (New York: Doubleday, 1968), p. 113.

90 It is interesting to note that Nabokov criticizes Dostoevsky's characters because 'they all are treated throughout the book they happen to be in like chessmen in a complicated chess problem' (*LRL*, p. 109). Else-where he notes: 'One feels that he does not see his characters physically,

that they are merely puppets, remarkable, fascinating puppets plunged into the moving stream of the author's ideas' (*LRL*, p. 129).

91 Interview conducted by Mossman, included in *SO*, p. 148.

92 'A Hanging', in *The Collected Essays, Journalism and Letters of George Orwell*, 4 vols., ed. Sonia Orwell and Ian Angus (London: Secker and Warburg, 1968), vol. I, pp. 44–8.

93 *Nabokov*, pp. 112–13. Hyde's entire discussion of this novel (pp. 109–15) is very illuminating. I am greatly indebted to this book, in which phrases like 'the truthfulness of art' appear without inverted commas.

94 Interview conducted by Alan Levy, *The New York Times Magazine*, 31 Oct. 1971, p. 38.

2. *Invitation to a Beheading* and *Bend Sinister*

1 References are to *Priglashenie Na Kazn'* (Paris, 1938; repr. Ann Arbor, Mich.: Ardis, 1979); and *Invitation to a Beheading*, trans. Dimitri Nabokov in collaboration with the author (London: Weidenfeld and Nicolson, 1960). I have included both page references in the text (the original comes first) when the novel is quoted (except here since there is no Russian Foreword). The translation is almost always literal (see Grayson, *Nabokov Translated*, pp. 119–24). Where it differs significantly from the original, I have noted and discussed the differences; otherwise, I have simply quoted the English. Since there is no need constantly to distinguish between the two versions, I have used the English title throughout.

2 Introduction to *Bend Sinister* (Harmondsworth: Penguin Books, 1974), p. 6. Nabokov's Introduction is not included in the Weidenfeld and Nicolson edition of the novel (1960), but for the sake of uniformity all references are to this edition. They too are included in the text. The Penguin Introduction is cited in the notes.

3 *Conclusive Evidence*, p. 217. The comment is not included in *Drugie Berega* or *Speak, Memory*.

4 Interview conducted by Allene Talmey, included in *SO*, p. 156.

5 Review of *Priglashenie Na Kazn'*, *Russkie Zapiski*, no. 13 (1939), pp. 198–9.

6 Review of *SZ*, no. 59 (containing a part of *Priglashenie Na Kazn'*), *PN*, 28 Nov. 1935, p. 3. See also his *Odinochestvo i Svoboda* (New York: Izdatel'stvo Imeni Chekhova, 1955), pp. 215–20.

7 'O Sirina', *Vozrozhdenie*, 13 Feb. 1937, p. 9. An abridged translation by Michael Walker can be found in *Nabokov*, ed. Alfred Appel, Jr and Charles Newman (London: Weidenfeld and Nicolson, 1971), pp. 96–101. I have quoted p. 98 of this translation.

8 Some exceptions that should be mentioned: Robert Alter, '*Invitation to a Beheading*: Nabokov and the Art of Politics', in *Nabokov*, ed. Appel and Newman, pp. 41–59; Douglas Fowler, *Reading Nabokov* (Ithaca,

N.Y.: Cornell Univ. Press, 1974), pp. 24–6, 38–44; and Hyde, *Nabokov*, pp. 129–33.

9 'The Alpha and Omega of Nabokov's Prison House of Language: Alphabetic Iconicism in *Invitation to a Beheading*', *Russian Literature*, 6 (1978), p. 362. This is the best article yet written on the novel.

10 *Crystal Land* (Berkeley: Univ. of California Press, 1972), pp. 96, 117.

11 Interview conducted by Appel, included in *SO*, p. 66. He put this suggestion as a question to Nabokov, who replied: 'Yes, possibly.'

12 'Nabokov: Homo Ludens', in *Nabokov*, ed. Quennell, p. 95.

13 'Reading Between the Lines and the Squares', *MFS*, 25 (1979), p. 425.

14 'Nabokov and Fictional Artifice', p. 444.

15 The phrase is used by Patricia Merivale in 'The Flaunting of Artifice in Vladimir Nabokov and Jorge Luis Borges', in *Nabokov*, ed. L. S. Dembo (Madison: Univ. of Wisconsin Press, 1967), pp. 209–24.

16 *Nabokov and the Novel* (Cambridge, Mass.: Harvard Univ. Press, 1980), pp. 54–5, 66.

17 'Macule' is the kind of exotic substitution that Nabokov sometimes liked to make when revising a translation. The Russian has *blik*, 'speck of light'. For some interesting examples of this kind of revision see Grayson, *Nabokov Translated*, pp. 193–208.

18 'Nabokov and the Art of Politics', pp. 54–5.

19 Preface to *Leaves of Grass* (1855), *Walt Whitman: The Complete Poems*, ed. Francis Murphy (Harmondsworth: Penguin Books, 1975), p. 759.

20 Lilly, 'Nabokov: Homo Ludens', p. 94.

21 Bader identifies the allusion in *Crystal Land*, p. 114.

22 *Nabokov* (Lausanne: Éditions l'Age d'Homme, 1979), p. 81.

23 Freud links dreams about failing examinations with sexual anxieties. He writes: 'Wilhelm Stekel, who put forward the first interpretation of dreams of Matriculation ("Matura"), was of the opinion that they regularly related to sexual tests and sexual maturity. My experience has often confirmed his view' (*The Interpretation of Dreams*, vol. IV of *The Complete Psychological Works of Sigmund Freud*, ed. and trans. James Strachey (London: The Hogarth Press and The Institute of Psycho-Analysis, 1953), p. 276).

24 *Nabokov*, p. 88.

25 Introduction to *Bend Sinister*, p. 6.

26 *Speak, Memory*, p. 298.

27 Interview conducted by Nicholas Garnham, included in *SO*, p. 118.

28 The author of a recent book on Nabokov argues: ' "Average reality" is the public realm shared by the individuals who make up a society. Contributing to this domain are the social concerns, political anxieties, and financial crises that plague every generation of men and women, consuming a great deal of their attention and energy ... This general world of common causes promotes the lowest common denominator – the average – of individual human consciousness. It is always being

added up and accounted for by the sociologist, the psychologist, and the reporter. Collective life is always a compromise, and the general notion of the "common man" only a caricature of the individual's specific nature' (Pifer, *Nabokov and the Novel*, p. 50).

29 Cedric Watts pointed this out to me in conversation.

30 Pifer, *Nabokov and the Novel*, pp. 89–90.

31 See the interview conducted by Martin Esslin, included in *SO*, pp. 112–13.

32 Interviews conducted by Appel and by Duffy and Sheppard, included in *SO*, pp. 85, 124. See also *Ada* (London: Weidenfeld and Nicolson, 1969), p. 314.

33 *Speak, Memory*, p. 203.

34 *Ibid.* p. 207.

35 See interviews conducted by Gold, Duffy and Sheppard, and Appel, included in *SO*, pp. 103–4, 127, 175; and Nabokov's contribution to 'Reputations Revisited', *TLS*, 21 June 1977, p. 66.

36 *War of the Worlds* (London: William Heinemann, 1898), pp. 2, 4.

37 *The First Men in the Moon* (London: Macmillan, 1904), p. 334.

38 *Speak, Memory*, p. 243. Surely 'bums' is an inappropriate Americanism in this distinctly English evocation of snobbery and elegance.

39 *Speak, Memory*, p. 243. The comment quoted is omitted from the Russian version of the autobiography.

40 Field points out that there are 'many facts and features in Vladimir Nabokov's life which have some precedent in the life of his father'. See his list in *Life in Part*, pp. 84–5. Of particular relevance here is the following: 'V. D. Nabokov believed in a state of patrician democracy which allows for the existence of an intellectual, monied elite. His son's belief in democracy as I understand it – and I am well aware that he himself would state the matter, already has in fact, in far more attractive and less blunt fashion – is the same.'

41 *V. D. Nabokov and the Russian Provisional Government, 1917*, ed. and trans. Virgil Medlin and Steven Parsons (New Haven, Conn.: Yale Univ. Press, 1976), p. 146.

42 *History of the Russian Revolution*, trans. Max Eastman (London: Victor Gollancz, 1965), p. 530. Trotsky often refers to V. D. Nabokov's admirably lucid account of events in that extraordinary year. The following passage is of particular interest: 'On the 27th [of February], Nabokov, already known to us as a member of the Kadet centre, and at that time working – a legalised deserter – at General Headquarters, went to his office as usual and stayed until three o'clock, knowing nothing of the events. Towards evening shots were heard on the Morskaia. Nabokov listened to them from his apartment. Armoured cars dashed along, individual soldiers and sailors ran past, sidling along the wall. The respected liberal observed them from the side windows of his vestibule. "The telephone continued to function, and my friends, I remember, kept me in touch with what was going on

during the day. At the usual time we went to bed." This man will soon become one of the inspirators of the revolutionary (!) Provisional Government, occupying the position of General Administrator. To-morrow [actually three days later, the second of March] an unknown man will approach him on the street – a book-keeper, perhaps, or a teacher – bow low and remove his hat [these are Trotsky's additions; Nabokov's account has the man simply shaking his hand], and say to him: "Thank you for all that you have done for the people." Nabokov, with modest pride, will relate the incident himself' (pp. 153–4). If V. V. Nabokov were reporting these incidents, he would praise his father for his display of aristocratic coolness and modesty. Trotsky is pointing out that the sang-froid is possible only because someone else is doing the fighting. Of course he conveniently omits saying that Nabokov had been fighting against the inequities of Tsarist autocracy during a long and distinguished public career.

43 Interview conducted by Gold, included in *SO*, p. 96.

44 *Speak, Memory*, p. 80. Field says that 'On the occasions when he himself was in the servant's [*sic*] quarters, Nabokov was most struck and even a little puzzled by the "odd smell"' (*Life in Part*, p. 102).

45 *Tyrants Destroyed and Other Stories*, trans. Dimitri Nabokov in collaboration with the author (London: Weidenfeld and Nicolson, 1975), p. 6. For 'ambition', the Russian has *gonor*, 'arrogance' ('Istreblenie Tiranov', *Vesna v Fial'ta i Drugie Rasskazy* (New York: Izdatel'stvo Imeni Chekhova, 1956), p. 168).

46 Interview conducted by Hughes, included in *SO*, p. 58.

47 Interview conducted by Pierre Domergues, *Les Langues Modernes*, Jan.–Feb. 1968, p. 102. He adds some examples: 'Mao, Nasser, Hitler, le beau barbu cubain dont le nom m'échappe, le mélancolique Kossyguine, le style pompier des écrits de Lénine, tout ça c'est tellement grotesque que ces faces à claques, ces pièces montées au beurre rance, deviennent appétissantes à force d'être repoussantes'.

48 *Tyrants Destroyed*, p. 2.

49 'Tyrants Destroyed', pp. 7, 18, 35.

50 *Letters*, p. 117.

51 See his *Conversations With Stalin*, trans. Michael Petrovich (London: Rupert Hart-Davis, 1962), p. 146.

52 Review of Robert Conquest, *The Great Terror*, Soviet Studies, 20 (1968–9), pp. 539–40.

53 Quoted in George Feifer, *Russia Close-Up* (London: Jonathan Cape, 1973), p. 224.

54 *Joseph Stalin* (London: Hutchinson, 1974), p. 436.

55 'Tyrants Destroyed', p. 36.

56 *A Russian Beauty and Other Stories*, trans. Dimitri Nabokov in collaboration with the author, except for the title story, which is translated by Simon Karlinsky (London: Weidenfeld and Nicolson, 1973),

p. 3. 'A Russian Beauty' was originally published as 'Krasavitsa', in *Soglyadatai* (Berlin, 1938; repr. Ann Arbor, Mich.: Ardis, 1978).

57 *Life in Part*, p. 201. Field records that at the age of seventy Nabokov still wanted to write about the Nazi concentration camps: 'There is a sense of responsibility about this theme which I think I will tackle one day. I will go to those German camps and *look* at those places and write a *terrible* indictment.'

58 *Nineteen Eighty-Four* (London: Heinemann Educational Books, 1965), pp. 292–3.

59 Northrop Frye points this out in *Anatomy of Criticism* (Princeton: Princeton Univ. Press, 1957), p. 238.

60 *Nineteen Eighty-Four*, p. 278.

61 Interview conducted by Gold, included in *SO*, p. 101.

62 Somewhere at the back of Nabokov's dislike for this kind of sweeping self-condemnation is of course Freud, denounced in the Foreword to *Invitation to a Beheading* for his 'grotesque world of communal guilt' (p. 7), and relegated to the bottom of a toilet in *Bend Sinister*: 'At the bottom of the bowl a safety razor blade envelope with Dr S. Freud's face and signature floated' (p. 77).

63 Ironically, sometimes it was people like Nabokov, émigrés who had left the Soviet Union soon after the Revolution, who were sent back, swept up indiscriminately in the obsession with appeasing Stalin simply because they happened to be living in Europe.

64 'Free – and a Bit Too Easy', *The Times*, 7 Apr. 1981, p. 12.

65 Quoted in Robert Conquest, *The Great Terror*, rev. edn (London: Macmillan, 1973), pp. 678–9, 668.

66 'Were the Intellectuals Duped? The Thirties Revisited', *Encounter*, 41, Dec. 1973, p. 30. See also Conquest, *The Great Terror*, pp. 665–84.

67 See, for example, the interview conducted by Gold, *Saturday Evening Post*, 11 Feb. 1967, p. 85; and *Ada*, p. 560.

68 *The Problem of Knowledge* (London: Macmillan, 1965), pp. 184–5.

69 *Letters*, p. 31.

70 I am indebted here to Richard Pipes's discussion of the meaning of Stalinist history in 'The Pock-Marked God', a review of several books on Stalin, *TLS*, 24 June 1974, pp. 625–7.

71 Interview conducted by Appel, included in *SO*, p. 76.

72 *Priglashenie Na Kazn'* has *tochka*, 'point', not 'spark', and *nash-chupat'*, 'find by feeling, groping', instead of 'discern'. *Vzygrat'*, 'begin to seethe', is translated as 'leap', *nakrenyat'sya*, 'heel over', as 'flash'.

73 Introduction to *Bend Sinister*, p. 7.

74 For example: John Wain, 'Nabokov's Beheading', review of *Invitation to a Beheading*, *The New Republic*, 141, 21 Dec. 1959, p. 19; Julian Moynahan, *Vladimir Nabokov* (Minneapolis: Univ. of Minnesota Press, 1971), p. 21; and Lee, *Nabokov*, p. 74.

75 'La Réponse de Kafka', in *Essais Critiques* (Paris: Éditions du Seuil, 1964), p. 140.
76 In a letter to his mother, quoted in Field, *Life in Part*, p. 181.
77 *LL*, p. 270.
78 For another example of Nabokov's view of Kafka as a critic of bourgeois inhumanity and a defender of the helpless individual, see the 'Kafkaesque' story Nabokov told his classes every year, a gruesome account of a brutal murder that he had read about in the newspaper, *LL*, pp. 266–7.
79 *Nineteen Eighty-Four*, p. 30.
80 'Introduction', in *Twentieth Century Interpretations of '1984'*, ed. Samuel Hynes, Jr (Englewood Cliffs, N.J.: Prentice-Hall, 1971), p. 16.
81 *Ibid.* p. 16.
82 'Soviet Rule and Russia's Future', a Supplement to *The New Commonwealth*, no. 15, 23 Jan. 1920, p. 7.
83 *Ibid.* p. 8.
84 *LRL*, p. 254.
85 *Nineteen Eighty-Four*, pp. 275–6.
86 *Ibid.* p. 271.
87 Introduction to *Bend Sinister*, p. 6.

3. *The Gift*

1 Simon Karlinsky, 'Nabokov's Russian Games', *NYTBR*, 18 Apr. 1971, p. 12.
2 Review of *SZ*, no. 66 (containing a part of *Dar*), *Vozrozhdenie*, 24 June 1938, p. 9.
3 'Vladimir Nabokov's Novel *Dar* as a Work of Literary Criticism: A Structural Analysis', *Slavic and East European Journal* (hereafter *SEEJ*), NS 7 (1963), pp. 284–90.
4 *Crystal Land*, p. 6.
5 *The Literature of Exhaustion* (Durham, N.C.: Duke Univ. Press, 1974), p. 63.
6 *Nabokov's Dark Cinema*, p. 298.
7 Introduction to *The Annotated Lolita*, p. xxx.
8 *Life in Art*, pp. 25–6.
9 *Nabokov*, p. 93.
10 *Nabokov*, p. 26. The portrayal of Chernyshevsky was too lifelike in the eyes of *Sovremennye Zapiski*'s editors. One of them, Mark Vishnyak, says in his memoirs that they rejected Chapter Four because 'In the opinion of the editors the life of Chernyshevsky was portrayed in the novel with such naturalistic – or physiological – detail that its artistic value became questionable' ('*Sovremennye Zapiski*': *Vospominaniya* (Bloomington: Indiana Univ. Publications, 1957), p. 254n).
11 Page references are to the Ardis edition of *Dar* (1975) and to the Weidenfeld and Nicolson edition of *The Gift* (1963), translated by

Michael Scammell in collaboration with the author. On the rare occasions when passages cited do differ significantly from the original, I have supplied my own translation of *Dar*. Except when distinctions are being made between the two versions, I have used the English title.

12 *Polnoe Sobranie Sochinenii*, 16 vols., ed. V. Ya. Kirpotin *et al.* (Moscow: Gosudarstvennoe Izdatel'stvo Khudozhestvennoi Literatury, 1939–53); vol. XIV, p. 11. All subsequent references are to this edition and are included in the text.

13 William Woehrlin's *Chernyshevskii: The Man and the Journalist* (Cambridge, Mass.: Harvard Univ. Press, 1971) contains a detailed discussion (pp. 75–86) of this diary. Interestingly enough, *The Gift* is not mentioned in this excellent biography of Chernyshevsky.

14 *Life in Art*, p. 244.

15 *Nabokov's Dark Cinema*, pp. 58–9.

16 *Vladimir Nabokov* (New York: Frederick Ungar, 1974), p. 39.

17 'Nabokov's *Gift*', review of *The Gift*, in *Standards* (New York: Horizon Press, 1966), p. 186.

18 '*Dar*: A Structural Analysis', p. 286.

19 *Reading Nabokov*, p. 167.

20 *The Italics Are Mine*, trans. Philippe Radley (London: Longmans, Green and Co., 1969), p. 566. Field confirms this: 'There is no doubt in my mind', he writes in his biography, 'that the imaginary dialogues between Godunov-Cherdyntsev and the poet Koncheev in *The Gift* represent the aesthetic positions of Nabokov and Khodasevich discoursing as spiritually friendly peers on the summit of Russian literature.' But he adds that 'Nabokov denies this emphatically, indignantly' (*Life in Part*, p. 218).

21 *V Poiskakh Nabokova* (Paris: La Presse Libre, 1979), p. 62.

22 *Polnoe Sobranie Sochinenii*, 13 vols., ed. N. F. Belchikov *et al.* (Moscow: Izdatel'stvo Akademii Nauk SSSR, 1953–9), vol. XII, p. 129.

23 It is true that these critics, because of the way they evaluated literature, often play right into Nabokov's hands. He quite rightly points out that Belinsky and Chernyshevsky placed the great, and some not so great, European writers higher than Gogol, for example. What he doesn't say is that it was their commitment to the view that the literary works of an undeveloped culture could not be equal in worth to those of an advanced one that necessitated this judgment. It is only fair to add that arguing that Belinsky had a low opinion of Gogol on the basis of this kind of evidence, as Fyodor does (pp. 284/241–2), is a little like collecting the negative remarks about Pushkin in Nabokov's *Eugene Onegin* commentary and using them to prove that he thought Pushkin overrated. As far as Chernyshevsky is concerned, he claimed that 'the most unconditional admirers of everything Gogol wrote, praising to the skies every one of his works, every line he wrote, do not sympath-

ize as keenly with him as we do, do not attribute to his work such enormous significance for Russian literature as we do' (vol. III, p. 10).

24 *Eugene Onegin*, 4 vols., rev. edn (London: Routledge and Kegan Paul, 1975), vol. II, pp. 151, 227. Alexander Gerschenkron points out the inconsistency in a review of Nabokov's *Onegin*, 'A Manufactured Monument?', *Modern Philology*, 63 (1965–6), p. 345.

25 See also vol. II, p. 437 and vol. III, p. 339. If Chernyshevsky were out to do a hatchet job on Pushkin's 'pure poetry' surely he would seize on a poem like 'Chern'', ('The Rabble'), with its claim that 'like the wind [the poet's] song is free, but then like the wind it is also barren', and its series of rhetorical questions about what possible use the poet can be to the common herd (*Polnoe Sobranie Sochinenii*, 16 vols., ed. V. D. Bonch-Bruevich *et al.* (Moscow: Izdatel'stvo Akademii Nauk SSSR, 1937–49), vol. III, p. 141), and denounce the author for his anti-social attitude. But he simply quotes these lines and says: 'Now it is possible to answer these very basic questions more calmly and more advantageously for the significance of Pushkin in the history of our development than Pushkin himself answered them' (vol. II, p. 474).

26 *Belinskij and Russian Literary Criticism* (Madison: Univ. of Wisconsin Press, 1974), p. 255. In regard to Chernyshevsky's criticism, Terras is almost as harsh as Nabokov; but in general his book is an excellent account of a large and complex subject, and I have found it very useful.

27 *Eugene Onegin*, vol. II, p. 167.

28 *Polnoe Sobranie Sochinenii*, vol. III, p. 247.

29 *Eugene Onegin*, vol. III, p. 288.

30 *Nabokov*, pp. 54, 102.

31 Interview conducted by Talmey, included in *SO*, p. 156.

32 *Letters*, p. 220. Compare his comments on Gogol the 'false humorist' which the public so admires, in *Nikolay Gogol*, pp. 29–32.

33 Actually Nabokov has mercifully edited Chernyshevsky's ramblings here; see vol. XV, p. 275.

34 Koncheev may be referring to this kind of misrepresentation when, in the second imaginary conversation he has with Fyodor, he charges him with 'reworking' some of his sources (pp. 380/321); but he seems to mean stylistic reworking only, and he adds that all the criticisms he has to make about *Chernyshevsky* are 'trivial' (pp. 381/322). For Chernyshevsky's real attitude to 'monographs', see his enthusiastic reviews of specialized studies of archaeology, church history, French publication laws, the way geometry is taught in military schools, Hungarian grammar, the relations between Slavic languages and Sanskrit, etc., in vol. II of the *Complete Works*.

35 Wallace he rated less highly: 'He acquired a considerable reputation by virtue of his excellent research, but for all its conscientiousness, it shows that he never became a first-class scientist' (vol. X, p. 748).

36 *Russian Thinkers*, ed. Henry Hardy and Aileen Kelly (London: The Hogarth Press, 1978), pp. 224–5.

37 *Pale Fire* (London: Weidenfeld and Nicolson, 1962), p. 152. Karlinsky was the first to point out the correspondence between Gradus and Chernyshevsky ('*Dar*: A Structural Analysis', p. 290n).

38 This sentence is not in *Dar*.

39 *Polnoe Sobranie Sochinenii*, 30 vols., ed. V. G. Bazanov *et al.* (Leningrad: Izdatel'stvo 'Nauka', 1972–   [publication not yet complete]) vol. XVIII, pp. 70–103. I am indebted here to Terras's discussion of this essay in *Belinskij and Russian Literary Criticism*, p. 223.

40 *Afanasy Afanasevich Fet: Stikhotvoreniya* (Moscow: Izdatel'stvo 'Khudozhestvennaya Literatura', 1970), p. 170.

41 See his reviews of Pisemsky, *Ocherki iz Krest'yanskago Byta*, and of Saltykov-Shchedrin, *Gubernskie Ocherki*, *Sobranie Sochinenii*, 8 vols., ed. N. V. Gerbel (St Petersburg: no publ., 1865–7), vol. VII, pp. 285, 251.

42 *Pis'ma*, 13 vols., ed. M. P. Alekseev *et al.* (Moscow: Izdatel'stvo Akademii Nauk SSSR, 1961–8), vol. II, p. 282; vol. V, p. 12.

43 Not everyone would agree with this qualification. Karlinsky sees 'the dogmatic authoritarian component' in the criticism of the Belinsky–Chernyshevsky school as the precursor of Lenin's 'fanaticism, cruelty and lack of all scruple' (Introduction to the *Letters*, p. 7). And Adam Ulam says that Chernyshevsky 'mirrors the mentality of the revolutionary: his cunning and naïveté, the ability to withstand and to inflict suffering, both the crudity and the elation of his vision of a better world' (*Lenin and the Bolsheviks* (London: Secker and Warburg, 1966), p. 70).

44 In *Nabokov*, ed. Appel and Newman, pp. 7–16.

45 'Nabokov and Chekhov', pp. 13, 14.

46 *Letters*, p. 321. In *Speak, Memory*, Goncharov is included in a list of minor Russian writers whom Nabokov calls 'stupefying bores (comparable to American "regional writers")' (p. 160).

47 This word is not in *Dar*, but the point is the same in both versions. Nabokov speaks slightingly in *Drugie Berega* (p. 120) of Aksakov's descriptions of butterfly hunting.

48 *Polnoe Sobranie Sochinenii*, 15 vols., ed. M. P. Alekseev *et al.* (Moscow: Izdatel'stvo Akademii Nauk SSSR, 1960–8), vol. IV, p. 124.

49 Hyde discusses *Journey to Arzrum* in *Nabokov*, pp. 21–3.

50 *Polnoe Sobranie Sochinenii*, vol. VIII, p. 469.

51 *O Teorii Prozy* (Moscow, 1929; repr. Ann Arbor, Mich.: Ardis, n.d.), p. 13.

52 *Polnoe Sobranie Sochinenii*, vol. VIII, pp. 452–3.

53 For example: 'The true exercise of Fyodor's gift requires that he forsake dead forms of perception, which are "unworthy of an artist"' (Ellen Pifer, 'No Frivolous Firebird: Character, Reality, Morality in Nabokov's Fiction', unpublished dissertation, Univ. of California, Berkeley, 1976, p. 155).

54 See also the account of Germans bathing in the Grunewald in *Speak,*

Memory, pp. 303–4. The same passage appears in *Conclusive Evidence*, pp. 233–4, but is somewhat toned town in *Drugie Berega*, pp. 260–1.

55 *PN*, 15 Feb. 1938, p. 3.

56 In a letter to a friend written in 1937, the year he finished *The Gift* and left Germany, Nabokov wrote: 'I have always been unable to abide Germans, the swinish German spirit, but in their present state of things (which, by the way, suits them rather well) life finally became absolutely unbearable there for me, and I don't say this simply because I am married to a Jewish woman' (quoted in Field, *Life in Part*, p. 201). He wrote Wilson during the Second World War: 'My ardent desire that Russia, in spite of everything, may defeat or rather utterly abolish Germany – so that not a German be left in the world, is putting the cart before the horse, but the horse is so disgusting that I prefer doing so' (*Letters*, p. 46). For an excellent summary of Nabokov's views on Germany, see Dieter Zimmer, 'L'Allemagne Dans l'Oeuvre de Nabokov', trans. Rudolf Boehm and Isabelle Micha, *L'Arc* no. 24 (Spring 1964), pp. 67–75.

57 Nabokov alters the epithets in the English translation in an attempt to sustain the energy created by the sound effects in the original. *Dar* has 'bezdarno-udarnaya, pritorno-ritoricheskaya, fal'shivo-vshivaya povest'' – 'feebly percussive, cloyingly rhetorical, falsely-lousy tale'. The Weidenfeld and Nicolson edition has 'trash' instead of the 'brash trash' that is in the American edition. This is presumably a printing error.

58 *Nabokov*, p. 25.

59 The chapter on *Dead Souls* in *Nikolay Gogol* contains many examples that illustrate this difference between the two writers.

60 The same incident is recounted in both English versions of Nabokov's autobiography (*Conclusive Evidence*, p. 85; *Speak, Memory*, p. 128), but omitted from *Drugie Berega*.

61 *Life in Part*, p. 76.

62 Interview conducted by John Wain, *The Observer*, 1 Nov. 1959, p. 21.

63 Significantly, Shakhovskaya, in the first full-length study of Nabokov in Russian, although extremely sympathetic to both him and his work, dwells on this aspect of Nabokov's Russia and stresses the difference between him and his great predecessors. She notes the absence of the Russian common people in his novels, calls his Russia a 'closed world', and even claims that his descriptions of nature are those of a Petersburgian, a 'dachnik': 'His landscapes are country-estate, not rural: a park, a lake, avenues and mushrooms – which namely dachniks love to gather (butterflies – that is another matter). But it is as if Nabokov never knew the smell of hemp, warmed by the sun, the cloud of chaff flying up from the threshing floor, the breathing of the earth after a flood, the knocking of the thresher on the threshing floor, sparks flying from the blacksmith's hammer, the taste of steaming milk, or the hunks of rye bread sprinkled with salt . . . Everything which Levin and Rostov knew,

which Tolstoy, Turgenev, Pushkin, Lermontov, Gogol, Bunin, every Russian writer belonging to the gentry or to the peasantry, with the exception of Dostoevsky, knew as part of himself' (*V Poiskakh Nabokova*, pp. 95, 93).

64 See his remarks in two letters from Switzerland written in 1836, *Polnoe Sobranie Sochinenii*, 14 vols., ed. N. L. Meshcheryakov *et al.* (Moscow: Izdatel'stvo Akademii Nauk SSSR, 1940–52), vol. XI, pp. 60, 61.

65 It is interesting to compare Koncheev's somewhat pessimistic forecast with Khodasevich's view of his own poetic legacy, expressed in a 1931 poem called 'Monument':

In me is the end, in me the beginning,
I who accomplished so little.
But still I am a durable link,
To me this happiness is given.

In the new great Russia
They will erect my two-faced idol.
At the intersection of two roads
Where there is time, wind and sand . . .

The original and a rhymed translation can be found in *Modern Russian Poetry*, ed. Vladimir Markov and Merrill Sparks (London: MacGibbon and Kee, 1966), pp. 406–7. Khodasevich's work was finally republished in the Soviet Union in 1974.

66 *Polnoe Sobranie Sochinenii*, vol. III, p. 424. The translation is Nabokov's from *Eugene Onegin*, vol. II, p. 311.

67 *Eugene Onegin*, vol. II, p. 311. In his Pushkin commentary, Nabokov goes so far as to claim that the first four stanzas should be put in inverted commas, and that the fifth is 'the artist's own grave voice repudiating the mimicked boast' (vol. II, p. 310). But as John Bayley points out, this would destroy the poem's ambivalence and 'the deadpan gravity of Pushkinian equivocation' (*Pushkin* (Cambridge: Cambridge Univ. Press, 1971), p. 305).

68 Although none of his novels has yet appeared in the Soviet Union, a few critical articles about Nabokov's work have been published there. Of particular interest here is one of two articles published in a University of Tartu journal, *Vtorichnye Modeliruyushchie Sistemy*, in 1979. It is devoted to the poetry and poetics of 'F. K. Godunov-Cherdyntsev' ('Nekotorye Zamechaniya o Poezii i Poetike F. K. Godunova-Cherdyntseva', pp. 45–8). In it the author, Mikhail Lotman, has some interesting things to say about the poetic idea born of rhyming *otchizna*, 'native land', and *priznan*, 'recognized', in Fyodor's poem about Russia (pp. 66/60). The irony of touching on this theme in an article about an author who is not mentioned by his real name, not 'recognized' by his 'native land', doubtless did not escape him.

69 *Poems and Problems* (London: Weidenfeld and Nicolson, 1972), pp. 108–11. Nabokov's own translation, *en regard* in the text.

70 Foreword to *Stikhi* (Ann Arbor, Mich.: Ardis, 1979), p. 3.

71 *Nabokov's Spectral Dimension* (Ann Arbor, Mich.: Ardis, 1981).

72 Anna Maria Salehar discusses the play on words in Zina's name in 'Nabokov's *Gift*: An Apprenticeship in Creativity', in *Things About Nabokov*, ed. Proffer, pp. 76–7.

73 Quoted in *Life in Part*, p. 34.

74 Nabokov doesn't always sound so isolated within émigré literature as he does in *The Gift*. In 1927, on the tenth anniversary of the revolution, he wrote of his fellow exiles: 'Although it is now clear to us how different we are, and although it sometimes seems as if not one, but a million Russias are wandering the world, at times wretched and spiteful, at times fighting among themselves, there is however something linking us, some common aspiration or common spirit, which a future historian will understand and evaluate' ('Yubilei', *Rul'*, 18 Nov. 1927, p. 2).

75 *Speak, Memory*, pp. 280, 282.

76 *Polnoe Sobranie Sochinenii*, vol. XII, p. 67.

4. *Lolita*

1 The words quoted are from Alfred Appel's discussion of 'Nabokov's Puppet Show' in his Introduction to *Vladimir Nabokov: The Annotated Lolita* (London: Weidenfeld and Nicolson, 1971), p. xxvi. All subsequent references are to this edition and will be included in the text.

2 *The Pooh Perplex* (London: Arthur Barker, 1964), p. 3.

3 Appel's edition is the one book that is indispensable for anyone interested in *Lolita*. Of the many excellent studies of the novel that have appeared, I am particularly indebted to: Lionel Trilling, 'The Last Lover: Vladimir Nabokov's *Lolita*', *Encounter*, 11, Oct. 1958, pp. 9–19; Gabriel Josipovici, '*Lolita*: Parody and the Pursuit of Beauty', *Critical Quarterly*, 6 (1964), pp. 35–48, repr. in *The World and the Book*, 2nd edn (London: Macmillan, 1979), pp. 201–20; Michael Bell, '*Lolita* and Pure Art', *Essays in Criticism*, 24 (1974), pp. 169–84; Fowler, *Reading Nabokov*; Hyde, *Nabokov*; and Merrill, 'Nabokov and Fictional Artifice', *MFS*, 25 (1979), pp. 439–69.

4 The comments I have isolated here represent the main thrust of Appel's argument concerning *Lolita*. To be fair, I should add that his introduction and notes are full of observations about the 'ostensible subject' and Nabokov's 'puppets' that suggest how seriously he takes these aspects of the book, and how undogmatic he is about the absolute nature of Nabokovian artifice. It is mainly a question of emphasis. My sense is that to call *Lolita* 'artifice or nothing' (p. xviii), 'fantastic, a-realistic, and involuted' (p. xviii), and 'as grandly labyrinthine and as much a work of artifice' as *Pale Fire* (p. lix), to call its characters parodies in the sense that they 'can possess no other "reality"' (p. xxvii) – this is to get

the emphasis wrong. Praise for Nabokov's 'verisimilitude' (p. lx) inevitably seems half-hearted when it comes after comments like these. Even Appel admits, in a 1974 article, that critics 'who stress Nabokov's artifice at the expense of the more traditional components of his novels' misrepresent works like *Lolita* ('The Road to *Lolita*, or The Americanization of an Émigré', *Journal of Modern Literature*, no. 4 (1974), p. 3). Merrill takes up point by point Appel's argument about *Lolita*'s 'involution', in 'Nabokov and Fictional Artifice', pp. 446–54.

5 *Crystal Land*, pp. 67, 79–80.

6 'The Tantalization of *Lolita*', *Studies in the Novel*, 11 (1979), p. 339.

7 *Nabokov*, p. 113.

8 Robert M. Ryley, 'Will Brown, Dolores, Colo.', *VNRN*, no. 3 (Fall 1979), p. 30.

9 Priscilla Mayer, Abstract of 'Nabokov's *Lolita* and Pushkin's *Onegin*: A Colloquy of Muses', *VNRN*, no. 7 (Fall 1981), p. 33. Allusions and parallels in *Lolita* tend to be worked fairly hard. 'A breeze from wonderland' (p. 133) and 'combing her Alice-in-Wonderland hair' (p. 266) are enough to make one critic search out all the possible links between Nabokov's book and Carroll's. The results are often unconvincing: 'Another plot similarity is the possible identification of Humbert with Humpty Dumpty and the White Knight, the former representing Humbert the Terrible; the latter, Humbert the Humble. Not only is Humpty Dumpty's name an echo of Humbert's, but he is a literary critic, an *isolato*, cultivated, and doomed to fall ... Significantly too, Humpty Dumpty asserts a subjective view of semantics. Words mean what he wants them to, and when Humbert tells Lolita that he is "her father" (*Lolita*, p. 152) he likewise reshapes language to his own private ends' (Elizabeth Prioleau, 'Humbert Humbert Through the Looking Glass', *Twentieth Century Literature*, 21 (1975), p. 435).

10 See, for example, J. C. M. Barnes, '*Lolita* – Technically Pornographic', *Books and Bookmen*, 4, Mar. 1959, p. 3; and C. K. Davis, '*Lolita*', *Books and Bookmen*, 4, Apr. 1959, p. 3. The year that everybody in England was talking about *Lolita*, 1959, the Olympia Press brought out William Burroughs's *The Naked Lunch*. Of particular interest is a sequence from a blue movie in which three characters take turns hanging each other as a means of sexual stimulation, with some spectacular and gruesome results. With books like this being published, all the definitions of 'pornography' and 'serious literature' would soon have to be rewritten.

11 *Letters*, p. 172. In a 1959 interview, Nabokov is quoted as saying that 'there should certainly be some forms of censorship, against commercial pornography' (Interview conducted by John Coleman, *Spectator*, 6 Nov. 1959, p. 619).

12 Quoted in Ross Wetzeon, 'Nabokov as Teacher', in *Nabokov*, ed. Appel and Newman, p. 243.

13 The references to Joyce are from Appel's own lecture notes at Cornell, quoted in *The Annotated Lolita*, p. lv.

14 *Lady Chatterley's Lover* (London: William Heinemann, 1961), p. 266.

15 *Ulysses* (London: The Bodley Head, 1960), p. 477.

16 *LL*, p. 287.

17 'Partial Magic in the *Quixote*', in *Labyrinths*, ed. James Irby, who is also the translator of this particular essay (Harmondsworth: Penguin Books, 1970), p. 231.

18 There exists a link between what has happened in Nabokov criticism and some positions taken by recent critical theorists. Compare, for example, the views expressed here about the content of *Lolita* with those of Roland Barthes on de Sade's novels (*Sade, Fourier, Loyola* (Paris: Éditions du Seuil, 1971)): 'La grandeur de Sade n'est pas d'avoir célébré le crime, la perversion, ni d'avoir employé pour cette célébration un langage radical; c'est d'avoir inventé un discours immense, fondé sur ses propres répétitions (et non sur celles des autres)' (p. 130). The content of his novels is dispensable: 'Le sadisme ne serait que le *contenu* grossier (vulgaire) du texte sadien' (p. 174). They instruct us, not in the arts of cruelty and degradation, but in the elements of a 'Sadian Grammar': 'il ne s'agit pas d'opérer ce qui a été représenté, il ne s'agit pas de devenir sadique ou orgiaque avec Sade . . .; il s'agit de faire passer dans notre quotidienneté des fragments d'intelligible (des "formules") issus du texte admiré (admiré précisément parce qu'il essaime bien); il s'agit de parler ce texte, non de l'agir, en lui laissant la distance d'une citation, la force d'irruption d'un mot frappé, d'une vérité de langage' (pp. 12–13).

But Barthes is not content with the breathtaking audacity of this purest of formalisms. Properly decoded, Sade turns out to have a content after all: 'Les aventures sadiennes ne sont pas fabuleuses: elles se passent dans un monde réel, contemporain de la jeunesse de Sade, à savoir la société de Louis XV' (p. 134). What seems like wild debauchery is actually moral allegory; and Sade is a social critic, more realistic than Balzac, because in Sade's group of libertines the salient features of class structure, that collection of exploiters and exploited, are reproduced more faithfully: 'cette société est construite comme une maquette, une miniature; Sade y *transporte* la division de classe; d'un côté les exploitants, les possédants, les gouvernants, les tyrans; de l'autre le *petit peuple*' (p. 135).

When carried out with Barthes's distinctive *brio*, this kind of criticism, even when it leaves us unconvinced, can revitalize any text. In less capable hands, it often seems a sterile exercise, and inevitably creates uneasy feelings about the implications of insisting that words don't really mean what they say. Then there are all those readers who actually enjoy taking their Sade straight. The Quilty who makes 'private movies out of *Justine* and other eighteenth-century sexcapades' (p. 300) may be reading his master less imaginatively than someone like Barthes, but it is this kind of reading that Sade would have wholeheartedly approved of. In rehabilitating an author like him, literary critics indirectly encourage the Quilty approach, because they have surrendered the right to pass aesthetic or moral judgment on what is, in its raw, untreated state, pretty wretched stuff.

19 'The Last Lover', p. 19.

20 'She Was a Child and I Was a Child', *Spectator*, 6 Nov. 1959, pp. 635–6.

21 I am indebted here to some comments made by Gabriel Josipovici on an earlier draft of this chapter.

22 *Men Without Art* (London: Cassell, 1934), pp. 175–6.

23 In a chapter devoted to Nabokov in a book called *Autobiographical Acts* (Baltimore: Johns Hopkins Univ. Press, 1976), Elizabeth Bruss points out that Humbert's description of himself as 'an exceptionally handsome male; slow-moving, tall, with soft dark hair and a gloomy but all the more seductive cast of demeanour' (p. 27) is Nabokov's way of having some fun at the expense of his conceited hero, and of mocking the whole notion that a first person narrator can be objective about himself. Yet this hardly justifies her conclusion that Humbert's attractiveness is as bogus as the stereotypes he models himself on (pp. 129–30), for simply by humorously acknowledging the hackneyed quality of his physical attributes he gives them a new status: 'Of course', he says, 'such announcements made in the first person may sound ridiculous. But every once in a while I have to remind my reader of my appearance much as a professional novelist, who has given a character of his some mannerism or a dog, has to go on producing that dog or that mannerism every time the character crops up in the course of the book' (p. 106). The immense appeal Humbert has for Lolita initially, his quite extraordinary hold on Charlotte, even the funny sad quick kiss in the hallway with Jean Farlow – without his singular attractiveness none of these makes sense.

24 For a discussion of the role of the 'superfluous man' in Nabokov, see Hyde, *Nabokov*, pp. 99–100. For a detailed exploration of Dostoevsky's influence on him, see Melvin Seiden, 'Nabokov and Dostoevsky', *Contemporary Literature*, 13 (1972), pp. 423–44.

25 *Notes From Underground [and] The Double*, trans. Jessie Coulson (Harmondsworth: Penguin Books, 1972), p. 114.

26 *Selected Writings of Edgar Allan Poe*, ed. David Galloway (Harmondsworth: Penguin Books, 1967), p. 138.

27 *Collected Poems, 1909–1962* (London: Faber and Faber, 1963), p. 98.

28 The literature on parody in *Lolita* is extensive, but its development has not fulfilled the expectations raised by those who first alerted readers to this aspect of Nabokov's fiction. Once the most exciting subject in Nabokov criticism, it now consists of ingenious but somewhat far-fetched attempts to add candidates to the list of novels that *Lolita* parodies. See, for example, Adam Gillon, 'Conrad's *Victory* and Nabokov's *Lolita*: Imitations of Imitations', *Conradiana*, 12 (1980),

pp. 51–71; or Richard Pearce, 'Nabokov's Black (Hole) Humor: *Lolita*
and *Pale Fire*', in *Comic Relief*, ed. Sarah Blacher Cohen (Urbana:
Univ. of Illinois Press, 1978), pp. 28–44, who claims that *Lolita* is a
parody of *Moby Dick*: 'If, on first thought, Humbert's nymphet
(especially as she is likened to a butterfly) makes an improbable white
whale, and the Humbert-Quilty double is a far cry from Ishmael-Ahab,
ponder a layer lower, reader – at least upon Humbert's historical,
anthropological, and scientific digressions, which realistically ground
and epically magnify the proportions of his nymphet and his quest'
(p. 33).

29 'The Tantalization of *Lolita*', p. 340.

30 'The Art of Persuasion in *Lolita*', *Poetics Today*, 1, parts 1–2 (1979),
p. 82.

31 There are relatively few dramatic scenes in the novel. It is interesting to
see what happens in *Lolita: A Screenplay* (New York: McGraw-Hill,
1974), written for the Kubrick film but mostly ignored by the director,
when Nabokov finds himself obliged to substitute such scenes for
Humbert's narration. In *Lolita*, he can take a comparatively unimportant event, like Humbert's discovery, just before she escapes from him,
that Lolita is ill, and have his hero report it in a way that conveys all of
his solicitousness and cruelty and sick desire in the space of a page or
two. Nabokov uses it to teach us something about human nature. The
same event in the dramatized version is reduced to stuff like this: 'My
poor darling! What a setback. Tsk-tsk. I know what we'll do. At the
next turnout I'll take your temperature. I have a thermometer in my
overnight bag ... [He takes it.] Ah, here we are. Good God, one
hundred and three. I must take you straight to a hospital' (pp. 177–8).
Crude attempts to flaunt the artifice of the fiction threaten to turn this
version of *Lolita* into a rather trivial authorial game. The delicate
balance between the comic and the serious in Humbert's last, desperate
attempt to keep Lolita by setting off on another journey is gone,
replaced by the bathos of self-referential slapstick. Quilty phones
Humbert and hints that he knows all about him, prompting the following exchange:

> Humbert: It's a hoax. It's a hoax. But that's immaterial. Rumors, he
> said. Oh, *mon Dieu!*
> Lolita: We must go away.
> Humbert: We must flee as in an old melodrama. Our safest bet is to go
> abroad.
> Lolita: Okay – let's go to Mexico. I was conceived there.
> Humbert: I'm sure I'll find a lecturing job there. Marvelous! I know a
> Spanish poet in Mexico City. He is full of black bulls and symbols,
> and as corny as a matador. But he is influential. (p. 168)

To stock Humbert's meditations with the author's *bêtes noires*, to
remake *Lolita* into 'late Nabokov' in this way, and to do it with dialogue
as feeble as this, seems unworthy of a great novelist. In the original,

Humbert's gibes at Freudianism make sense; they are a plausible part of his strange psychological make-up. In *Lolita: A Screenplay*, they are gratuitous. Here he is dictating one of his 'Baudelaire and Poe' lectures: 'Other commentators, commentators of the Freudian school of thought. No. Commentators of the Freudian prison of thought. Hm. Commentators of the Freudian nursery-school of thought . . .' etc. (pp. 70–1). It was not a question of Nabokov's lacking talent as a dramatist. It was just that this serious comic novel refused to be turned into a foolish play, refused to live when deprived of Humbert's crucial narrative voice. The attempt to assert dictatorial control over his aesthetic object failed, and the real *Lolita* slipped away from him. Perhaps this should be seen as encouraging.

32 '*Lolita*: The Springboard of Parody', in *Nabokov*, ed. Dembo, p. 128.

33 Not everyone would agree with this reading. Douglas Fowler argues that the fact that Lolita dismisses her romance with Humbert as if it were 'a bit of dry mud caking her childhood' (p. 274) proves that 'the brainless and lobotomized triumph through sheer indifference' (*Reading Nabokov*, p. 164); and Jonathan Raban says of the scene: 'Humbert sees his masterpiece, his Lolita, transformed into a surburban slut called Mrs Richard F. Schiller' ('Transparent Likenesses: New Novels', review of *Transparent Things*, *Encounter*, 41, Sept. 1973, p. 74).

34 In a 1964 interview that is not often quoted, Nabokov said: 'I don't think *Lolita* is a religious book, but I do think it is a moral one. And I do think that Humbert Humbert in his last stage is a moral man because he realizes that he loves *Lolita* [italicized in the text of the interview] like any woman should be loved. But it is too late, he has destroyed her childhood. There is certainly this kind of morality in it' (Interview conducted by Douglas M. Davis, *The National Observer*, 29 June 1964, p. 17).

35 Interview conducted by Garnham, included in *SO*, p. 115.

36 'The Morality of *Lolita*', *Kenyon Review*, 28 (1966), pp. 363–4.

37 Interview conducted by Duval-Smith, included in *SO*, p. 16.

38 Michael Bell remarks on this in '*Lolita* and Pure Art', p. 182. My argument in this section owes a great deal to this article.

39 '*Lolita* and Pure Art', p. 182.

40 *Letters*, pp. 285, 296.

41 'Partial Magic in the *Quixote*', p. 70.

42 'Up From Ultraism', trans. Norman Thomas di Giovanni in collaboration with the author, *NYRB*, 15, 13 Aug. 1970, p. 3.

5. *Ada*

1 I am of course indebted to all those critics who have helped to shed some light on the novel's daunting obscurities and have written so insightfully about it. Of particular importance are: Appel, '*Ada* Des-

cribed', in *Nabokov*, ed. Appel and Newman, pp. 160–86; D. Barton Johnson, 'Nabokov's *Ada* and Puškin's *Eugene Onegin*', *SEEJ*, NS 15 (1971), pp. 316–23; Karlinsky, 'Nabokov's Russian Games', *NYTBR*, 8 Apr. 1971, pp. 2, 10, 12, 14, 16, 18; Proffer, '*Ada* as Wonderland: A Glossary of Allusions to Russian Literature', in *Things About Nabokov*, ed. Proffer, pp. 249–79; and Brian Boyd, 'Nabokov and *Ada*', unpublished dissertation, Univ. of Toronto, 1979. Nabokov's own helpful 'Notes to *Ada*' (by 'Vivian Darkbloom') are appended to the Penguin edition of the novel (1971), pp. 463–77.

The most significant exception to the general emphasis on formal matters is the chapter on *Ada* in Douglas Fowler's *Reading Nabokov*; I have tried to indicate in the notes just where he has anticipated what I have to say. He describes the novel as 'naked Nabokoviana' (p. 188), and argues that 'all mimetic and dramatic interest in *Ada* has been sacrificed' (p. 186), and that, with a few minor exceptions, 'The situations in the novel are not convincing, and neither are the characters' (p. 186). This kind of overstatement illustrates the dangers of using an arbitrary set of criteria to judge the book. I have tried to judge *Ada* by the standards Nabokov set himself.

2 Carol Johnson, 'Nabokov's *Ada*: Word's End', review of *Ada*, *Art International*, 13 Oct. 1969, p. 42.

3 Alfred Kazin, 'In the Mind of Nabokov', review of *Ada*, *Saturday Review*, 10 May 1969, p. 28.

4 Elizabeth Dalton, '*Ada* or Nada', review of *Ada*, *Partisan Review*, 37 (1970), p. 155.

5 'Prospero's Progress', *Time*, 23 May 1969, p. 82.

6 'Nabokov's Waterloo', review of *Ada*, *TLS*, 2 Oct. 1969, p. 1121.

7 Interview conducted by Appel, included in *SO*, p. 91.

8 *Ada, or Ardor: A Family Chronicle* (London: Weidenfeld and Nicolson, 1969), p. 75. All subsequent references are to this edition and will be included in the text.

9 'Ode on a Grecian Urn', *Keats: Poetical Works*, 2nd edn, ed. H. W. Garrod (London: Oxford Univ. Press, 1958), pp. 260–2.

10 'We Need One Another', in *Phoenix*, ed. Edward McDonald (London: William Heinemann, 1936), p. 193.

11 Some reviewers complained about this aspect of *Ada*: see, for example, Morris Dickstein, 'Nabokov's Folly', *The New Republic*, 160, 28 June 1969, p. 28; and D. J. Enright, 'Pun-Up', *The Listener*, 82, 2 Oct. 1969, p. 457. It is also discussed by Fowler, *Reading Nabokov*, pp. 178–9.

12 *Nabokov Translated*, pp. 115–16.

13 *Nabokov and the Novel*, pp. 150–1.

14 Cf. Donald Morton: 'As in *Lolita*, a similar but even higher miracle of art occurs in *Ada*, for Nabokov makes the reader forego his repugnance toward incest and "not care" also. How Nabokov manages this feat is one of the book's most interesting aspects' (*Nabokov*, p. 132).

15 See Appel, 'Ada Described', p. 162; Alex de Jonge, 'Figuring Out Nabokov', *TLS*, 16 May 1975, p. 526; and Couturier, *Nabokov*, p. 40.

16 'Extraterritorial', in *Nabokov*, ed. Appel and Newman, p. 124.

17 'Nabokov's *Ada* as Science Fiction', *Science Fiction Studies*, 2 (1975), p. 78.

18 'Van Loves Ada, Ada Loves Van', review of *Ada*, *The New Yorker*, 2 Aug. 1969, p. 72. Other possibilities: '[Incest] symbolizes … the relation between the scientific and artistic parts of Nabokov's sensibility' (Stark, *Literature of Exhaustion*, p. 105); and: 'In Nabokov's Eden, the act of incest embodies that creative principle of inbreeding which nurtures both nature and art' (Pifer, *Nabokov and the Novel*, p. 147).

19 It is interesting to note that Aquinas disapproved of incest because he thought that 'if the love of husband and wife were combined with that of brother and sister, mutual attraction would be so strong as to cause unduly frequent intercourse' (Bertrand Russell, *History of Western Philosophy* (London: George Allen and Unwin, 1961), p. 451).

20 Many readers find the novel too long. Nabokov says in one of his recently published lectures: 'A publisher once remarked to me that every writer had somewhere in him a certain numeral engraved, the exact number of pages which is the limit of any one book he would ever write. My number, I remember, was 385' (*LRL*, p. 251).

21 *Nabokov*, p. 199.

22 *Figures III* (Paris: Éditions du Seuil, 1972), p. 185.

23 Jonathan Culler uses this phrase in summarizing a structuralist approach to character in the modern novel. See his *Structuralist Poetics* (London: Routledge and Kegan Paul, 1975), p. 231. This book has been very useful to me.

24 Dickstein, 'Nabokov's Folly', p. 27.

25 See Proffer, '*Ada* as Wonderland', p. 268, for a short list of Russian authors who have used a duel in their fiction. Fowler accuses Nabokov of having 'skimmed the fantasies from his own adolescence' here, and insists that the duel 'is not meant as a parody, since it has no comic, and hence anticlimactic, twist. It is played straight, and the humor is, alas, unintentional' (*Reading Nabokov*, pp. 180–1).

26 *Style* (New Haven, Conn.: Yale Univ. Press, 1974), p. 62.

27 Richard Patteson, 'The Viewer and the View: Perception and Narration in Nabokov's English Novels', unpublished dissertation, Univ. of Pennsylvania, 1975, p. 207.

28 See Laurence Lerner, *Love and Marriage* (London: Edward Arnold, 1979), p. 34.

29 Nabokov points out the resemblance (*LRL*, p. 103), but he doesn't think Dostoevsky represents much of an advance.

30 *Sémantique Structurale* (Paris: Librairie Larousse, 1966), p. 176.

31 In the Preface to *Anthologie de l'Humour Noir* (Paris: Jean-Jacques Pauvert, 1966), p. 21.
32 *Structuralist Poetics*, p. 159.
33 Appel, '*Ada* Described', p. 181.
34 Bobbie Ann Mason, *Nabokov's Garden* (Ann Arbor, Mich.: Ardis, 1974), p. 113.
35 '*Ada* Described', pp. 171, 172. Daniel Albright argues that 'All great novels try, in a sense, to sum up and terminate the genre of the novel, but the claims of *Ada* are better than those of many' (*Representation and the Imagination* (Chicago: Univ. of Chicago Press, 1981), p. 76).
36 *LL*, p. 4.
37 But D. Barton Johnson, in '*Ada* and *Eugene Onegin*', does make a convincing case for seeing two stanzas (3: 13, 14) of Pushkin's poem as a source for Nabokov's novel. The general point is that the reader soon realizes that deciphering Ada's allusions is usually its own reward, that there is no 'meaning' waiting at the other end to clear everything up, no context that profoundly enriches the novel. Lermontov's 'Demon' doesn't really explain Nabokov's. Both like young girls, but that is all they have in common. The one from Antiterra is only a dingy old satyr compared to Lermontov's splendid Hyperion. 'Zhivago' becomes 'Mertvago' several times in *Ada*, but no one's perception of Pasternak's novel or of Nabokov's seems to have been seriously affected. And those who go to *Childhood, Boyhood, and Youth* believing that, as one critic has it, Part I of *Ada* is Nabokov's 'completion of Tolstoy's reminiscences' (Appel, '*Ada* Described', p. 170) will find that Tolstoy is not 'pre-Nabokov' in quite the way that this remark suggests. I should add that many critics would disagree about the importance of the allusions, e.g., Sissela Bok: 'The literary references ... seem to tie the work to major poetical traditions, to provide depth and resonance, and increased wealth of shading, and perspective' ('Redemption Through Art in Nabokov's *Ada*', *Critique*, 12 (1971), p. 118).
38 I have drawn here on Culler's discussion of parody in *Structuralist Poetics*, pp. 152–4.
39 'Victorian Modernists: Fowles and Nabokov', *Journal of Narrative Technique*, 3 (1973), p. 108.
40 *Ibid.*, p. 116.
41 I am not sure that the nineteenth-century novel is the main object of Nabokov's parody. When Robert Alter suggests that in *Ada* the plot is 'from one point of view comprised of a string of stock scenes from the traditional novel – the young man's return to the ancestral manor, the festive picnic, the formal dinner, a midnight blaze on the old estate, the distraught hero's flight at dawn from hearth and home as the result of a misunderstanding, the duel, the hero's profligacy in the great metropolis, and so forth' ('Nabokov's Ardor', review of *Ada*, *Commentary*, 48, Aug. 1969, p. 48), he alerts us to the fact that the object of *Ada*'s parodic plot is often the romance of popular fiction. Nabokov's extrav-

agant, voluptuous emotional excesses are modelled, not on something
in George Eliot or Stendhal or Tolstoy, but on the fictional forms that
have always appealed to a large public, from the 'penny dreadful' to the
modern soap opera. Nabokov himself suggests this in *Ada* when he
writes: 'What constricted his heart? Why did he pass his tongue over his
thick lips? Empty formulas befitting the solemn novelists of former days
who thought they could explain everything' (p. 475). The rhetorical
questions and melodramatic double-takes suggest that when Nabokov
says 'novel' here he has certain kinds of popular romance in mind.

42 Couturier, *Nabokov*, p. 47.
43 *Le Plaisir du Texte* (Paris: Éditions du Seuil, 1973), p. 102.
44 *S/Z* (Paris: Éditions du Seuil, 1970), p. 146.
45 Figure borrowed from the Preface to Northrop Frye's *The Critical Path*
    (Bloomington: Indiana Univ. Press, 1971), p. 7. Critics continue to
    deny that Nabokov's novels are full of his ideas, e.g., Charles Ross:
    'Although there are pleasures to reading *Speak, Memory* in conjunction
    with Nabokov's novels, the final effect of Nabokov's interviews from
    the 1960s and 1970s collected in *Strong Opinions* and Andrew Field's
    biography *Nabokov: His Life in Part* is to forever divorce the man from
    his work, despite the similarity between the artist's hyperbole . . . and
    the private man's polemics' ('An Editor's Preface', *MFS*, 25 (1979),
    p. 393); or they maintain that these ideas are inaccessible, e.g., Coutur-
    ier: 'Sachant pertinemment qu'il ne pourra jamais écrire une écriture
    entièrement "aphone", a-discursive, il s'ingénie de manière quasi per-
    verse à multipler [sic] les voix, à les superposer, et nous rend incapable
    de les identifier, de les débrouiller' (*Nabokov*, pp. 23–4).
46 The year *Ada* was published, 1969, Nabokov answered an interviewer's
    question about his idea of time by quoting Van Veen, adding: 'I have
    not decided yet if I agree with him in all his views on the texture of time.
    I suspect I don't.' Two years later he said: 'My conception of the texture
    of time somewhat resembles its image in Part Four of *Ada*.' In yet
    another 1971 interview, he made no distinction between his views and
    those of his character, and talked at some length about time, using
    Van Veen's ideas and vocabulary (Interviews conducted by James
    Mossman, Paul Sufrin, and Kurt Hoffman, included in *SO*, pp. 143,
    184, 185–6).
47 *Nikolay Gogol*, p. 145. Physicists see the relation of the two men rather
    differently. Max Born describes Einstein's 'indebtedness' this way:
    'Since Euclidean geometry failed, Einstein could have fallen back on
    some other definite non-Euclidean geometry. There are systems of this
    sort worked out by Lobatschweski (1829) [he mentions others] . . . If we
    would choose a special non-Euclidean geometry of this kind to repre-
    sent the physical world we would simply be substituting one evil for
    another. Einstein went back to the physical phenomena, namely, the
    concept of space-time coincidence or the event represented by a world
    point' (*Einstein's Theory of Relativity*, rev. edn prepared with the

collaboration of Gunther Liebfried and Walter Biem (New York: Dover Publications, 1962), p. 334).

48 I have borrowed here from the account of the special theory of relativity in George Abell's *Exploration of the Universe*, 3rd. edn (New York: Holt, Rinehart and Winston, 1975), pp. 186–90. Nabokov would not have been impressed by this kind of evidence. He once said: 'While not having much physics, I reject Einstein's slick formulae; but then one need not know theology to be an atheist' (Interview conducted by Garnham, included in *SO*, p. 116). Douglas Fowler was the first to point out the weakness of Nabokov's case against the new physics. He says that it shows 'how powerfully Nabokov desires to dismiss from *his* world everything that is esthetically inadmissible' (*Reading Nabokov*, p. 200).

49 *Life in Part*, p. 87.

50 E.g., Field, *Life in Art*, pp. 264–5.

51 *The Genesis of Secrecy* (Cambridge, Mass.: Harvard Univ. Press, 1979), p. 144.

52 Nabokov's gibes at Freud are perhaps responsible for some of the ersatz psychoanalysis he has been subjected to on the basis of *Ada*: 'Nabokov's work eliminates *mind* and seems almost willffully [*sic*] dumb. His introjected authoritarian knowledge screens ideas with allusion, meaning with synonym, poetic relationship with anecdotal reference. One wants to say, how lucky to have had a loving mother permit all those words! But those words don't tell all and aren't usable for fucking mother with. [new paragraph] They are usable for creating culture with, love and beauty with embarrasing [*sic*] balls, Aphrodite affirmed but also defaced: the image of the boy running around Europe in search of his penis seems to be funny, I doubt whether Nabokov finds it funny' (Jerald Zaslove, 'Nabokov in Context', *Recovering Literature*, vol. 1, no. 3 (1972), p. 25).

53 *Boswell's Life of Johnson*, 6 vols., ed. George Birbeck Hill and L. F. Powell (Oxford: Clarendon Press, 1934), vol. III, p. 305.

54 'Frank Kermode's *The Sense of an Ending*', *Critical Quarterly*, 16 (1974), p. 313.

55 A similar passage appears in an interview conducted by Gold, included in *SO*, p. 101.

56 Appel points this out in '*Ada* Described', p. 185n.

57 Critics who have tried to rationalize Nabokov's peremptory dismissals of all sorts of novelists have not had much success. Stendhal, Balzac, Céline, Sartre, Aksakov, Goncharov, Leskov, Saltykov, Dostoevsky, Gorky, Pasternak, Mann, George Eliot, Conrad, Lawrence, James, Dreiser, Faulkner – the heterogeneous nature of this list suggests what a difficult task is in store for anyone who tries to explain what distinguishes these writers from the ones Nabokov approves of. Simon Karlinsky argues that 'Nabokov invariably finds uncongenial those writers who subjugate themselves to the prevalent normative poetics of

their age . . .; writers who rely too much on readymade conventions and formulae (as Stendhal and Conrad did, to his way of thinking); or those who strive for effects which are emotional rather than artistic (such as Dostoevsky and Faulkner)' (Introduction to the *Letters*, pp. 16–17). I think the examples sit rather uneasily in the parentheses.

58 Interview conducted by Duval-Smith, included in *SO*, p. 18.

6. *Pale Fire*, *Transparent Things*, and *Look at the Harlequins!*

1 *The Genesis of Secrecy*, p. 126.
2 'Reading Criticism', *PMLA*, 91 (1976), p. 804.
3 Robert Alter, *Partial Magic* (Berkeley: Univ. of California Press, 1975), p. 186.
4 'Vladimir Nabokov's *Pale Fire*', *Encounter*, 19, Oct. 1962, pp. 71, 81.
5 *Partial Magic*, p. 190.
6 Interview conducted by Garnham, included in *SO*, p. 119.
7 'Remembering Nabokov', in *Nabokov*, ed. Quennell, p. 24.
8 *Pale Fire* (London: Weidenfeld and Nicolson, 1962), pp. 42–3. All subsequent references are to this edition and will be included in the text.
9 *Life in Art*, p. 320.
10 *Crystal Land*, p. 37.
11 *Life in Art*, pp. 321–2.
12 *Partial Magic*, pp. 214–15.
13 *The Annotated Lolita*, p. 111.
14 *The Literature of Exhaustion*, p. 69.
15 If we take a look at *Solus Rex*, a fragment often referred to as a prototype for *Pale Fire* (see, for example, Field, *Life in Art*, pp. 292–7; and Nina Berberova, 'The Mechanics of *Pale Fire*', in *Nabokov*, ed. Appel and Newman, especially pp. 155–9), we can see Nabokov struggling with the same kind of problem. There he tries to keep everything – nonsense, satire, and mimesis – and succeeds with none of them. The court scenes in this distant northern land are too bound up with the real to become pure romantic absurdity; the royal decadence and the political machinations are too silly to have any genuine satiric bite. He wants to overlap his narratives, to join this story with the encounter between Sineusov and Falter in 'Ultima Thule', subordinating dramatic suspense to something else, but he has not yet found what that something else might be. The hybrid that results is surprisingly aimless for Nabokov. He tries to proceed without using his hero's obsession to organize events (the protagonist, K., is just a nonentity in exile) but he cannot find an alternative, and probably abandoned the novel, his last attempt to write fiction in Russian, as a result.
16 *Representation and the Imagination*, p. 85. The chapter on Nabokov in this book is brilliant. Field sees the novel's aesthetic allegory differently: 'In the relationship between John Shade and Charles Kinbote, Nabokov has given us the best and truest allegorical portrait of "the

literary process" that we have or are likely ever to get, and the Shade-Kinbote relationship also happens to be a completely fictional but very apt paradigm of Nabokov's relationship to his own various fictional worlds' (*Life in Art*, pp. 316–17).

17 *Partial Magic*, p. 215.

18 I have borrowed here from A. D. Nuttall's discussion of *Tristram Shandy* in *A Common Sky* (London: Chatto and Windus for Sussex Univ. Press, 1974), pp. 53–4.

19 Cedric Watts pointed this out to me in conversation.

20 'An Essay on Man', *The Poems of Alexander Pope*, ed. John Butt (London: Methuen, 1963), p. 515. For discussions of the relations between Nabokov's novel and Pope's poem see McCarthy, '*Pale Fire*', p. 74; John O. Lyons, '*Pale Fire* and the Fine Art of Annotation', in *Nabokov*, ed. Dembo, pp. 157–64; and Merrill, 'Nabokov and Fictional Artifice', *MFS*, 25 (1979), pp. 459–60. Merrill (p. 461) makes the point about Nabokov's undercutting Shade's affirmation.

21 There is a parallel here with the argument of the Russian critics who celebrated Gogol as a realist who created nightmare worlds because the Russia of his time was a nightmare world.

22 Jacques Ehrmann, '*Homo Ludens* Revisited', *Yale French Studies*, no. 41 (1968), p. 55. For a detailed discussion of these questions see Richard Lanham, 'Games, Play, Seriousness', '*Tristram Shandy*' (Berkeley: Univ. of California Press, 1973), pp. 37–51, to which I am indebted here.

23 E.g., Robert Martin Adams: '*Pale Fire* no more affirms or denies anything, including the potentiality of its own cosmos, than does the *Wake* – it is simply an achieved book' (*Afterjoyce* (New York: Oxford Univ. Press, 1977), p. 156).

24 Alex de Jonge suggests a plausible intermediate position here: 'Nabokov is both delicate and tentative in his presentation of pattern. Moreover, he is a novelist, not a metaphysician; and it is an essential characteristic of novels that they question and challenge the propositions they advance through irony and ambiguity. The very fact that he makes such ample use of flawed or deranged characters suggests that the insights they arrive at are open to question. Perhaps, rather than affirm through his fictions that the world is ordered and patterned, he interrogates it in the hope that it might be' (Nabokov's Uses of Pattern', in *Nabokov*, ed. Quennell, p. 68).

25 See his *Understanding Media* (London: Routledge and Kegan Paul, 1964), pp. 33–40.

26 For example, Strother Purdy: 'This study is so detailed, brings out identifications buried so deep in the narrative, appeared so soon after publication of the novel, and worked such an effective puff for it, that it looks like a plant. Until it is proved to be otherwise, I intend to take it as commentary, and explanation, from the source' ('*Solus Rex*: Nabokov and the Chess Novel', *MFS*, 14 (1968), p. 391n).

Several people have asked me if Alfred Appel is Nabokov's invention.
27 '*Pale Fire*', p. 71.
28 *Life in Art*, p. 315.
29 Bader, *Crystal Land*, p. 34.
30 Hyde, *Nabokov*, p. 174.
31 Philip R. Hughes, 'The Knight Moves of the Mind: Nabokov's Use of Illusion to Transcend the Limits of Life and Art', unpublished dissertation, Boston Univ., 1974, p. 68n.
32 Joseph M. Nassar, 'The Russian in Nabokov's English Novels', unpublished dissertation, State Univ. of New York, 1977, pp. 95, 97.
33 For some discussions of this question, see Lyons, '*Pale Fire*', and Clarence Brown, 'Nabokov's Pushkin and Nabokov's Nabokov', in *Nabokov*, ed. Dembo, pp. 157–64, 195–208; and Anthony Burgess, 'Pushkin and Kinbote', review of *Eugene Onegin, Encounter*, 24, May 1965, pp. 74–8.
34 *Eugene Onegin*, vol. III, p. 177. The following remarks are also relevant: 'What is History? Dreams and dust. How many ways are there for a novelist of dealing with history? Only three. He can court the elusive Muse of verisimilitude by doing his best to unearth and combine all pertinent facts and details; he can frankly indulge in farce or satire by treating the past as a parody of the present; and he can transcend all aspects of time by entrusting a mummy selected at random to the sole care of his genius – provided he has genius' ('Mr Masefield and Clio', *The New Republic*, 9 Dec. 1940, p. 808).
35 *Eugene Onegin*, vol. III, p. 178.
36 *The Annotated Lolita*, p. 39.
37 *Transparent Things* (London: Weidenfeld and Nicolson, 1973), p. 39. All references are to this edition and will be included in the text.
38 See, for example, Jonathan Raban, 'Transparent Likenesses: New Novels', *Encounter*, 41, Sept. 1973, p. 76.
39 *Theory of Fiction: Henry James*, ed. James Miller, Jr (Lincoln: Univ. of Nebraska Press, 1972), p. 219.
40 *Nabokov*, p. 205.
41 Interview conducted by Gold, included in *SO*, p. 95.
42 Interview conducted by Appel, included in *SO*, p. 69.
43 *The Letters of Philip Dormer Stanhope, 4th Earl of Chesterfield*, 6 vols., ed. Bonamy Dobrée (London: Eyre and Spottiswoode, 1932), vol. IV, p. 1209.
44 Nabokov enjoys this kind of lexical deflection. In another passage, Hugh, reading proof, trips over 'balanic', a word that stumps him and no doubt sends most readers to the dictionary, where they find 'of or relating to the glans of the penis or of the clitoris' (*Webster's Third*). Then comes a reference to a 'nebris', a fawnskin worn by Dionysus, then one to the 'Reign of Cnut', with a coy suggestion that the letters of the last word should be transposed (p. 75). Fragments of a stimulating orgy we never get to read about? Perhaps: but whatever the desired

effect, the immediate one is puzzlement. Like a collection of naughty puns in Esperanto, these oblique references don't justify the search they occasion.

45 The same deliberate trivialization is used for Armande's death scene: 'What a fall! What a silly Julia! What luck that Mr Romeo still gripped and twisted and cracked that crooked cricoid as X-rayed by the firemen and mountain guides in the street. How they flew! Superman carrying a young soul in his embrace!' (p. 81). The humour here does not exist alongside the horror, it pre-empts it altogether. Appel notes that death is everywhere in the novel, and that 'Only authorial comedy can transfigure and transcend all the dread in Nabokov's gay "pocket requiem" ' (*Nabokov's Dark Cinema*, p. 298). He may be right, but there is no more dread in this crucial scene than there is metaphysical anguish in *The Two Ronnies*. Nabokov now sees all the old themes as a little bit silly.

46 Unpublished interview, included in *SO*, pp. 194, 196.

47 'Long Novels and Short Stories', review of *Transparent Things*, *The Hudson Review*, 26 (1973–4), p. 228.

48 Robert Alter, 'Mirrors For Immortality', review of *Transparent Things*, *Saturday Review*, 11 Nov. 1972, p. 74.

49 Michael Rosenblum, 'Finding What the Sailor Has Hidden: Narrative as Patternmaking in *Transparent Things*', *Contemporary Literature*, 19 (1978), p. 231.

50 Unpublished interview, included in *SO*, p. 195. Hyde has some perceptive things to say about *Transparent Things* as a portrait of the ageing author (*Nabokov*, pp. 201–6).

51 Dimitri Nabokov claims that his father's 'openness to and trust of others, a goodness bordering sometimes on ingenuousness', allowed 'certain scoundrels' to get close to him: 'How funny – and how wretched – the grudging concession of a recent biographer: "He is, I reckon, a good man, oh, in a peculiar way perhaps, and with certain lapses, but a good man none the less." . . . I shall, however, follow Father's example and not pursue polemics with the unworthy. It is far better to let lying dogs sleep' ('On Revisiting Father's Room', in *Nabokov*, ed. Quennell, pp. 128–9). This response conveys that streak of fierce protectiveness which runs in the family. The portrayal of Nabokov in Field's book is on the whole very sympathetic.

52 *Charles Dickens* (London: Methuen, 1906), p. 66.

53 *Figures III*, p. 109. Christine Brooke-Rose has written an excellent essay using Genette's structural analyses to help explain the *nouveau nouveau roman*, 'Transgressions: An Essay-Say on the Novel Novel Novel', *Contemporary Literature*, 19 (1978), pp. 378–407, to which I am indebted here.

54 *Figures III*, p. 91.

55 *Structuralist Poetics*, p. 135.

56 From the blurbs on the cover of one of the paperback editions of *Ada* (Greenwich, Conn.: Fawcett Publications, 1971).

57 Unpublished interview, included in *SO*, pp. 195–6.
58 *Philosophical Investigations*, trans. G. E. M. Anscombe, 2nd. edn (Oxford: Basil Blackwell, 1958), p. 18. A recent book on the *Philosophical Investigations* glosses the passage this way: 'Meaning is not a spiritual activity, nor are we free, as it were, in the domain of the mind, to mean what we wish by whatever sign we use. Meaning something by an utterance requires that the symbol employed be either predetermined as a signal (as in a code) or else possess the appropriate articulations. Whether I can mean so-and-so by uttering such-and-such depends on the general use of the sentence uttered and its relation to those sentences which would, in the language, express what I meant. It is not just a question of "who is master"!' (G. P. Baker and P. M. S. Hacker, *Wittgenstein*, vol. I (Chicago: Univ. of Chicago Press, 1980), p. 217).
59 *Nabokov*, p. 60.
60 *Look at the Harlequins!* (London: Weidenfeld and Nicolson, 1975), pp. 47–8. All future references are to this edition and will be included in the text.
61 'Nabokov's Beheading', *The New Republic*, 161, 21 Dec. 1959, p. 18.
62 *The Annotated Lolita*, p. 11.
63 *Nabokov*, pp. 217–18.
64 'Things About *Look at the Harlequins!*', in *Things About Nabokov*, ed. Proffer, p. 295.
65 'Nabokov as His Own Half-Hero: *Look at the Harlequins!*', *NYTBR*, 13 Oct. 1974, p. 2.
66 *The Annotated Lolita*, p. 19.
67 To a critic's suggestion that *Ada* translates into fiction 'the two principal loves' of Nabokov's life, 'his first serious affair' as a youth and 'his long and happy marriage' (Matthew Hodgart, 'Happy Families', review of *Ada*, *NYRB*, 12, 22 May 1969, p. 3), Nabokov responded: 'I do object violently to your seeing in reunited Van and Ada (both rather horrible creatures) a picture of my married life. What the hell, Sir, do you know about my married life? I expect a prompt apology from you' (Letter to the Editor, *NYRB*, 13, 10 July 1969, p. 36).
68 *Oeuvres*, 2 vols., ed. Jean Hytier (Paris: Éditions Gallimard, 1960), vol. II, p. 894.
69 'Out of Style', *New Statesman*, 89, 25 Apr. 1975, pp. 555–6.

Select bibliography

ABBREVIATIONS

MFS	*Modern Fiction Studies*
NYRB	*The New York Review of Books*
NYTBR	*The New York Times Book Review*
PMLA	*Publications of the Modern Language Association of America*
PN	*Poslednie Novosti*
SEEJ	*The Slavic and East European Journal*
SO	*Strong Opinions*
SZ	*Sovremennye Zapiski*
TLS	*The Times Literary Supplement*
VNRN	*The Vladimir Nabokov Research Newsletter*

The most complete bibliography of Nabokov's works is Andrew Field's *Nabokov: A Bibliography* (New York: McGraw-Hill, 1973). It is far from ideal – its errors and omissions are currently being corrected in *VNRN* – but everyone who works on Nabokov is immensely indebted to Field. Samuel Schuman's *Vladimir Nabokov: A Reference Guide* (Boston: G. K. Hall, 1979) is an excellent annotated bibliography of the secondary material. It is being regularly supplemented by checklists in *VNRN*. The selected bibliography and the excerpts from émigré criticism of Nabokov's work in Grayson, *Nabokov Translated*, are extremely useful. The Nabokov volume in the 'Critical Heritage' series (London: Routledge and Kegan Paul, 1982), edited by Norman Page, is a good record of how his work has been reviewed. What follows is a list of works cited and a selected list of other material that I found helpful in the preparation of this book. Works by Nabokov are in chronological order. Dates in square brackets indicate the year in which a book or article first appeared.

PRIMARY SOURCES CITED IN THE TEXT

Novels, Short Stories, and Poems

'Osa'. *Rul'*, 24 June 1928, p. 2.
Korol', Dama, Valet. Berlin, 1928; repr. Ann Arbor, Mich.: Ardis, 1979.
Kamera Obskura. Berlin, 1933; repr. Ann Arbor, Mich.: Ardis, 1978.
Otchayanie. Berlin, 1936; repr. Ann Arbor, Mich.: Ardis, 1978.
Soglyadatai. Paris, 1938; repr. Ann Arbor, Mich.: Ardis, 1978.

Laughter in the Dark. Trans. Vladimir Nabokov [1938]. London: Weidenfeld and Nicolson, 1961.

Priglashenie Na Kazn'. Paris, 1938; repr. Ann Arbor, Mich.: Ardis, 1979.

Bend Sinister [1947]. London: Weidenfeld and Nicolson, 1960.

Dar [1952]. 2nd edn Ann Arbor, Mich.: Ardis, 1975.

Vladimir Nabokov: The Annotated Lolita [1955]. Ed. Alfred Appel, Jr. London: Weidenfeld and Nicolson, 1971.

Vesna v Fial'ta i Drugie Rasskazy. New York: Izdatel'stvo Imeni Chekhova, 1956.

Invitation to a Beheading. Trans. Dimitri Nabokov in collaboration with the author. London: Weidenfeld and Nicolson, 1960.

Pale Fire. London: Weidenfeld and Nicolson, 1962.

The Gift. Trans. Michael Scammell in collaboration with the author. London: Weidenfeld and Nicolson, 1963.

Despair. Trans. Vladimir Nabokov. London: Weidenfeld and Nicolson, 1966.

King, Queen, Knave. Trans. Dimitri Nabokov in collaboration with the author. London: Weidenfeld and Nicolson, 1968.

Ada, or Ardor: A Family Chronicle. London: Weidenfeld and Nicolson, 1969.

Poems and Problems. London: Weidenfeld and Nicolson, 1972.

Transparent Things. London: Weidenfeld and Nicolson, 1973.

A Russian Beauty and Other Stories. Trans. Dimitri Nabokov in collaboration with the author, except for the title story, which is translated by Simon Karlinsky. London: Weidenfeld and Nicolson, 1973.

Lolita: A Screenplay. New York: McGraw-Hill, 1974.

Look at the Harlequins! London: Weidenfeld and Nicolson, 1975.

Tyrants Destroyed and Other Stories. Trans. Dimitri Nabokov in collaboration with the author. London: Weidenfeld and Nicolson, 1975.

Interviews

'U V. V. Sirina'. Interview conducted by Andrey Sedykh in *PN*, 3 Nov. 1932, p. 2.

'Talk With Mr Nabokov'. Interview conducted by Harvey Breit in *NYTBR*, 1 July 1951, p. 17.

'Small World of Vladimir Nabokov'. Interview conducted by John Wain in *The Observer*, 1 Nov. 1959, p. 21.

'Nabokov'. Interview conducted by John Coleman in *Spectator*, 6 Nov. 1959, p. 619.

Interview conducted by some New York journalists in June 1962. Included in *SO*, pp. 3–8.

'Vladimir Nabokov on His Life and Work'. Interview conducted by Peter Duval-Smith in *The Listener*, 68, 22 Nov. 1962. Included in *SO*, pp. 9–19.

'Playboy Interview: Vladimir Nabokov'. Interview conducted by Alvin Toffler in *Playboy*, Jan. 1964. Included in *SO*, pp. 20–45.

'On the Banks of Lake Leman Mr Nabokov Reflects on *Lolita* and *Onegin*'. Interview conducted by Douglas M. Davis in *The National Observer*, 29 June 1964, p. 17.

Film interview conducted by Robert Hughes for the Television 13 Educational Program, 1965. Included in *SO*, pp. 51–61.

'The Artist in Pursuit of Butterflies'. Interview conducted by Herbert Gold in *Saturday Evening Post*, 240, 11 Feb. 1967, pp. 81–5.

'An Interview With Vladimir Nabokov'. Interview conducted by Alfred Appel, Jr in *Nabokov*, ed. Dembo. Included in *SO*, pp. 62–92.

'The Art of Fiction XL'. Interview conducted by Herbert Gold in *The Paris Review*, no. 41 (Oct. 1967). Included in *SO*, pp. 93–107.

'Entretien Avec Vladimir Nabokov'. Interview conducted by Pierre Domergues in *Les Langues Modernes*, Jan.–Feb. 1968, pp. 92–102.

'Nabokov on Nabokov and Things'. Interview conducted by Martin Esslin in *NYTBR*, 12 May 1968. Included in *SO*, pp. 108–14.

'The Strong Opinions of Vladimir Nabokov'. Interview conducted by Nicholas Garnham in *The Listener*, 10 Oct. 1968. Included in *SO*, pp. 115–19.

'Prospero's Progress'. Article by Martha Duffy and Ron Sheppard based on an interview with Nabokov, *Time*, 23 May 1969. Interview included in *SO*, pp. 120–30.

'To Be Kind, To Be Proud, To Be Fearless'. Interview conducted by James Mossman in *The Listener*, 23 Oct. 1969. Included in *SO*, pp. 141–52.

'Vladimir Nabokov Talks About Nabokov'. Interview conducted by Allene Talmey in *Vogue*, Dec. 1969. Included in *SO*, pp. 153–8.

'Conversations With Nabokov'. Interview conducted by Alfred Appel, Jr in *Novel: A Forum on Fiction*, Spring 1971. Included in *SO*, pp. 159–76.

'Vladimir Nabokov, 72 Today, Writing a New Novel'. Interview conducted by Alden Whitman in *The New York Times*, 23 Apr. 1971. Included in *SO*, pp. 177–80.

'Understanding Nabokov – A Red Autumn Leaf is a Red Autumn Leaf, Not a Deflowered Nymphet'. Interview conducted by Alan Levy in *The New York Times Magazine*, 31 Oct. 1971, pp. 20–2, 24, 28, 30, 32, 36, 38, 40–1.

Radio interview conducted by Paul Sufrin for Swiss Broadcast, 1971. Included in *SO*, pp. 183–4.

Film interview conducted by Kurt Hoffman for *Bayerischer Rundfunk*, 1971. Included in *SO*, pp. 185–93.

Unpublished interview, 1972. Included in *SO*, pp. 194–6.

'Checking in With Vladimir Nabokov: An Interview With the Master'. Interview conducted by Gerald Clark in *Esquire*, 84, July 1975, pp. 67–9, 131, 133.

Miscellaneous

Review of A. Bulkin, *Stikhotvoreniya*. *Rul'*, 25 Aug. 1926, p. 5.

Review of Sergey Rafalovich, *Terpkiya Budni* and *Simon Volkhv*. *Rul'*, 19 Jan. 1927, p. 4.

Review of Dimitry Kobyakov, *Gorech'* and *Keramika*, and Evgeny Shakh, *Semya Na Kamne*. *Rul'*, 11 May 1927, p. 4.

'Novye Poety'. Review of six émigré poets. *Rul'*, 31 Aug. 1927, p. 4.

'Yubilei'. *Rul'*, 18 Nov. 1927, p. 2.

Review of Vladislav Khodasevich, *Sobranie Stikhov*. *Rul'*, 14 Dec. 1927, p. 5.

'Tri Knigi Stikhov'. Review of Boris Bozhnev, *Fontan*, Dovid Knut, *Vtoraya Kniga Stikhov*, and *Stikhotvorenie: Poeziya i Poeticheskaya Kritika*. *Rul'*, 23 May 1928, p. 4.

Review of Aleksey Remizov, *Zvezda Nadzvezda*. *Rul'*, 14 Nov. 1928, p. 4.

Review of *Volya Rossii*, no. 2. *Rul'*, 8 May 1929, p. 4.

Review of A. Damanskaya, *Zheny*. *Rul'*, 25 Sept. 1929, p. 5.

Review of Aleksandr Kuprin, *Elan*. *Rul'*, 23 Oct. 1929, p. 5.

'Torzhestvo Dobrodeteli'. *Rul'*, 5 Mar. 1930, pp. 2–3.

'Molodye Poety'. Review of Antonin Ladinsky, *Chernoe i Goluboe*, and *Perekrestok 2*, an anthology of poems. *Rul'*, 28 Jan. 1931, pp. 2–3.

Review of Boris Poplavsky, *Flagi*. *Rul'*, 11 Mar. 1931, p. 5.

Review of Nina Berberova, *Poslednie i Pervye*. *Rul'*, 23 July 1931, p. 5.

'Mr Masefield and Clio'. Review of John Masefield, *Basilissa, a Tale of The Empress Theodora*. *The New Republic*, 9 Dec. 1940, pp. 808–9.

Nikolay Gogol [1944]. London: Weidenfeld and Nicolson, 1973.

Conclusive Evidence (later retitled *Speak, Memory: A Memoir*). New York: Harper and Brothers, 1951.

Drugie Berega. New York: Izdatel'stvo Imeni Chekhova, 1954.

'On a Book Entitled *Lolita*'. Afterword to *Lolita* [1957]. *The Annotated Lolita*, pp. 313–19.

Foreword to *Invitation to a Beheading*, pp. 5–7 [1960].

Foreword to *The Gift*, pp. 7–9 [1963].

Introduction to *Bend Sinister* [1964]. Harmondsworth: Penguin Books, 1974, pp. 5–11.

Eugene Onegin. A Novel in Verse by Alexandr Pushkin. Translated from the Russian, with a commentary, by Vladimir Nabokov. 4 vols. [1964]. Rev. edn, London: Routledge and Kegan Paul, 1975.

Speak, Memory: An Autobiography Revisited. London: Weidenfeld and Nicolson, 1967.

Foreword to *King, Queen, Knave*. London: Weidenfeld and Nicolson, 1968, pp. v–ix.

Letter to the Editor. *NYRB*, 13, 10 July 1969, p. 36.

'Anniversary Notes'. Nabokov's comments on the *Tri-Quarterly* issue (no. 17, Winter 1970) devoted to him. Included in *SO*, pp. 284–303.

Foreword to *Glory*. London: Weidenfeld and Nicolson, 1972, pp. ix–xiv.

Strong Opinions. London: Weidenfeld and Nicolson, 1974.

'Reputations Revisited'. *TLS*, 21 June 1977, p. 66.

The Nabokov–Wilson Letters: Correspondence Between Vladimir Nabokov and Edmund Wilson, 1940–1971. Ed. Simon Karlinsky. London: Weidenfeld and Nicolson, 1979.

Lectures on Literature. Ed. Fredson Bowers. London: Weidenfeld and Nicolson, 1980.

Lectures on Russian Literature. Ed. Fredson Bowers. London: Weidenfeld and Nicolson, 1982.

OTHER PRIMARY SOURCES

'Kembridzh'. *Rul'*, 28 Oct. 1921, p. 2.

Article on the poems of Rupert Brooke. *Grani*, no. 1 (1922), pp. 213–31.

Review of Rikhard Demmel, *Volshebnyi Solovei*. *Rul'*, 30 Mar. 1924, p. 7.

Review of A. Znosko-Borovsky, *Kapablanka i Alekhin*. *Rul'*, 16 Nov. 1927, p. 4.

Review of Raisa Blokh, *Moi Gorod*. *Rul'*, 7 Mar. 1928, p. 4.

Review of Vladimir Pozner, *Stikhi Na Sluchai*. *Rul'*, 24 Oct. 1928, p. 4.

'Pamyati Yu. I. Aikhenvalda'. *Rul'*, 23 Dec. 1928, p. 5.

'Literaturnoe Obozrenie'. Review of Ivan Bunin, *Izbrannye Stikhi*. *Rul'*, 22 May 1929, pp. 2–3.

Review of Irina Odoevtseva, *Isol'da*. *Rul'*, 30 Oct. 1929, p. 5.

Review of Vladimir Piotrovsky, *Beatriche*. *Rossiya i Slavyanstvo*, 11 Oct. 1930, p. 3.

'Literaturnyya Zametki: O Vosstavshikh Angelakh'. Review of *Volya Rossii*, nos. 7 and 8. *Rul'*, 15 Oct. 1930, pp. 2–3.

'Les Écrivains et l'Époque'. *Le Mois*, June–July 1931, pp. 137–9.

'Pamyati A. M. Chernago'. *PN*, 13 Aug. 1932, p. 3.

'Pouchkine, ou Le Vrai et le Vraisemblable'. *La Nouvelle Revue Française*, 1 Mar. 1937, pp. 362–78.

'Diaghilev and a Disciple'. Review of Serge Lifar, *Serge Diaghilev: An Intimate Biography*. *The New Republic*, 18 Nov. 1940, pp. 699–700.

'Crystal and Ruby'. Review of Shota Rustaveli, *The Knight in the Tiger's Skin*. *The New Republic*, 25 Nov. 1940, pp. 733–4.

'Prof. Woodbridge in an Essay on Nature Postulates the Reality of the World'. Review of Frederick Woodbridge, *An Essay on Nature*. *The New York Sun*, 10 Dec. 1940, p. 15.

'Homes for Dukhobors'. Review of J. F. C. Wright, *Slava Bohu, The Story of the Dukhobors*. *The New Republic*, 13 Jan. 1941, pp. 61–2.

'Faint Rose, or The Life of an Artist Who Lived in an Ivory Tower'. Review of John Rothenstein, *Life and Death of Conder*. *The New York Sun*, 21 Jan. 1941, p. 11.

'Mr Williams' Shakespeare'. Review of Frayne Williams, *Mr Shakespeare of the Globe*. *The New Republic*, 19 May 1941, p. 702.

'Belloc Essays – Mild But Pleasant'. Review of Hilaire Belloc, *The Silence of the Sea and Other Essays*. *NYTBR*, 23 Nov. 1941, p. 26.

'Cabbage Soup and Caviar'. Review of *A Treasury of Russian Life and Humor*, ed. John Cournos, and *A Treasury of Russian Literature*, ed. Bernard Guerney. *The New Republic*, 17 Jan. 1944, pp. 92–3.

'Lolita's Creator: Author Nabokov, a Cosmic Joker'. Article based on an interview with Nabokov. *Newsweek*, 25 June 1962, pp. 51–4.

'Portrait de Nabokov'. Interview conducted by Sylvia Lannes in *L'Express*, 30 June 1976, pp. 22–5.

'Vladimir Nabokov'. Interview conducted by George Feifer in *Saturday Review*, 27 Nov. 1976, pp. 20–4, 26.

'A Blush of Colour – Nabokov in Montreux'. Interview conducted by Robert Robinson for *The Book Programme*, BBC. Published in *The Listener*, 24 Mar. 1977. Repr. in *Nabokov*, ed. Quennell, pp. 119–25.

SECONDARY SOURCES CITED IN THE TEXT

Abell, George. *Exploration of the Universe*. 3rd edn, New York: Holt, Rinehart and Winston, 1975.

Adamovich, Georgy. Review of *SZ*, no. 48 (containing a part of *Podvig*). *PN*, 11 Feb. 1932, p. 2.

Review of *SZ*, no. 59 (containing a part of *Priglashenie Na Kazn'*). *PN*, 28 Nov. 1935, p. 3.

'Perechityvaya *Otchayanie*'. *PN*, 5 Mar. 1936, p. 3.

Odinochestvo i Svoboda. New York: Izdatel'stvo Imeni Chekhova, 1955.

Adams, Robert Martin. *Afterjoyce: Studies in Fiction After 'Ulysses'*. New York: Oxford Univ. Press, 1977.

Albright, Daniel. *Representation and the Imagination: Beckett, Kafka, Nabokov, and Schoenberg*. Chicago: Univ. of Chicago Press, 1981.

Alter, Robert. 'Nabokov's Ardor'. Review of *Ada*. *Commentary*, 48, Aug. 1969, pp. 47–50.

'*Invitation to a Beheading*: Nabokov and the Art of Politics'. In *Nabokov*, ed. Appel and Newman, pp. 41–59.

'Mirrors For Immortality'. Review of *Transparent Things*. *Saturday Review*, 11 Nov. 1972, pp. 72–6.

Partial Magic: The Novel as a Self-Conscious Genre. Berkeley: Univ. of California Press, 1975.

Amis, Kingsley. 'She Was a Child and I Was a Child'. Review of *Lolita*. *Spectator*, 6 Nov. 1959, pp. 635–6.

Amis, Martin. 'Out of Style'. Review of *Look at the Harlequins!* *New Statesman*, 89, 25 Apr. 1975, pp. 555–6.

Anon. 'Nabokov's Waterloo'. Review of *Ada*. *TLS*, 2 Oct. 1969, p. 1121.

Anon. 'What Made Humbert Run'. Review of *The Annotated Lolita*. *TLS*, 25 Feb. 1972, p. 213.

Appel, Alfred, Jr. '*Lolita*: The Springboard of Parody'. In *Nabokov*, ed. Dembo, pp. 106–43.

Introduction to *The Annotated Lolita*, ed. Appel, pp. xv–lxxi.

'*Ada* Described'. In *Nabokov*, ed. Appel and Newman, pp. 160–86.

Nabokov's Dark Cinema. New York: Oxford Univ. Press, 1974.

'The Road to *Lolita*, or The Americanization of an Émigré'. *Journal of Modern Literature*, 4 (1974), pp. 3–31.

'Remembering Nabokov'. In *Nabokov*, ed. Quennell, pp. 11–33.

Appel, Alfred, Jr, and Charles Newman, eds. *Nabokov: Criticism, Reminiscences, Translations, and Tributes*. London: Weidenfeld and Nicolson, 1971. First published in *Tri-Quarterly*, no. 17 (Winter 1970).

Ayer, A. J. *The Problem of Knowledge*. London: Macmillan, 1965.

Bader, Julia. *Crystal Land: Artifice in Nabokov's English Novels*. Berkeley: Univ. of California Press, 1972.

Baker, G. P. and P. M. S. Hacker. *Wittgenstein: Understanding and Meaning*, vol. I. Chicago: Univ. of Chicago Press, 1980.

Barnes, J. C. M. '*Lolita* – Technically Pornographic'. Letter to the Editor. *Books and Bookmen*, 4, Mar. 1959, p. 3.

Barth, John. *Lost in the Funhouse*. New York: Doubleday, 1968.

Barthes, Roland. 'La Réponse de Kafka'. In *Essais Critiques*. Paris: Éditions du Seuil, 1964, pp. 138–42.

S/Z. Paris: Éditions du Seuil, 1970.

Sade, Fourier, Loyola. Paris: Éditions du Seuil, 1971.

Le Plaisir du Texte. Paris: Éditions du Seuil, 1973.

Bayley, John. *Pushkin: A Comparative Commentary*. Cambridge: Cambridge Univ. Press, 1971.

'Under Cover of Decadence: Nabokov as Evangelist and Guide to the Russian Classics'. In *Nabokov*, ed. Quennell, pp. 42–58.

Belinsky, V. G. *Polnoe Sobranie Sochinenii*. 13 vols. Ed. N. F. Belchikov *et al*. Moscow: Izdatel'stvo Akademii Nauk SSSR, 1953–9.

Bell, Michael. '*Lolita* and Pure Art'. *Essays in Criticism*, 24 (1974), pp. 169–84.

Berberova, Nina. *The Italics Are Mine*. Trans. Philippe Radley. London: Longmans, Green and Co., 1969.

Berlin, Isaiah. *Russian Thinkers*. Ed. Henry Hardy and Aileen Kelly. London: The Hogarth Press, 1978.

Bok, Sissela. 'Redemption Through Art in Nabokov's *Ada*'. *Critique*, 12 (1971), pp. 110–20.

Borges, Jorge Luis. *Labyrinths*. Ed. James Irby. Trans. James Irby *et al*. Harmondsworth: Penguin Books, 1970.

'Up From Ultraism'. Trans. Norman Thomas di Giovanni in collaboration with the author. *NYRB*, 15, 13 Aug. 1970, pp. 3–4.

Born, Max. *Einstein's Theory of Relativity*. Rev. edn prepared with the collaboration of Gunther Liebfried and Walter Biem. New York: Dover Publications, 1962.

Boswell, James. *Boswell's Life of Johnson*. 6 vols. Ed. George Birkbeck Hill and L. F. Powell. Oxford: Clarendon Press, 1934.

Boyd, Brian. 'Nabokov and *Ada*'. Unpublished dissertation, Univ. of Toronto, 1979.

Breton, André. Preface to *Anthologie de l'Humour Noir*. Paris: Jean-Jacques Pauvert, 1966, pp. 9–22.

Brooke-Rose, Christine. 'Transgressions: An Essay-Say on the Novel Novel Novel'. *Contemporary Literature*, 19 (1978), pp. 378–407.

Brown, Clarence. 'Nabokov's Pushkin and Nabokov's Nabokov'. In *Nabokov*, ed. Dembo, pp. 195–208.

Bruss, Elizabeth. *Autobiographical Acts: The Changing Situation of a Literary Genre*. Baltimore: Johns Hopkins Univ. Press, 1976.

Burgess, Anthony. 'Pushkin and Kinbote'. Review of *Eugene Onegin*. *Encounter*, 24, May 1965, pp. 74–8.

Chernyshevsky, N. G. *Polnoe Sobranie Sochinenii*. 16 vols. Ed. V. Ya. Kirpotin *et al.* Moscow: Gosudarstvennoe Izdatel'stvo Khudozhestvennoi Literatury, 1939–53.

Chesterton, G. K. *Charles Dickens*. London: Methuen, 1906.

Conquest, Robert. *The Great Terror: Stalin's Purges of the Thirties*. Rev. edn. London: Macmillan, 1973.

Couturier, Maurice. *Nabokov*. Lausanne: Éditions l'Age d'Homme, 1979.

Crews, Frederick. *The Pooh Perplex: A Student Casebook*. London: Arthur Barker, 1964.

Culler, Jonathan. *Structuralist Poetics: Structuralism, Linguistics, and the Study of Literature*. London: Routledge and Kegan Paul, 1975.

Dalton, Elizabeth. '*Ada* or Nada'. Review of *Ada*. *Partisan Review*, 37 (1970), pp. 155–8.

Davis, C. K. '*Lolita*'. Letter to the Editor. *Books and Bookmen*, 4, Apr. 1959, p. 3.

Dembo, L. S., ed. *Nabokov: The Man and His Work*. Madison: Univ. of Wisconsin Press, 1967. First published in *Wisconsin Studies in Contemporary Literature*, no. 8 (Spring 1967).

Dickstein, Morris. 'Nabokov's Folly'. Review of *Ada*. *The New Republic*, 160, 28 June 1969, pp. 27–9.

Djilas, Milovan. *Conversations With Stalin*. Trans. Michael Petrovich. London: Rupert Hart-Davis, 1962.

Dostoevsky, Fyodor. *Notes From Underground [and] The Double*. Trans. Jessie Coulson. Harmondsworth: Penguin Books, 1972.

   Polnoe Sobranie Sochinenii. 30 vols. Ed. V. G. Bazanov *et al.* Leningrad: Izdatel'stvo 'Nauka', 1972–   [publication not yet complete].

Druzhinin, A. V. *Sobranie Sochinenii*. 8 vols. Ed. N. V. Gerbel. St Petersburg: [no publ.] 1865–7,

Ehrmann, Jacques. '*Homo Ludens* Revisited'. *Yale French Studies*, no. 41 (1968), pp. 31–57.

Eliot, T. S. *Collected Poems, 1909–1962*. London: Faber and Faber, 1963.

Enright, D. J. 'Pun-Up'. Review of *Ada*. *The Listener*, 82, 2 Oct. 1969, pp. 457–8.

Feifer, George. *Russia Close-Up*. London: Jonathan Cape, 1973.

Fet, A. A. *Stikhotvoreniya*. Moscow: Izdatel'stvo 'Khudozhestvennaya Literatura', 1970.

Field, Andrew. *Nabokov: His Life in Art. A Critical Narrative*. London: Hodder and Stoughton, 1967.

Nabokov: His Life in Part. London: Hamish Hamilton, 1977.

Fowler, Douglas. *Reading Nabokov*. Ithaca, N.Y.: Cornell Univ. Press, 1974.

Freud, Sigmund. *The Interpretation of Dreams*. Vol. 4 of *The Complete Psychological Works*, ed. and trans. James Strachey. London: The Hogarth Press and The Institute of Psycho-Analysis, 1953.

Frye, Northrop. *Anatomy of Criticism: Four Essays*. Princeton: Princeton Univ. Press, 1957.

The Critical Path: An Essay on the Social Context of Literary Criticism. Bloomington: Indiana Univ. Press, 1971.

Gass, William. 'Upright Among Staring Fish'. *Saturday Review*, NS 1, Jan. 1973, pp. 35–6.

Genette, Gérard. *Figures III*. Paris: Éditions du Seuil, 1972.

Gerschenkron, Alexander. 'A Manufactured Monument?' Review of *Eugene Onegin*. *Modern Philology*, 63 (1965–6), pp. 336–47.

Gillon, Adam. 'Conrad's *Victory* and Nabokov's *Lolita*: Imitations of Imitations'. *Conradiana*, 12 (1980), pp. 51–71.

Gogol, N. V. *Polnoe Sobranie Sochinenii*. 14 vols. Ed. N. L. Mesh-cheryakov *et al.* Moscow: Izdatel'stvo Akademii Nauk SSSR, 1940–52.

Grayson, Jane. *Nabokov Translated: A Comparison of Nabokov's Russian and English Prose*. Oxford: Oxford Univ. Press, 1977.

Green, Martin. 'The Morality of *Lolita*'. *Kenyon Review*, 28 (1966), pp. 352–77.

Greimas, A. J. *Sémantique Structurale: Recherche de Méthode*. Paris: Librairie Larousse, 1966.

Hingley, Ronald. *Joseph Stalin: Man and Legend*. London: Hutchinson, 1974.

Hodgart, Matthew. 'Happy Families'. Review of *Ada*. *NYRB*, 12, 22 May 1969, p. 3.

Hughes, Philip R. 'The Knight Moves of the Mind: Nabokov's Use of Illusion to Transcend the Limits of Life and Art'. Unpublished dissertation, Boston Univ., 1974.

Hyde, G. M. *Vladimir Nabokov: America's Russian Novelist*. London: Marion Boyars, 1977.

Hyman, Stanley Edgar. 'Nabokov's *Gift*'. Review of *The Gift*. In *Standards: A Chronicle of Books For Our Time*. New York: Horizon Press, 1966, pp. 184–8.

Hynes, Samuel Jr, ed. 'Introduction'. In *Twentieth Century Interpretations of '1984'*. Englewood Cliffs, N.J.: Prentice-Hall, 1971, pp. 1–19.

Johnson, Carol. 'Nabokov's *Ada*: Word's End'. Review of *Ada*. *Art International*, 13, Oct. 1969, pp. 42–3.

Johnson, D. Barton. 'Nabokov's *Ada* and Puškin's *Eugene Onegin*'. *SEEJ*, NS 15 (1971), pp. 316–23.

'The Alpha and Omega of Nabokov's Prison House of Language: Alphabetic Iconicism in *Invitation to a Beheading*'. *Russian Literature*, 6 (1978), pp. 347–64.

de Jonge, Alex. 'Figuring Out Nabokov'. Review of some critical books on Nabokov. *TLS*, 16 May 1975, pp. 526–7.

'Nabokov's Uses of Pattern'. In *Nabokov*, ed. Quennell, pp. 59–72.

Josipovici, Gabriel. '*Lolita* and the Pursuit of Beauty'. *Critical Quarterly*, 6 (1964), pp. 35–48. Repr. in *The World and the Book: A Study of Modern Fiction*. 2nd edn, London: Macmillan, 1979, pp. 201–20.

Joyce, James. *Ulysses*. London: The Bodley Head, 1960.

Juliar, Michael. 'Notes From a Descriptive Bibliography'. *VNRN*, no. 8 (Spring 1982), pp. 20–7.

Kaplan, Fred. 'Victorian Modernists: Fowles and Nabokov'. *Journal of Narrative Technique*, 3 (1973), pp. 108–20.

Karlinsky, Simon. 'Vladimir Nabokov's Novel *Dar* as a Work of Literary Criticism: A Structural Analysis'. *SEEJ*, NS 7 (1963), pp. 284–90.

'Nabokov and Chekhov: The Lesser Russian Tradition'. In *Nabokov*, ed. Appel and Newman, pp. 7–16.

'Nabokov's Russian Games'. *NYTBR*, 18 Apr. 1971, pp. 2, 10, 12, 14, 16, 18.

'Dear Volodya, Dear Bunny; or Affinities and Disagreements'. Introduction to *The Nabokov-Wilson Letters*, pp. 1–25.

Kazin, Alfred. 'In the Mind of Nabokov'. Review of *Ada*. *Saturday Review*, 10 May 1969, p. 28.

Keats, John. *Keats: Poetical Works*. 2nd edn. Ed. H. W. Garrod. London: Oxford Univ. Press, 1958.

Kermode, Frank. *The Genesis of Secrecy: On the Interpretation of Narrative*. Cambridge, Mass.: Harvard Univ. Press, 1979.

Khodasevich, Vladislav. 'Knigi i Lyudi'. Review of *Kamera Obskura*. *Vozrozhdenie*, 3 May 1934, pp. 3–4.

'O Sirine'. *Vozrozhdenie*, 13 Feb. 1937, p. 9. An abridged translation (by Michael Walker) appears in *Nabokov*, ed. Appel and Newman, pp. 96–101.

Review of *SZ*, no. 66 (containing a part of *Dar*). *Vozrozhdenie*, 24 June 1938, p. 9.

'Monument'. In *Modern Russian Poetry*. Ed. Vladimir Markov and Merrill Sparks. London: MacGibbon and Kee, 1966, pp. 406–7.

Lanham, Richard. '*Tristram Shandy*': The Games of Pleasure*. Berkeley: Univ. of California Press, 1973.

Style: An Anti-Textbook. New Haven, Conn.: Yale Univ. Press, 1974.

Lawrence, D. H. 'We Need One Another'. In *Phoenix: The Posthumous Papers of D. H. Lawrence*. Ed. Edward McDonald. London: William Heinemann, 1936, pp. 188–95.

Lady Chatterley's Lover. London: William Heinemann, 1961.

Lee, L. L. *Vladimir Nabokov*. Twayne United States Author Series No. 266. Boston: G. K. Hall and London: George Prior, 1976.

Lerner, Laurence. *Love and Marriage: Literature and Its Social Context*. London: Edward Arnold, 1979.

Levin, Bernard. 'Free – and a Bit Too Easy'. *The Times*, 7 Apr. 1981, p. 12.

Lewis, Wyndham. *Men Without Art*. London: Cassell, 1934.

Lilly, Mark. 'Nabokov: Homo Ludens'. In *Nabokov*, ed. Quennell, pp. 88–102.

Lotman, Mikhail. 'Nekotorye Zamechaniya o Poezii i Poetike F. K. Godunova-Cherdyntseva'. *Vtorichnye Modeliruyushchie Sistemy*, Univ. of Tartu (Estonia, USSR), 1979, pp. 45–8.

Lyons, John O. '*Pale Fire* and the Fine Art of Annotation'. In *Nabokov*, ed. Dembo, pp. 157–64.

McCarthy, Mary. 'Vladimir Nabokov's *Pale Fire*'. *Encounter*, 19, Oct. 1962, pp. 71–84.

McLuhan, Marshall. *Understanding Media: The Extensions of Man*. London: Routledge and Kegan Paul, 1964.

Mason, Bobbie Ann. *Nabokov's Garden: A Guide to 'Ada'*. Ann Arbor, Mich.: Ardis, 1974.

Mayer, Priscilla. Abstract of 'Nabokov's *Lolita* and Pushkin's *Onegin*: A Colloquy of Muses'. *VNRN*, no. 7 (Fall 1981), pp. 33–4.

Medlin, Virgil, and Steven Parsons, eds. and translators. *V. D. Nabokov and the Russian Provisional Government, 1917*. New Haven, Conn.: Yale Univ. Press, 1976.

Megerle, Brenda. 'The Tantalization of *Lolita*'. *Studies in the Novel*, 11 (1979), pp. 338–48.

Merivale, Patricia. 'The Flaunting of Artifice in Vladimir Nabokov and Jorge Luis Borges'. In *Nabokov*, ed. Dembo, pp. 209–24.

Merrill, Robert. 'Nabokov and Fictional Artifice'. *MFS*, 25 (1979), pp. 439–69.

Miller, James Jr., ed. *Theory of Fiction: Henry James*. Lincoln: Univ. of Nebraska Press, 1972.

Morton, Donald. *Vladimir Nabokov*. New York: Frederick Ungar, 1974.

Moynahan, Julian. *Vladimir Nabokov*. Minneapolis: Univ. of Minnesota Press, 1971.

Muchnic, Helen. 'Jeweler at Work'. Review of *Details of a Sunset and Other Stories*. *NYRB*, 23, 27 May 1976, pp. 22–4.

Nabokov, Dimitri. 'On Revisiting Father's Room'. In *Nabokov*, ed. Quennell, pp. 126–36.

Nabokov, V. D. 'Soviet Rule and Russia's Future'. A Supplement to *The New Commonwealth*, no. 15, 23 Jan. 1920, pp. 1–8.

Nabokov, Vera. Foreword to *Stikhi*. Ann Arbor, Mich.: Ardis, 1979, pp. 3–4.

Nassar, Joseph M. 'The Russian in Nabokov's English Novels'. Unpublished dissertation, State Univ. of New York, 1977.

Nelson, Cary. 'Reading Criticism'. *PMLA*, 91 (1976), pp. 801–15.

Nove, Alec. Review of Robert Conquest, *The Great Terror*. *Soviet Studies*, 20 (1968–9), pp. 536–42.

Nuttall, A. D. *A Common Sky: Philosophy and the Literary Imagination*. London: Chatto and Windus for Sussex Univ. Press, 1974.

Orwell, George. *Nineteen Eighty-Four*. London: Heinemann Educational Books, 1965.

'A Hanging'. In *The Collected Essays, Journalism and Letters of George Orwell*. 4 vols. Ed. Sonia Orwell and Ian Angus. London: Secker and Warburg, 1968, vol. I, pp. 44–8.

Osokin, Sergey. Review of *Priglashenie Na Kazn'*. *Russkie Zapiski*, no. 13 (1939), pp. 198–9.

Osorgin, Mikhail. Review of *Korol', Dama, Valet*. *PN*, 4 Oct. 1928, p. 3.

Review of *Kamera Obskura*. *SZ*, no. 54 (1934), pp. 458–60.

Patteson, Richard F. 'The Viewer and the View: Perception and Narration in Nabokov's English Novels'. Unpublished dissertation. Univ. of Pennsylvania, 1975.

'Nabokov's *Look at the Harlequins!*: Endless Re-Creation of the Self'. *Russian Literature Triquarterly*, no. 14 (Winter 1976), pp. 84–98.

Pearce, Richard. 'Nabokov's Black (Hole) Humor: *Lolita* and *Pale Fire*'. In *Comic Relief: Humor in Contemporary American Literature*. Ed. Sarah Blacher Cohen. Urbana: Univ. of Illinois Press, 1978, pp. 28–44.

Pifer, Ellen. 'No Frivolous Firebird: Character, Reality, Morality in Nabokov's Fiction'. Unpublished dissertation, Univ. of California at Berkeley, 1976.

Nabokov and the Novel. Cambridge, Mass.: Harvard Univ. Press, 1980.

Pipes, Richard. 'The Pock-Marked God'. Review of some books on Stalin. *TLS*, 24 June 1974, pp. 625–7.

Poe, Edgar Allan. *Selected Writings of Edgar Allen Poe*. Ed. David Galloway. Harmondsworth: Penguin Books, 1967.

Poirier, Richard. 'Nabokov as His Own Half-Hero: *Look at the Harlequins!*' Review of *Look at the Harlequins!* *NYTBR*, 13 Oct. 1974, pp. 2–4.

Pope, Alexander. *The Poems of Alexander Pope*. Ed. John Butt. London: Methuen, 1963.

Prescott, Peter. 'Prof. Nabokov'. Review of *Lectures on Literature*. *Newsweek*, 20 Oct. 1980, p. 96.

Prioleau, Elizabeth. 'Humbert Humbert Through the Looking Glass'. *Twentieth Century Literature*, 21 (1975), pp. 428–37.

Pritchard, William. 'Long Novels and Short Stories'. Review of *Transparent Things* (and other novels). *The Hudson Review*, 26 (1973–4), pp. 225–40 (227–8).

Proffer, Carl R. '*Ada* as Wonderland: A Glossary of Allusions to Russian Literature'. In *Things About Nabokov*, ed. Proffer, pp. 249–79.

'Things About *Look at the Harlequins!*' In *Things About Nabokov*, ed. Proffer, pp. 295–301.

Proffer, Carl R., ed. *A Book of Things About Vladimir Nabokov*. Ann Arbor, Mich.: Ardis, 1974.

Purdy, Strother. '*Solus Rex*: Nabokov and the Chess Novel'. *MFS*, 14 (1968), pp. 379–95.

Pushkin, A. S. *Polnoe Sobranie Sochinenii*. 16 vols. Ed. V. D. Bonch-Bruevich *et al*. Moscow: Izdatel'stvo Akademii Nauk SSSR, 1937–49.

Quennell, Peter, ed. *Vladimir Nabokov: A Tribute*. London: Weidenfeld and Nicolson, 1979.

Raban, Jonathan. 'Transparent Likenesses: New Novels'. Review of *Transparent Things* (and other novels). *Encounter*, 41, Sept. 1973, pp. 74–8 (75–6).

Rosenblum, Michael. 'Finding What the Sailor Has Hidden: Narrative as Patternmaking in *Transparent Things*'. *Contemporary Literature*, 19 (1978), pp. 219–32.

Ross, Charles R. 'An Editor's Preface'. *MFS*, 25 (1979), pp. 391–5.

Ross, Charles R., ed. *MFS*, 25, no. 3 (Autumn 1979), pp. 387–554. Special Issue: Vladimir Nabokov.

Rowe, W. W. *Nabokov's Spectral Dimension*. Ann Arbor, Mich.: Ardis, 1981.

Russell, Bertrand. *History of Western Philosophy and Its Connection With Political and Social Circumstances From the Earliest Times to the Present Day*. London: George Allen and Unwin, 1961.

Russell, Charles. 'The Vault of Language: Self-Reflective Artifice in Contemporary American Fiction'. *MFS*, 20 (1974), pp. 349–59.

Ryley, Robert M. 'Will Brown, Dolores, Colo.'. *VNRN*, no. 3 (Fall 1979), p. 30.

Salehar, Anna Maria. 'Nabokov's *Gift*: An Apprenticeship in Creativity'. In *Things About Nabokov*, ed. Proffer, pp. 70–83.

Sartre, Jean-Paul. 'Vladimir Nabokov: *La Méprise*'. Review of *Despair*. In *Situations I*. Paris: Gallimard, 1947, pp. 58–60.

Scholes, Robert. *Fabulation and Metafiction*. Urbana: Univ. of Illinois Press, 1979.

Seiden, Melvin. 'Nabokov and Dostoevsky'. *Contemporary Literature*, 13 (1972), pp. 423–44.

Shakhovskaya, Zinaida. *V Poiskakh Nabokova*. Paris: La Presse Libre, 1979.

Sheidlower, David I. 'Reading Between the Lines and the Squares'. *MFS*, 25 (1979), pp. 413–25.

Shklovsky, Viktor. *O Teorii Prozy*. Moscow, 1929; repr. Ann Arbor, Mich.: Ardis, n.d.

Stanhope, P. D. *The Letters of Philip Dormer Stanhope, 4th Earl of Chesterfield*. 6 vols. Ed. Bonamy Dobrée. London: Eyre and Spottiswoode, 1932.

Stark, John O. *The Literature of Exhaustion: Borges, Nabokov, and Barth*. Durham, N.C.: Duke Univ. Press, 1974.

Steiner, George. 'Extraterritorial'. In *Nabokov*, ed. Appel and Newman, pp. 119–27.

Stuart, Dabney. '*The Real Life of Sebastian Knight*: Angles of Perception'. *Modern Language Quarterly*, 29 (1968), pp. 312–28.

Nabokov: The Dimensions of Parody. Baton Rouge: Louisiana State Univ. Press, 1978.

Suagee, Stephen. 'An Artist's Memory Beats All Other Kinds'. In *Things About Nabokov*, ed. Proffer, pp. 54–62.

Swanson, Roy. 'Nabokov's *Ada* as Science Fiction'. *Science Fiction Studies*, 2 (1975), pp. 76–88.

Tamir-Ghez, Nomi. 'The Art of Persuasion in *Lolita*'. *Poetics Today: Theory and Analysis of Literature and Communication*, 1, Parts 1–2 (1979), pp. 65–83.

Terras, Victor. *Belinskij and Russian Literary Criticism: The Heritage of Organic Aesthetics.* Madison: Univ. of Wisconsin Press, 1974.

Trilling, Lionel. 'The Last Lover: Vladimir Nabokov's *Lolita*'. *Encounter*, 11, Oct. 1958, pp. 9–19.

Trotsky, Leon. *History of the Russian Revolution.* Trans. Max Eastman. London: Victor Gollancz, 1965.

Tsetlin, M. Review of *Korol', Dama, Valet. SZ*, no. 37 (1928), pp. 536–8.

Turgenev, I. S. *Polnoe Sobranie Sochinenii.* 15 vols. Ed. M. P. Alekseev *et al.* Moscow: Izdatel'stvo Akademii Nauk SSSR, 1960–8.

Pis'ma. 13 vols. Ed. M. P. Alekseev *et al.* Moscow: Izdatel'stvo Akademii Nauk SSSR, 1961–8.

Ulam, Adam B. *Lenin and the Bolsheviks: The Intellectual and Political History of the Triumph of Communism in Russia.* London: Secker and Warburg, 1966.

Updike, John. 'Van Loves Ada, Ada Loves Van'. Review of *Ada. The New Yorker*, 2 Aug. 1969, pp. 67–75.

Introduction to *Lectures on Literature*, pp. xvii–xxvii.

Valéry, Paul. *Oeuvres.* 2 vols. Ed. Jean Hytier. Paris: Gallimard, 1960.

Vishnyak, Mark. '*Sovremennye Zapiski*': *Vospominaniya.* Bloomington: Indiana Univ. Publications, 1957.

Wagner, Geoffrey. 'Vladimir Nabokov and the Redemption of Reality'. *Cimarron Review*, 10 (1970), pp. 16–23.

Wain, John. 'Nabokov's Beheading'. Review of *Invitation to a Beheading. The New Republic*, 161, 21 Dec. 1959, pp. 17–19.

Whitman, Walt. *Walt Whitman: The Complete Poems.* Ed. Francis Murphy. Harmondsworth: Penguin Books, 1975.

Watson, George. 'Were the Intellectuals Duped? The Thirties Revisited'. *Encounter*, 41, Dec. 1973, pp. 20–30.

Webster, Richard. 'Frank Kermode's *The Sense of an Ending*'. *Critical Quarterly*, 16 (1974), pp. 311–24.

Weidlé, Wladimir. '20 Let Evropeiskoi Literatury'. *PN*, 10 Feb. 1939, p. 3.

Wells, H. G. *War of the Worlds.* London: William Heinemann, 1898. *The First Men in the Moon.* London: Macmillan, 1904.

Wetzeon, Ross. 'Nabokov as Teacher'. In *Nabokov*, ed. Appel and Newman, pp. 240–6.

Wittgenstein, Ludwig. *Philosophical Investigations*. 2nd edn. Trans. G. E. M. Anscombe. Oxford: Basil Blackwell, 1958.

Woehrlin, William F. *Chernyshevskii: The Man and the Journalist*. Cambridge, Mass.: Harvard Univ. Press, 1971.

Zaslove, Jerald. 'Nabokov in Context'. *Recovering Literature*, 1, no. 3 (1972), pp. 23–8.

Zimmer, Dieter E. 'L'Allemagne Dans l'Oeuvre de Nabokov'. Trans. Rudolf Boehm and Isabelle Micha. *L'Arc* (Nabokov Special Issue), no. 24 (Spring 1964), pp. 67–75.

OTHER SECONDARY SOURCES

Adamovich, Georgy. Review of *SZ*, no. 41 (containing a part of *Zashchita Luzhina*). *PN*, 13 Feb. 1930, p. 3.

Review of *SZ*, no. 46 (containing a part of *Podvig*). *PN*, 4 June 1931, p. 2.

Review of *SZ*, no. 51 (containing a part of *Kamera Obskura*). *PN*, 2 Mar. 1933, p. 3.

'Sirin'. *PN*, 4 Jan. 1934, p. 3.

Review of *SZ*, no. 55 (containing a part of *Otchayanie*). *PN*, 24 May 1934, p. 2.

Review of *SZ*, no. 56 (containing a part of *Otchayanie*). *PN*, 8 Nov. 1934, p. 3.

Review of *SZ*, no. 58 (containing a part of *Priglashenie Na Kazn'*). *PN*, 4 July 1935, p. 2.

Review of *Russkie Zapiski*, no. 2 (containing 'Oblako, Ozero, Bashnya'). *PN*, 16 Dec. 1937, p. 3.

Review of *Russkie Zapiski*, Aug.–Sept. 1938 (containing 'Istreblenie Tiranov'). *PN*, 15 Sept. 1938, p. 3.

Adams, Robert Martin. 'Passion Among the Polyglots'. Review of *Ada*. *The Hudson Review*, 22 (1969–70), pp. 717–24.

Amis, Martin. 'The Sublime and the Ridiculous'. In *Nabokov*, ed. Quennell, pp. 73–87.

Anderson, Quentin. 'Nabokov in Time'. Review of *Despair*. *The New Republic*, 154, 4 June 1966, pp. 23–8.

Bitsilli, P. M. 'Vozrozhdenie Allegorii'. *SZ*, no. 61 (1936), pp. 191–204. Trans. Dwight Stephens in *Nabokov*, ed. Appel and Newman, pp. 102–18.

Review of *Priglashenie Na Kazn'* and *Soglyadatai*. *SZ*, no. 68 (1939), pp. 474–7. Trans. D. Barton Johnson in *Things About Nabokov*, ed. Proffer, pp. 63–9.

Burgess, Anthony. 'Poet and Pedant'. *Spectator*, 218, 24 Mar. 1967, pp. 336–7.

Chernyshev, A., and V. Pronin. 'Vladimir Nabokov, Vo-Vtorykh i Vo-Pervykh'. *Literaturnaya Gazeta*, 4 Mar. 1970, p. 13.

Donoghue, Denis. 'Bright Brute'. Review of *King, Queen, Knave*. *The Listener*, 80, 10 Oct. 1968, p. 480.

Foster, Ludmila A. 'Nabokov in Russian Émigré Criticism'. *Russian Literature Triquarterly*, no. 3 (Spring 1972), pp. 330–41. Repr. in *Things About Nabokov*, ed. Proffer, pp. 42–53.

'Nabokov's Gnostic Turpitude: The Surrealistic Vision of Reality in *Priglašenie Na Kazn''*. In *Mnemozina–Studia Litteraria Russica in Honorem Vsevolod Setchkarev*. Ed. Joachim Baer and Norman Ingham. Munich: Wilhelm Fink, 1974, pp. 117–29.

Gove, Antonia F. 'Multilingualism and Ranges of Tone in Nabokov's *Bend Sinister*'. *Slavic Review*, 32 (1973), pp. 79–90.

Grabes, H. *Fictitious Biographies: Vladimir Nabokov's English Novels*. Trans. Pamela Gliniars in collaboration with the author. The Hague: Mouton, 1977.

Graff, Gerald. *Literature Against Itself: Literary Ideas in Modern Society*. Chicago: Univ. of Chicago Press, 1979.

Hughes, Robert P. 'Notes on the Translation of *Invitation to a Beheading*'. In *Nabokov*, ed. Appel and Newman, pp. 284–92.

Johnson, D. Barton. 'Contrastive Phonoaesthetics, or Why Nabokov Gave Up Translating Poetry as Poetry'. In *Things About Nabokov*, ed. Proffer, pp. 28–41.

Kantor, M. 'Bremya Pamyati'. *Vstrechi*, no. 3 (Mar. 1934), pp. 125–8.

Kermode, Frank. 'Aesthetic Bliss'. Review of *Bend Sinister*. *Encounter*, 14, June 1960, pp. 81–6.

'Zemblances'. Review of *Pale Fire*. *New Statesman*, 64, 9 Nov. 1962, pp. 671–2.

Khodasevich, Vladislav. Review of *Zashchita Luzhina*. *Vozrozhdenie*, 11 Oct. 1930, p. 2.

Literaturnye Stat'i i Vospominaniya. New York: Izdatel'stvo Imeni Chekhova, 1954.

King, Bruce. '*Lolita*: Sense and Sensibility at Midcentury'. *Geste (Lolita* Special Issue), no. 5 (Mar. 1959), pp. 3–9.

Klemtner, Susan Strehle. 'To "Special Space": Transformotions in *Invitation to a Beheading*'. *MFS*, 25 (1979), pp. 427–38.

Lerner, Laurence. *The Truthtellers: Jane Austen, George Eliot, D. H. Lawrence*. New York: Schocken Books, 1967.

Levinton, G. A. 'Poeticheskii Bilingvism i Mezh'yazykovie Vlianiya'. *Vtorichnye Modeliruyushchie Sistemy*, Univ. of Tartu (Estonia, USSR), 1979, pp. 30–3.

Macdonald, Dwight. 'Virtuosity Rewarded, or Dr Kinbote's Revenge'. Review of *Pale Fire*. *Partisan Review*, 29 (1962), pp. 437–42.

McDonald, James L. 'John Ray, Jr, Critic and Artist: The Foreword to *Lolita*'. *Studies in the Novel*, 5 (1973), pp. 352–7.

Matlaw, Ralph, ed. *Belinsky, Chernyshevsky, and Dobrolyubov: Selected Criticism*. New York: E. P. Dutton, 1962.

Nakhimovsky, A. D. 'Linguistic Study of Nabokov's Russian Prose'. *SEEJ*, NS 21 (1977), pp. 78–87.

Novik, Al. Review of *Zashchita Luzhina*. *SZ*, no. 45 (1931), pp. 514–17.

Nuttall, A. D. *'Crime and Punishment': Murder as Philosophic Experiment*. Edinburgh: Scottish Academic Press for Sussex Univ. Press, 1978.

Oates, Joyce Carol. 'A Personal View of Nabokov'. *Saturday Review*, NS, 1, Jan. 1973, pp. 36–7.

Osorgin, Mikhail. Review of *Podvig*. *PN*, 27 Oct. 1932, p. 3.

Pilsky, Petr. Review of *SZ*, no. 58 (containing a part of *Priglashenie Na Kazn'*). *Segodnya*, 5 July 1935, p. 3.

Pjatigorsky, A. M. 'A Word About the Philosophy of Vladimir Nabokov'. *Wiener Slawistischer Almanach*, 4 (1979), pp. 5–17.

Proffer, Carl R. 'From *Otchaianie* to *Despair'*. *Slavic Review*, 27 (1968), pp. 258–67.

Keys to 'Lolita'. Bloomington: Indiana Univ. Press, 1968.

'A New Deck For Nabokov's Knaves'. In *Nabokov*, ed. Appel and Newman, pp. 293–309.

Robbe-Grillet, Alain. 'Note Sur la Notion d'Itinéraire Dans *Lolita'*. *L'Arc*, no. 24 (Spring 1964), pp. 37–8.

Schapiro, Leonard. 'Lenin After Fifty Years'. In *Lenin: The Man, the Theorist, the Leader: A Reappraisal*. Ed. Leonard Schapiro and Peter Reddaway. London: Pall Mall Press, 1967, pp. 3–22.

Schuman, Samuel. *'Lolita*: Novel and Screenplay'. *College Literature*, 5 (1978), pp. 195–204.

Shapiro, Gavriel. 'Khristianskie Motivy, ikh Ikonografiya i Simvolika, v Romane Vladimira Nabokova *Priglashenie Na Kazn''*. *Russian Language Journal*, 33 (1979), pp. 144–62.

Stacy, R. H. 'Reaction'. In his *Russian Literary Criticism*. Syracuse: Syracuse Univ. Press, 1974, pp. 231–55.

Stainchamps, Ethel. 'Nabokov's Handling of English Syntax'. *American Speech*, 36 (1961), pp. 234–5.

Stegner, Page. *Escape Into Aesthetics: The Art of Vladimir Nabokov*. New York: Dial Press, 1966.

'Parody's End'. Review of *Look at the Harlequins! Atlantic Monthly*, 234, Nov. 1974, pp. 98, 103–4.

Struve, Gleb. 'Tvorchestvo Sirina'. *Rossiya i Slavyanstvo*, 17 May 1930, p. 3.

Russkaya Literatura v Izgnanii: Opyt Istoricheskogo Obzora Zarubezhnoi Literatury. New York: Izdatel'stvo Imeni Chekhova, 1956.

Tanner, Tony. *City of Words: American Fiction 1950–1970*. London: Jonathan Cape, 1971.

Tekiner, Christina. 'Time in *Lolita*'. *MFS*, 25 (1979), pp. 463–9.

Terapiano, Yury. Review of *Kamera Obskura*. *Chisla*, no. 10 (1934), pp. 287–8.

Toynbee, Philip. 'This Bright Brute is the Gayest'. Review of *King, Queen, Knave*. *NYTBR*, 12 May 1968, pp. 4–5.

Trilling, Lionel. *The Liberal Imagination: Essays on Literature and Society*. London: Mercury Books, 1961.

Venturi, Franco. *Roots of Revolution: A History of the Populist and Socialist Movements in Nineteenth Century Russia*. Trans. Francis Haskell. London: Weidenfeld and Nicolson, 1960.

Vesterman, William. 'Why Humbert Shoots Quilty'. *Essays in Literature*, 5 (1978), pp. 85–93.

Watts, Cedric. 'Janiform Novels'. *English*, 24 (1975), pp. 40–9.

Conrad's 'Heart of Darkness': A Critical and Contextual Discussion. Milan: Mursia International, 1977.

Weber, Alfred. 'Nabokov's *Ada*: A Style and Its Implications'. *Recovering Literature*, vol. I, no. 1 (1972), pp. 54–65.

Weidlé, Wladimir. Review of *SZ*, no. 42 (containing a part of *Zashchita Luzhina*). *Vozrozhdenie*, 12 May 1930, p. 3.

Review of *SZ*, no. 44 (containing *Soglyadatai*). *Vozrozhdenie*, 30 Oct. 1930, p. 2.

Weiler, Rudolf. 'Nabokov's Bodies: Description and Characterization in His Novels'. Unpublished dissertation, Univ. of Zurich, 1976.

Wills, Garry. 'The Devil and *Lolita*'. *NYRB*, 21, 21 Feb. 1974, pp. 4–6.

Zaitsev, K. 'Buninskii Mir i Sirinskii Mir'. *Rossiya i Slavyanstvo*, 8 Nov. 1929, p. 3.

Review of *SZ*, no. 44 (containing *Soglyadatai*). *Rossiya i Slavyanstvo*, 15 Nov. 1930, p. 4.

Index